WHO GETS WHAT?

Who Gets What?

The Hardening of Class Inequality in the Late Twentieth Century

John Westergaard

Polity Press

First published in 1995 by Polity Press
in association with Blackwell Publishers.

Editorial office:
Polity Press
65 Bridge Street
Cambridge CB2 1UR, UK

Marketing and production:
Blackwell Publishers, the publishing imprint of Basil Blackwell Ltd
108 Cowley Road
Oxford OX4 1JF, UK

Basil Blackwell Inc.
238 Main Street
Cambridge, MA 02142, USA

ISBN 0 7456 0107 3

British Library Cataloguing-in-Publication Data

A CIP catalogue record for this book is available from the British Library.

Library of Congress Cataloging-in-Publication Data

Westergaard, John H.
    Who gets what? : the hardening of class inequality in the late
twentieth Century / John Westergaard.
    Includes bibliographical references and index.
    ISBN 0–7456–0107–3
    1. Social classes. 2. Equality. 3. Marxian economic.
4. Economic Policy. I. Title.
    HT609.W45 1995
    305. 5—dc20   94–19317
                                                                              CIP

Typeset in 10 on 12 pt Palatino
by Pure Tech Corporation, Pondicherry, India
Printed in Great Britain by T. J. Press, Padstow, Cornwall

This book is printed on acid-free paper.

Contents

Acknowledgements

This book draws in part on earlier work of mine, which it aims to consolidate and extend. But only a few pieces of the text build directly on previously published material: thus my argument in chapter 2 on a paper that appeared in 1977; and the framework of my analysis in part II of the book, especially in chapter 5, on an article first published in 1978. While both pieces are now comprehensively revised, curtailed here and much expanded there, I am grateful to the original publishers – Lawrence & Wishart and the Merlin Press respectively – for permission to make such use of these two articles. Part III (chapters 7–11) can, I suppose, be seen as a long updating postscript to the book called *Class in a Capitalist Society* (1975), which I wrote in very different times with the outstanding help of Henrietta Resler: I take this opportunity to record, with sorrow, her tragically early death only a few years later. A much condensed version of this part of the present book formed three lectures I gave at Hitotsubashi University in Tokyo in December 1992 (Westergaard, 1993), a Japanese translation of which with subsequent discussion is in preparation for book-form publication by Aoki, Tokyo: I have gained valuable collegial stimulus and encouragement from this experience.

I have, as ever, far more debts of gratitude than I can record. Among the friends and colleagues I want to thank especially are Anthony Arblaster, Rosemary Crompton, Ralph Miliband, Iver Hornemann Møller, Iain Noble, Andrew Tylecote, Alan Walker and Masao Watanabe, either because they have read and commented valuably on some part of the text and/or because, even perhaps unknown to themselves, their work and ideas have informed, stimulated or challenged me while writing. I could easily extend the list and fear that here, as also in my references to relevant literature, I omit more names deserving acknowledgement than I manage to include. I am very grateful to Tony Giddens and Gill Motley for their long-suffering patience with my tardiness; and I much appreciate also the former's comments, and those of an anonymous reader, on drafts of the text. I am very grateful, too, to staff in the office of my Department – Sylvia Parkin and others – and to Jill Kerkhoff and Tina Wood for their shares in typing a densely written manuscript. Let me, finally, also thank the University of Sheffield and the Department of Sociological Studies here for continuing to allow me a room to work in, and other facilities essential to completion of this book, well after my formal retirement.

J.H.W.

Sheffield, Autumn 1993

To Hanne and Camilla

Introduction

Three themes run through this book: the persistence of class inequality in present society, indeed its remarkable hardening in recent years; the varying role of public policy in modifying or accentuating it; and the key place which concerns with distribution of welfare and with social justice warrant in analysis of it. I look at recent trends to sharper class inequality, and their paradoxical coincidence in time with much commentary asserting the terminal decline of matters of class, most directly in part III of the book. Readers keen to take a short cut to that topic can go more or less straight there, to chapters 7–11, as each of the three parts into which the main text divides may be read as fairly self-contained, some essential cross-references apart. Nonetheless the nature of the analysis in part III, and many features of the evidence in its support, presuppose consideration of the book's complementary themes, which come in parts I and II. These concern some theoretical aspects to the study of class first – the importance there of questions about 'who gets what'; and then the shifting sands of public policy, economic and social, as significant parameters of class structure throughout the second half of the twentieth century.

I should make the conception of class I adopt explicit from the start. I take class to signify a set of social divisions that arise from a society's economic organization. Whatever the form of this organization, it involves arrangements for command over deployment of key and scarce resources. The first step in class analysis, then, is to identify the character and sources of such power: who commands, how and how far, to what ends and to whose benefit? The last of these questions is highly salient, so I shall argue; and it leads immediately to the next step. Where prime command is concentrated in relatively few hands, benefit from the deployment of scarce resources will be skewly spread: to privilege commanders, and to make for multiple divisions in share of benefit among others. Here class analysis becomes a matter of mapping the contours of disparity of benefit among people at large. It is no simple matter, even given good information, because disparity of benefit comes in different forms whose patterns will rarely coincide neatly: inequality of rights over property of course; but also inequality of income especially, because real income and its incidence over individual life-cycles is crucial for social experience; inequalities of security, of personal autonomy in and out of work, of opportunity for self-advancement or risk of loss, of health or sickness. But in so far as these diverse manifestations of economic inequality coincide to mark off much the same people from each other on most counts, it makes good shorthand sense to term them divisions of class, rough though their boundaries will usually be. It is essential for all sociological understanding to map such divisions, moreover, since the sharper they are the more they set distinctly different terms for people's everyday life experiences and prospects: divergent conditions, and varying configurations of limit and latitude, for social relationships.

That applies in my view even regardless of how people in this or that rough class location, by the twin criteria of involvement or not in command and extent of shares in benefit, see their situation and may or may not react to it. Differences of class location undoubtedly tend to make for differences of outlook as well as of life-style. But whether and then how people in low location, for example, resent their shorter straws and may seek some resolution in consequence – say by pursuit of individual ambition (within the law or in breach of it), or by no more than sullen nonconformity, or by some form of collective action with class-fellows (even just voting) to change the unequal order in their own favour – these are issues for a third step in class analysis. They cannot, in all logic, be considered before the two first steps have been taken.

Of course it was concern with class mobilization for common cause that gave classical Marxism the political fire in its belly – on an assumption that, in capitalist societies by contrast with all previous ones, subordinate class 'being-in-itself' would in due course translate into class 'action-for-itself', to wholesale overturn of the ruling order. And from this, as from the potency for structural change it ascribed to contradictions of economic interest even before capitalism, classical Marxism drew also its own distinctive fourth purpose for class analysis: to explain the large movements in human history. These are claims well-nigh impossible to sustain. But grant freely that Marxism's grand explanatory ambition went to dogmatic excess; that while indeed very significant among the causes of large-scale change, economic contradictions are not the unique *primus motor* of all societal history; nor of the two crucial transitions in that history, of which the second – from agrarianism to industrialism – has been compellingly described as the result of 'a near miraculous concatenation of circumstances' (Gellner, 1988). Note just as freely that there has been no lasting socialist revolution anywhere at the hands of a mass wage-earner working class. Yet the basic purposes of class analysis stand nonetheless, so long as inequality stays firmly built into the disposition of economic resources. Even free of both mono-causal material determinism and confidence in capitalist collapse, comprehensive sociological agendas still have to keep three items high in place: the character and sources of power embedded in economic organization; the disparities of human life experience that arise in consequence; and the ways in which, politically and otherwise, people act out their varieties of class-shaped experience.

Readers inclined to schematic typification of theories may, reasonably enough, regard the front place I give here to power as 'Marxist'. But the importance I then immediately attach to disparities of life experience – inequalities of economic life chance – may strike them as 'Weberian'. Labelling on these lines implies a dichotomization of approaches to class analysis which I think unwarranted. But it is familiar from much literature, which takes Marxist approaches to put distinctive and overriding emphasis on command versus subordination in processes of production as *the* defining feature of class division. In this view, then, a schema to map the class structure of modern capitalist societies is Marxist if, and only if, it marks the boundaries between classes by more or less exclusive reference to the contrasts of role or function in a system of production geared overall to profit optimization and capital accumulation. What in Marxist logic comprehensively determines class location is here supposed to be what 'economically active' people *do*: whether they exercise prime command towards growth and accumulation of profit; or they take some more limited part in control by way of auxiliary authority, work supervision or coordinating service; or they merely supply labour to effects directed and pulled together from above. On Marxist agendas so stereotypically conceived, questions about what people *get* are quite subsidiary by contrast. Answers to them – about the distribution of income, security, opportunity and so on – may follow more or less closely from the pattern of disparate functions in processes of production. But they are not supposed to matter, in their own right, for mapping the economic divisions of class structure in a manner faithful to Marxism. Approaches which do assign such intrinsic importance to questions about 'who gets what' – to detailed inquiry into how benefit of outcome from production is distributed – are then labelled Weberian; and by Marxists who themselves adopt the dichotomy, they are liable to be scorned as heretical.

The conception of class which I set out earlier implies that I see no merit in such schematics. I also regard the point as one of more than pernickety scholarly detail. Those Marxists who dismiss concern with distributive benefit as peripheral to concern with role in the command structure of production thereby blunt the force which class analysis otherwise has to gain from their insights. Non-Marxists who accept the dichotomization have concomitantly been all the more ready to deny that force, when they have then taken Marxism to be near-blind to commonsensical notions of social inequality. This is why, in the first chapter, it is my aim precisely to clear away any assumption that close attention to distributive benefit and disadvantage is inherently out of tune with Marxism; and to uphold instead the contention, which runs through this book, that the consequences of unequal economic power by way of unequal personal experiences and prospects in life must be central to class analysis of whatever theoretical persuasion. I use as my means to this end, in chapter 1, critique of a debate among Marxists in the 1970s and 1980s about 'class boundaries'. But while the immediate subject of this debate was how to place the 'new middle classes', my interest is much less in conclusions on that score than in such conceptions of class as the debate brought into play. And I revive the debate for reconsideration now, not especially to highlight Marxist approaches in themselves; but because its leading participants clearly exemplified that class-analytical preoccupation with the order of production *tout court* – to neglect of the order of distribution as a mere by-product – which I think both stultifying and erroneously ascribed to the inherent logic of all Marxism.

Such near-exclusive concentration on production, so I shall argue, has nothing to say about the class locations of most people who are not 'economically active'; or it can say something there only by resort to interpretative devices which themselves, in the main, are hard to square with a single-minded 'production orientation'. It implies characterization of the class structure as a range just of 'positions' – in paid work or in control of it – with little or no complementary reference to the ways in which people are recruited to positions, may move between them, and exit from them. So it allows scant attention to people's lifetime economic experiences and prospects, beyond work as well as in it: scant attention, for example, to contrasts between career-enhanced and job-confined life circumstances. In defining class location as a matter of productive role by itself without express reference to income, moreover, it may have helped to give leeway for implausible current assertions that disparities of 'consumer power' – which turn largely on income, after all – are somehow now disconnected from class inequality. Not least, and in odd juxtaposition with classical Marxism's ultimate political concerns, it brushes aside the part which people's shares in the proceeds of production play in the formation of class interests. Marxism in politics, no less than reformist social democracy and trade unionism whenever aimed beyond narrow sectional advantage, has looked towards social justice; and equity of distribution, provision for fair shares, figures centrally in notions of social justice. But the reality of unfair shares as a source of social tension and political challenge slips out of sight, if class demarcations are defined without distinct attention to distributive outcomes from the order of production.

It may seem an odd quirk that one-sided 'production orientation' flourished notably in some Marxist class analysis – never all – at a time when issues of distributive justice and injustice had acquired quite high political visibility. This was in and just before the 1970s when, in Britain and many other western countries, post-war economic boom was turning to 'stagflation'; when rebellious moods were sliding from the exuberant iconoclasm of the late 1960s to more diffuse but also wider-spread distrust of authority and established organization; when trade unions and shopfloor workers, still but now less securely in a seller's market, had come to press industrial action with greater militancy. Disillusion with the familiar order of power and political process mingled with distributive discontent. But in practice pressures for 'fairer shares' made the running: demands for higher pay in wage-earning work, most obviously; for housing, when homeless people took to squatting; for widening and more certainty of educational opportunities, an issue then once again prominent in political programmes where middle-class parental anxieties added weight to moves for new access-friendly reform.

Mounting concern then both about labour 'indiscipline' and about how to sustain economic growth on a durable basis led governments to extend earlier, now so-called corporatist, arrangements for macroeconomic management. These were by intention cross-class arrangements; they involved tripartite cooperation between state, collectively organized business, and trade unions; they grew out of tensions over equity in distribution as well as over efficiency in production, but in turn came to highlight the former. It is those features of the framework of economic policy, together with their free-market aimed reversal from around 1980, which form the subject of chapters 2 and 3. One purpose of these is to illustrate the general thesis from chapter 1 by showing how tripartite corporatism revolved indeed around dilemmas of class-distributive justice: both directly, in policy efforts to contain pressures from labour; and indirectly, in measures to secure the foundations of an economic growth without whose continuation it was feared that conflicts over share-out might increase further. Public policy there sought to resolve popular discontents without class confrontation and, as I shall argue against variously opposed views, without sacrifice of basic capitalist prescriptions for production and distribution. But the circle proved hard to square; and I shall also suggest here (in chapter 3) that, when cooperation-directed tripartism gave way to rampant laissez-faire, this was because it encapsulated internal strains, both between and within classes, which it could not well bridge. Yet the free-marketeering now ascendant looks no more stable an alternative policy. It has as yet signally failed to yield the steady buoyancy of economic growth which was supposed to be its hallmark. But it has dramatically sharpened class inequalities. Overt strife on that score has been, in fact, subdued rather than encouraged by recurrent recession. But latent tensions may then prove the harder to contain, if and when growth does recover enough to boost popular confidence in more active assertion of demands for fairer shares.

If the last point is speculative, not so the widening of class inequalities since the late 1970s, for which chapters 8–10 set out the main evidence. That evidence is in striking discord with much current commentary, the character of which I review beforehand in chapter 7. And as fashionable conjecture about a definitive demise of a class has been triggered especially, in Britain, by electoral decline of the Labour Party, I turn in chapter 11 to the subject of politics and class. My aim there is to demonstrate that, while matters of class have indeed come to figure only weakly in institutional political processes, disquiet and resentment over inequality continue to figure strongly in popular perceptions of today's socio-economic order. This certainly marks a notable defeat, so far, for radical-right policy in another of its goals: the goal, through 're-education' backed by experience of market realities, to wean people away from judgements of the world in class terms, and from assumptions that it is a proper business of government to provide for fairer shares.

There is realism to stubborn popular beliefs that government action can change the distribution of shares in socio-economic welfare, if also to parallel disheartened beliefs that there is little positive to be practically expected now on this score from current politics. The gross hardening of class disparities since about 1980 has in fact been much a result of the shifts of policy framework so sharply exemplified by radical-right steerage of government in Britain. Shifts of economic climate, worldwide, have played a potent part too; but their inequality-enlarging effects have been formidably enhanced by deliberate political action inspired by market mania, privatizing passion and skinflint aims for public provision of welfare. While post-war policy settlements for 'social reconstruction' set in motion no continuous trend to steadily fairer shares once their initial impetus was spent, they and the measures of tripartite corporatism which followed them can now be seen at least to have held off the polarizing impact, on economic class structure, of which market forces proved capable under much looser rein in the two end-decades of the twentieth century.

Public policy thus sets significant surrounding terms for patterns and changes of class division. This is why matters of policy loom large in the book, and come before comprehensive attention to that persistence of class inequality to which recent government action-cum-inaction has added sharp extra bite. Following discussion of varying appoaches to macro-economic management in chapters 2–3, the next three chapters look into the scope, limits and shifts of 'welfare state' provision. The conceptual theme here concerns the diverse notions of distributive justice that appear embodied in public measures for welfare: my focus is on the question how far, if and when at all, these contravene the generally unspoken rules for distribution which capitalist organization of the economy implies. Practical pursuit of this issue entails, of course, examination of a variable mix of measures: state-endorsed private measures, as well as those that are plainly public; measures ordinarily defined to be matters of economic policy, as well as those conventionally relegated to the category of social policy. And the range of measures reviewed extends, not least, to 'counter-measures' taken in Britain since the late 1970s, on government premises – in major part misconceived, so I argue – that accumulated welfare state provision has indeed put property and market workings in jeopardy.

In so joining issues of public policy to issues of class structure, I hope in this book to help bridge an analytical divide which I think wider than it should be. Subject specialization and disciplinary organization in much of the academic world tend to earmark matters of class generally for sociologists' attention, while any more than loose concern with policy is liable to be assigned to separate specialists. The latter to boot often subdivide only too distinctly into experts on 'economic' and on 'social' policy, in part-reflection of ministerial demarcation of government functions and priorities. To try to straddle boundaries of this sort entails, of course, the risk of knowing too little about one or even each of the fields that merit joining. But on just the grounds I have outlined, class analysis and analysis of policy, social-cum-economic, have excellent cause to trespass on one another's territory – and both of them across other fences, such as those around politics – however vulnerable the results may then be to specialist correction.

While these rather platitudinous remarks about excess of disciplinary self-enclosure apply to a good deal of academic work everyday, there are more exceptions than I could even begin to list here. Let me note, however, that the Marxist tradition – in very principle if not in consistent practice – offers one set of exceptions. It does so because it has taken all that is social, political and cultural to be formed out of what it describes as economic. Insupportable though this appears as a causal theorem, it has the substantial virtue of turning eyes to the diverse connections between matters which conventional subject specialization tends to disconnect. Yet while panoramic of perspective in that sense, Marxism has been too prone at times to narrow its sights in another sense: to close itself off inside its own spheres of discourse, to sidestep engagement with alternative 'bourgeois' perceptions. I have made comments already that similarly found fault with this and that line of Marxist analysis; and critique recurs at several points of the main text, both in chapter 1 and later. Yet I still regard my own approach as primarily – today most unfashionably – Marxist: at least as better described that way than any other shorthand way. So these things may need a little concluding elaboration here.

Some follow-through of fault-finding first. When one-sided 'production orientation' was prominent in tone-setting versions of Marxist class analysis, this involved indeed a purist determination to stay free of influence from conceptual paradigms – here any with a fair streak of 'distribution orientation' – seen as alternative and so deemed un-Marxist. Theoretical self-insulation in this manner was common in several of the new schools of Marxism which made academic headway in the West at the time, from the mid-1960s and for about a decade and a half on. These included in the first place the varieties of 'structuralism' exemplified by Louis Althusser and Nicos Poulantzas in France; and, if with less impact in Britain, various strands of 'state derivation' and 'capital logic' theory from Germany (cf. for example, Holloway and Picciotto, 1978). Work in one or another of such modes commonly relied on a language and style of abstraction that seemed calculated to obscure, and so to fence it off within its own patch. That effect tended to follow, too, from the leading 'problematics' set. These were to return in depth to classical Marxist texts, and just from their logic to refine the parameters for understanding of the modern world, rather than to set Marxist against rival interpretations and treat both as sources of hypotheses to be tested. Inclined also to embrace a wider mood then for 'anti-positivist' demotion of empirical inquiry – in a manner that inflated sensible caution about quantification into near-total rejection – neo-Marxism of this sort thus came close to a perversely relativistic view of knowledge; and to judgement of theory by definitive reference only to its self-consistency, internally and with this or that reading of the founding father's work. Often, moreover, it involved a form of grand theorizing, curiously akin to earlier and conservative Parsonianism, that described effects as 'functions' and so seemed to equate them with causes.

Did this then help to give Marxist analysis the bad name now so apparent from its widespread re-relegation to places low down or right off current social scientific agendas? In some part no doubt. But dogmatism and pretentious abstraction, intellectual navel-gazing and leanings towards relativism, are not sins to which only Marxism is liable; they look, for example, well to the fore in many of the 1980s' and 1990s' speculations in postmodernism. Nor has impatience with those features of some of the 1960s' and 1970s' neo-Marxisms been confined to critics from quite opposed perspectives; indeed my own dissent here comes in rather mild terms compared with that voiced – already long ago – by several other Marxists (for instance, Miliband, 1970; Thompson, 1978; Glass 1979). Moreover, the diverse brands of both new and older Marxism which acquired some prominence in the mid-1960s to mid-1970s have much of positive social scientific substance to their credit, all too readily forgotten now. They never came to hold the academic sway that orthodox mythology has ascribed to them; not even in sociology, where their bird's-eye vision contested the ground of innovation with the worm's-eye vision of symbolic interactionism and ethnomethodology. But they did much for a time to set fresh agendas to horizon-widening effects. It was, for example, Marxist work which led the way then into exploration of 'the big state'; which set new models for the study of world economic networks, development and dependency; which injected concerns with power and powerlessness into a 'new criminology'. These and more now became matters for varieties of extended 'class analysis', in good part cross-disciplinary, to the salience of which most scholarship before had been tone-deaf.

Reasonably enough for theory which had made grand claims to forecast human future, Marxism must have lost credibility more from its failures of prophecy than from any other analytical foibles. But the point is moot how far this can go by itself to explain its current eclipse on the academic, and not just the political, scene. A vision of popular socialist revolution to come may have seemed more realistic in the late

1960s than before. Yet it faded quickly: sooner than did social scientific interest in the new currents of Marxist thought, within several of which confidence in that vision had in any case already given way to agnosticism, despair or evasiveness. Since then, of course, the collapse of the Soviet regime has been widely proclaimed to mark a definitive end to all prospects of socialism. But even aside from the paradoxical self-assurance which sometimes colours such prophecy now in bourgeois mood, there is no ready logic to be found just here for defection from Marxist analysis, when most western proponents of the latter had quite long seen little in Soviet reality to call socialist anyway. The continuing drama of events east, from the late 1980s, probably matters in this context much more for the fact that few social scientists of whatever persuasion had expected anything so overwhelming and precipitate: just as few had anticipated the full impact of world economic convulsions from the mid-1970s onwards, or that ascendancy of the political right which has so far mainly gone with them. Much interpretation à la mode has taken all this to be evidence of a pervasive lack of predictability and structure to 'postmodern' society. As a prime exemplar of structural analysis, Marxism has then seemed liable for prime consignment to academic oblivion.

Even compound failures of foresight, however, are no proof of structureless flux. There is in fact plenty of 'structure' – of tenacity, consistency and interconnection of pattern – to the class inequality with which this book is concerned: to its sources, shape and persistence; to its shifts of incidence over time, and its recent hardening in clear linkage with changes of policy and economic climate; to much, also, in the ways that people diversely affected see these things, judge them, and take account of them if and when they vote. But visible structure in such senses does not signify predetermination of events in action, whether short-term or even in some hypothetical 'final outcome'. Marxism certainly has to abandon any still surviving faith in that, and in formulaic readings from past to future. Yet shorn of this, shorn of a good deal else of which my comments earlier have been critical – shorn too, I might add, of the labour theory of value and the 'law' of declining profit – Marxism still has more than enough to put into class analysis for its firm rehabilitation against current disdain.

Freed of dogmatism, Marxism yet retains an essential emphasis on the sources of inequality, in the command structure of economic activities, which full attention to the results for distributive welfare should complement but not supplant. Its insistence on the formidable potential for political conflict, societal change and resistance to change inherent in divisions of economic power and life circumstance has proved a signal lead into social understanding, though not the masterkey to historical explanation that Marx and his most dedicated followers thought it to be. To shrug this aside in respect of the known past is to ignore, for example, the highly visible imprint of cleavages of class interest on all western politics throughout the last couple of centuries, albeit to reformist rather than revolutionary effects. To deny it salience in respect of the uncertain present and the unknown future often involves alternative emphasis on other, indeed long-potent cleavages – of ethnicity and between nation-states especially – but then risks neglect of the ways in which concerns of class still intertwine with those. Moreover, taken as seriously as it warrants, Marx's distinction between class 'in itself' and 'for itself' continues to make good methodological sense, because it directs attention to negative cases significant for systematic research. When thus the economic inequalities of class harden but popular political allegiances seem to turn centre-right, there is more understanding to be gained by identifying this as a distinct puzzle for sustained inquiry than from seeing it as a manifestation of indecipherable flux-without-order, or as just another instance of politics following its own odd ways. The former leads to analysis aimed at general explanation; the latter in either version to little more than episodic description.

This is all very summary; and I intend no more. It amounts to a claim for Marxism, not as some fount of eternal wisdom, let alone the sole fount; yet as one indispensable set of prescriptions for priorities in class analysis, and as one continuingly significant source of hypotheses or hunches to be explored by empirical research. I will add just one further point. This is that Marxism – again not uniquely, but quite unmistakably – embodies radical aspirations for social justice, anger over denial or bland concealment of injustice. I make no apology for the presence of those concerns in this book. Priorities in social science cannot be free of influence from value judgements, though the latter must then be tamed by respect for facts.

Part I
Theoretical Preliminaries and the Changing Framework of Economic Policy

1 Production, Distribution and Class Boundaries

Class cartography and the middle classes

Class division has, I suggest, three faces. It arises from inequalities of command over scarce economic resources. It acquires tangible force as a set of consequent inequalities of people's conditions and prospects in life. It finds in turn social, cultural and political expression in a wide diversity of forms. The latter range from the ritual gradations of respect and contempt, the patterns of ambition and deference, the demarcations of life-style and life-outlook between people of different class-place, which sociologists often bracket together as matters of 'status'; to the views people have of the class structure and their own situations within it, and the ways in which they may or may not then seek to join with others, and against further others, to change or to defend the class order as they see it: matters concerning perceptions of class 'interest', and action or inaction towards class 'mobilization'. But leave aside here what appears on this large third face of class. The first and the second faces are proper – and logically prior – subjects for close observation in their own right, wherever they show distinct disparities of economic power and welfare to people's life experiences and social relationships.

That, in summary, is the notion of class which runs through this book. My aim in the first chapter is to set down a few theoretical markers. These will be in no way comprehensive; and they will involve no general review of rival conceptions of class or competing approaches to its study. They will instead focus, quite narrowly, on the relationship between what I have called the first and second faces of class division: between inequality of power and inequality of welfare as the material axes of class structure. It may seem little more than banal to suggest, as I do, that the two must figure closely together in all attempts to map the contours of class. While inequalities of power play a prime formative role, they are relatively elusive as objects of direct investigation, in some part evident only from the inequalities of condition and opportunity they generate; the latter represent the most substantial as well as visible way in which class division has everyday impact and comes to be experienced. Yet straightforward though many readers may find the point, it has been denied or set aside in some important theoretical work. This has been so in such versions of Marxism as have insisted that class position in modern capitalist societies must be defined as a matter essentially of place in the command structure of production only: place in the distributive order of welfare and ill-fare is then seen as just a by-product, with little significance of its own for location on class maps. It has, moreover, been quite common for many other writers to take this brand of Marxism as prototypical of all Marxism: to regard overriding concern with command-in-production as a defining feature of Marxist class analysis, to the necessary marginalization of 'Weberian' concern with benefit-from-distribution in the form of unequal life chances.

I shall look critically here at these ideas and argue instead that all class analysis, whatever its theoretical inspiration, needs to take issues of distributive benefit just as fully on board as issues of power over production: questions about 'who gets what' as much as questions about 'who does what'. My way to that conclusion will be to review a debate among Marxists, from the 1970s on, about class boundaries. I look at this controversy because it very clearly exemplified the 'production orientation' I have outlined, an approach which leading participants commonly brought to bear on the business of class mapping otherwise in question among them. My interest here is more in that than in the immediate focus of the debate, though this was important enough. It concerned a set of the more intractable problems posed for Marxism over many years before, but ever more visibly: that the 'middle classes', far from being squeezed out between concentrated capital and mass labour, are growing both in numbers and maybe in detachment from either side. On this issue turn also that of the growth of 'big government', which employs many people of the new middle classes; and the prospects of any socialist transformation ever, when the numbers of the industrial wage-earning class originally assigned to carry it forward are declining apace.

The term 'middle class' itself begs the question of the debate. Taken literally, it would imply that the groups, categories, positions in the class structure at issue really all are 'in the middle'. Yet the term makes sense as preliminary shorthand, because that is how they look at first sight. By conventional classification they comprise two clusters. The 'old middle classes' are the self-employed and employers of relatively few employees who make up the classical petite bourgeoisie. Far fewer than they were once, they have not vanished, and in the service economies of the late twentieth century have even been finding new if often insecure footholds. The 'new middle classes' run to much larger numbers: the focus of the boundary debate has been on them.

These are people – or the positions occupied by people – who are employees yet whose circumstances in or from work separate them from, and place them 'above', other hired labour. Convention equates them with non-manual employees, though even cursory reflection should raise much doubt about the way convention includes, at either end, both plainly subordinate 'white-collar' workers and chief business executives. But even excluding those, the cluster would remain large, still growing and very diverse – 'classes' in the plural, if classes at all. Moreover, if the cluster may be trimmed to exclude significant fringe categories, it needs conceptual expansion and differentiation – as analysis does for any segment of the class structure – to take account, not just of the positions of people currently employed in places within the range, but also of the situation over long years of life of people whose circumstances and roles turn on their own sometime, or others' current or sometime, employment within the range.

The need to include dependent children for many purposes with their parents is obvious; but the inclusion of spouses with their partners, if definitions and counts go by households, is uncontentious only if the spouse has hardly ever engaged in paid work, or both partners are employed in fairly similar positions within the range. People who have spent much of their working lives in employment though currently out of work – unemployed, retired or whatever – can again, quite reasonably, be included for many purposes according to their places as they were before: their situation now will take much of its character from, and will in turn illuminate, the circumstances of their past employment. But the links between past and present – between role or rewards in employment and conditions of existence out of it – then need to be traced. Conversely, some of the people currently employed in a particular place within the range may be likely to stay there only briefly: such transients cannot readily be assigned membership of a 'class' merely by reference to what they do or get just now.

These points are worth noting here for two reasons. First, they have come more to the fore in recent years. The much increased share of married women in employment – and the sustained feminist pressure for proper recognition of its significance – have highlighted issues about the place in class analysis of women, gender relations and the domestic economy of households (for example, Crompton and Mann, 1986; Goldthorpe, 1983, and following debate; Pahl, 1984; McRae, 1986; Bonney, 1988a and b). Recessions and restructuring of the labour market have marginalized a growing number of people, with no foothold or only a shaky one in paid work, but all the more on that score to be explicitly counted in class analysis (for instance, Craig et al., 1985; Gallie, 1988a; Harris, 1987; Westergaard et al., 1989). Research on occupational mobility has shown that, for all the barriers that continue to make individual opportunity highly unequal, there is considerable movement – for men up more than down – in the course of working life; and that, again for men, low-grade white-collar employment in particular is often a stepping-stone in one direction or another rather than a fixed place (for example, Goldthorpe, 1987; Stewart et al., 1980; Westergaard and Resler, 1975, pp. 82–3).

Second, some of these points were long overlooked in the debate among Marxists about class boundaries. I suspect that this came in good part from a leading preoccupation with production at the expense of distribution. If people's class positions are to be defined in essence by the nature and role of the money-generating work they do, that for one thing seems to leave people who do no such work out on a limb. For another, priority of attention to roles in production over distributive outcomes comes readily to imply a focus on *positions* and their interrelations rather than on the unequal experiences of the *people* who fill them. The class structure is liable to be seen in one guise only: as a complex set of interdependent economic functions – functions of strategic command, day-to-day control, mediation, subordinate supply of labour – with little or no reference to the recruitment of people to those functions; without much attention to their lifetime experiences of success or adversity, affluence or hardship, influence, autonomy or dependence, security or insecurity, in engagement – or lack of access to engagement – with the system of production. Yet people's experiences in these senses must be of central importance, especially if a main point of class cartography is to identify the ways in which that system may give rise to politically potent group conflicts of interest. 'Structuration' by the pattern of personal life-courses surely matters for class mobilization or its inhibition (Giddens, 1973; also Westergaard and Resler, 1975; Goldthorpe, 1987).

These points, however, do not take away from the fact that the debate about class boundaries began with a sound problematic. How was the growth of the 'middle classes' to be taken into full account within a tradition which had ruled this sort of development to be only an evanescent phenomenon? Marx had certainly foreseen a proliferation of supervisory, technical, commercial and accounting functions ostensibly intermediate between capital and routine labour: this in necessary consequence of the growing scale and concentration of capital. But he had also anticipated that class polarization would proceed nonetheless, because the bulk of the new functions would involve subordinate roles and conditions of employment progressively aligning their incumbents with other hired labour; while the minority in the top echelons would be so closely associated with capital control and exploitation as to be effectively at one with it. The latter forecast – applied to the high executives, board members and key consultants of modern corporations, usually employees in name but prime wielders of capital power in fact – has indeed proved sound. The former forecast has not. Even within private enterprise, at least mid-level management, technical and commercial staff remain distinct from waged labour by role, status and rewards. Moreover, Marx had not foreseen the phenomenal growth of administrative, professional and semi- professional employment in government and public services.

There is no cause for surprise that, when Marxists turned to these issues, they put the roles of 'middle-class' employment in the productive system at the head of their analysis. Capitalism, in Marxist theory, is a 'mode of production'; and in any such mode, classes are formed, first, out of the parts which their members play in the predominant 'relations of production'. In the capitalist mode, capital and labour acquire their inherently opposed characters through their mutual relationships in production for capital accumulation. But there is cause – for Marxists too – to raise eyebrows when the necessary starting point in production often became the be-all and end-all of analysis. For in original Marxist theory, clearly, any mode of production is a mode also of distribution. Classes are in mutual opposition, actual or potential, as commanders and commanded in the economic system for output; but also as drawers of unequal shares in the proceeds. Command carries all important weight in determining the share-out: the main causal chain runs from production to distribution. But the conflicts of interest embedded in the system turn on the inequities of distribution no less. The issue of who has and who has not surely cannot be set aside.

Marx did not set it aside; if he had, exploitation would not have loomed as large in what he wrote as it did. The lead in the new class boundaries debate, however, was taken by Marxists who seemed to turn a wilfully blind eye to the issue. I shall take only three examples to illustrate this. But they represent a trend of thought that spread far among their fellows – far enough indeed for non-Marxists still commonly to regard it as endemic to all Marxism. And a later line of qualification – to be sketched in the third of my examples – went only part of the conceptual way to make amends.

Exploitation, deprivation and welfare shares

With work originally published in 1974, Nicos Poulantzas was perhaps the first very plainly to build so production-preoccupied a reading of Marxist axioms into resolving the problem of present-day boundaries (Poulantzas, 1975; also 1977). His argument started from the distinction between 'productive' and 'unproductive' labour; and with the contention that only the former category qualifies for inclusion in the working class. 'Productive' workers yield the surplus which capital appropriates. By contrast, 'unproductive' workers – including in Marx's own time domestic servants not least – take away from the surplus because they are paid out of it. So, however dependent their condition and low their share of income and opportunity, 'unproductive' workers form no part of the working class.

The distinction between productive and non-productive labour had 'textual authority', if not so clearly its application to class analysis. The next step in Poulantzas's argument was highly contentious, even if assessed solely by the criterion of fidelity to Marx. This was to count labour as productive only if employed in material production. The effect was by one stroke of the pen to compress 'the working class' to minority and still diminishing proportions. State employees were ruled out of it by and large; but private employees, too, fall outside the class of labour if their contribution to surplus does not take material form. Clerks and salespeople, stock-keepers and book-keepers, administrative personnel and advertising staff, may all contribute to the profit appropriated by capital because their work helps to keep the enterprise running or to sell the end-product. The end-product itself may be entirely material, though services can equally well yield profit for private appropriation. No matter: even when such people have entirely subordinate jobs, with poor wages and conditions to match, the assertion that only direct involvement in material production counts would leave them outside the working class. Poulantzas, moreover, put in another stroke of the pen to cut out even semi-manual employees whose work can be said to involve direct material production. Technicians and workfloor supervisors would not qualify because their work gives them a share in the knowledge through which capital control is exercised. So, in the end, this solution to the boundary problem mirrored everyday simplistic convention by firmly disqualifying all white-collar and white-blouse workers. It went beyond it in also disqualifying a fair number of workers-by-hand, to say nothing of those outside paid work.

Here was 'embourgoisement' with a vengeance, though the political implications would constitute no valid argument in rebuttal if the analysis made sense otherwise. In all reason it did not, even to the eyes of most Marxists; and Poulantzas's prescription did not catch on to inspire a new school. It might therefore be allowed to rest now, except that the grounds on which it has to be rejected bear upon a feature of Poulantzas's argumentation that survived dismissal of its detail. This was the narrow-sighted focus on production from which he began.

There is, first, no cause at all in Marxist logic to attach the label 'working class' only to materially productive labour. Intangible services as well as tangible goods are produced for profit; and material production itself requires input of a variety of immaterial services before profit can be realized by commodity sale. So if the working class is taken to include all those, at least, whose work contributes to profit yet gives them no matching share in it, then this class must include non-manual workers, service workers, technical staff and a range of related employees: provided only that their labour helps to make a surplus much of which other and privileged hands cream off. Significantly, the working class will then also include people whose work makes only an indirect contribution to profit-making. That point gives wide leeway for inclusion especially of workers in the public sector, if their work can reasonably be taken to help in making – by boosting, maintaining or protecting – an overall surplus for privileged appropriation with at best only a limited share for themselves.

Of course there is then also wide leeway for uncertainty in practical application. The issues here turn on two questions: what constitutes a contribution, notably an indirect contribution, to profit-making, and what constitutes effective sharing, or exclusion from sharing, in the proceeds? Answers to the first question require analysis of the parts played by different kinds of work, particularly in public employment, either in direct generation of profit for privileged appropriation or in keeping the economic system as a whole viably geared to profit accumulation. That itself is a formidable task of analysis – to which modern Marxist examination of 'the state' has had much to contribute. But the answers forthcoming will still be limited by a preceding assumption: that only work – or at least some sort of productive role – qualifies people for inclusion in the 'working class'.

The notion of work here may be extended to unpaid labour – on the part of women in particular – in domestic activity that can be seen to help 'maintain and reproduce' the active labour force. (For a concise summary of the relevant 'domestic labour debate' and its later ramifications, see for example, Bryson, 1992, chapter 13.) And as an analytical category 'work' can be stretched even to include the unemployed, on the ground that they make up a 'reserve army of labour' needed in a capitalist economy both at times of labour shortage and to keep the active workforce disciplined. These roles outside employment can still, plausibly, be described as 'productive'. But it is hardly possible to extend the notion still further to include, for example, those who have permanently retired or those who, well within working age, nowadays find themselves durably without chance of employment. The initial emphasis on productive role as the key to class cartography leaves them off the map: ostensibly with some logic, in first-shot Marxist terms, because they produce nothing, even indirectly, from which a surplus can be extracted.

By contrast, answers to the second question – what constitutes sharing or not sharing in the surplus? – need not and should not be tied down by a presupposition that the question concerns only those who make a direct or indirect contribution to production. True, Marxist class analysis starts with employers' extraction of profit from their workers' labour. But it has already conceded that surplus is appropriated in other ways too, once it allows that a 'reserve army of labour' and multitudes of 'housewives' contribute non-employed to a surplus which benefits capital in general rather than any particular employer; or that many public employees, through work that services the economy and its social framework, help to make a surplus which again goes to no particular employer. The first point to note here then is that, in aggregate, the surplus open to privileged appropriation is the product not just of individual enterprises, each yielding a profit distinctly its own for its shareholders, controllers or proprietors. It comes also from the larger workings of the economic and social system.

A second point follows immediately. If surplus at the end of the day is part-product of the system as a whole, then the question of who shares in it – and how much – concerns its distribution among all participants in the system: among all members of the society, whether at the time and as individuals they contribute to generation of the surplus directly, indirectly, or not at all. When they have to eke out an existence on low incomes, the old and the sick, the unemployed and the non- employed, are no less significantly cut out of benefit from the surplus than are rank-and-file wage-earners. They are not, it is true, 'exploited' in the specific sense that matters for analysis of the capitalist labour process; and the money to support them comes in large measure now from public funds that draw on business profit as well as labour earnings. Yet they are plainly deprived and dependent, substantially excluded from the gains of 'the system'. This condition of deprivation, dependency and exclusion they have in common with – and experience indeed in sharper form than – wage-earners whose work helps to produce the surplus. They are surely, on those grounds, either part and parcel of the working class or – as some commentary now has it – even an 'underclass' below the working class. But the grounds here require close attention to distribution as well as production. Focus on the latter only, and you leave such people by analytical default in a classless vacuum.

A third point reinforces this conclusion. The 'surplus' is no longer – if it ever was – susceptible of simple identification. It arises from a complex interplay of public agencies and policies with private enterprise. State activity both goes in part to support profit-making in the long run, and takes some part of profit away in a succession of shorter runs. Pressures from labour, actual and feared, have both made for much of this extension of public policy and, varyingly, hemmed in the space for private profit-making. But just how far shares in the overall surplus have shifted in consequence is hard to say. Even as a matter of direct return to capital, moreover, business profit cannot simply be read off company balance sheets. The accountants' books, and the published statistics that draw on their figures, understate it in a variety of ways.

Dividends, interest to creditors and undistributed profits make up only some of the total business surplus. Undervaluation of assets and of future profitability may come to light from time to time – during take-over bids, for example – in the form of reported capital gains; but not on a regular and comprehensive basis. Significant parts of the surplus privately appropriated figure as costs in the books. These include the salaries and honoraria of directors and top executives, on a formal par with wages but in reality a share for controllers in profit; the perks that go with them, underrecorded as income to the recipients but progressively larger and more sophisticated up the top rungs of the managerial scale; the consultancy fees and special inducements paid to well-placed outside companies and agents, which count as outgoings in the payers' ledgers but again often as 'wages', if at all, for those who get them. Other business practices, such as internal transfer-pricing by multinational corporations and inflation of research and development costs by contractors to government, provide examples again of the means by which private profit may be boosted yet kept out of full sight.

Not only all this, but business surplus comes into recognizable being only when a commodity or service is sold. There are no ready means to identify the specific profits generated at each point of the chain of activities that go before market realization. So the quantity and incidence even of direct 'exploitation' cannot be pinned down precisely link for

link. On all the counts enumerated above, exploitation, like deprivation in the larger sense, will be visible in its full range only as substantial exclusion from the global surplus of a capitalist economy: in practice
as a matter of the size of share in the aggregate of welfare produced.

The question of who gets what must then be as central to class
mapping as the question of who does what. There is another very
good reason why attention to shares in the outcome is important side
by side with attention to roles in the process that goes beforehand.
This concerns the place of 'interest' in notions of class. Class takes
pride of place in Marxist social inquiry because class situation is
seen there as a prime source of interest formation; so of overt or latent
group conflict, and in turn of potential changes of socio-economic
structure. The question of class interest in such change is the question of who, by the nature of that structure and in long-run likelihood,
will be for it, against it, or neither very obviously. Answers must
depend in large measure on who, plausibly, will benefit, who not,
and who neither very obviously. Benefit, to complete the point,
must surely be weighed in terms of conditions of livelihood at least as
much as in terms of roles in production. When Marx expected workers
of the world to unite in the fullness of time to shake off their chains,
he certainly saw those chains as forged from the subordination they
shared in work under capital's command. But he also saw their interest in losing them as charged from the deprivation in life circumstances they had in common as a result. Marx's vision of the future has
proved too sanguine; yet the point of principle stands. If one key
purpose of class analysis is to untangle the structurally embedded
group interests that bear upon continuity or change of the established
order, then divisions of economic condition signify in their own right;
not just as effects which illustrate the divisions of economic function
and power that are their prime cause. The commonsense meaning to
the question 'who will be better off from change?' is crucial.

Indeed, interest formation as the key to class definition loomed large
in the most cogent frontal attack on Poulantzas's thesis from a Marxist (Wright, 1976). Curiously, however, neither the author then or later,
nor some other commentators who similarly put conflicts of interest
high on the agenda of the boundaries debate, ventured to turn the
spotlight as fully on distribution as logic then required.

Global capital versus collective worker

To take a notable British example, Rosemary Crompton and John
Gubbay in *Economy and Class Structure* (1977) nailed their colours

firmly at the time to the mast of production-centred class analysis. Like Wright they differed from Poulantzas on two significant scores especially. First, they found no mileage to any crass distinction between 'productive' and 'unproductive' labour for understanding class division. Second, they directed attention forcefully to the many places in the class structure of production that have ambivalent features – 'structural ambiguities' in their words, attached to 'contradictory class locations' in Wright's words – which tend to pull incumbents of those places two ways: to partial alignment in structural logic with capital; yet at the same time also to alignment with labour. Here again was realism. Where Poulantzas had assigned very large numbers of people – or places – indiscriminately to a 'petty bourgeois' limbo, analysis in this alternative mode required scrutiny of the diverse mixtures of roles associated with ostensibly middle-class work.

The key to unravelling these mixtures, Crompton and Gubbay argued, was to be found in a dichotomy of basic productive functions that marks capitalist economies. Drawing in part on Carchedi (1975) they set off the function of 'global capital' against that of the 'collective worker'. The former embraces all activities that go into directing economic enterprise towards the distinctive objective of capitalism: the appropriation and accumulation of surplus. The latter function includes, besides immediately productive work in plainly subordinate roles, a range of activities necessary for 'coordination' in any complex economy. There is, however, no simple dichotomy of actual jobs to match the conceptual dichotomy of functions. Over a wide range between two poles, many non-manual and even some manual occupations mix a part in mere coordination with another part in control for surplus accumulation. They mix a labour role with a capital role; and the ratios of the mixture vary. The range runs in the private sector from the classically marginal places of foremen and supervisors to management proper and supporting professional staff; and it has been stretched sideways by the growth of public-sector employment, whose activities bear indirectly, diversely and contradictorily on surplus accumulation for capital.

Recognition of this multiplicity of 'structural ambiguities' took class analysis a good step forward, but still little beyond the territory of production relations. Crompton and Gubbay in 1977 were as yet insistent in their dismissal of distribution – 'exchange relations' – as of no more than second-order importance. True, they acknowledged that 'the production process and the exploitation process are *fused together*'; and they allowed conditions of living and opportunity to figure in the analysis at a number of points: yet in principle only as features following from, and to be explained by, roles in production.

The key part played by production in determining class overall was assumed to give it a virtually exclusive part in defining the detailed configuration of class.

This could make good enough sense, if class boundaries drawn by reference to the relations of production coincide pretty well with boundaries drawn by reference to inequalities from distribution. And there is quite a degree of coincidence; yet not a sufficient degree. For one thing, boundary drawing with only production in mind either misses out the durably non-employed; or it can include them only by resort to conceptual back-doors that raise problems I shall discuss later. For another thing, even when it comes to people who are actively employed, there is no easy fit at all points between the lines of class indicated from a production-centred perspective and the lines suggested when the outcomes of distribution are brought into play. The fit is good, of course, at the narrow top and at the broad bottom. At the top in the dominant private sector, command to capital ends comes together with high privilege. And at the base of both private and public sectors, the total exclusion of routine labour from control to any end goes together with low or limited pay, conditions and opportunities. But between those two opposites – not in dispute anyway – there are real problems, above and beyond the difficulties of effectively distinguishing work in 'control' from work in mere 'coordination'. Take the case of such managerial and professional employment as may be shown to involve no control on behalf of global capital, only coordination of the sort needed in any complex economy. This sort of work should, by the theory, take its incumbents into labour's class bag; and indeed they can, reasonably, be ascribed an interest in acquiring a part in command over the ultimate ends of their work from which, as mere coordinators, they are excluded. That exclusion they share with routine workers. Yet even as mere coordinators, they will usually also enjoy a variable mix of advantages – in pay, perks, promotion prospects and the like – over routine workers. That must surely tell against assigning the two groups more or less on a par to the same class bag.

The example is no doubt more relevant to public-sector than to private-sector employment. Even low-level supervision in private business may, arguably, involve a small ingredient of 'control' – that is, on behalf of global capital – inasmuch as the enterprise as a whole is indisputably directed to capital ends. But, at any level, public-sector work is more ambiguous of function *vis-à-vis* capital. Some central government departments or sections within them can perhaps readily be ascribed an overriding if indirect contribution to the purposes of global capital. To that extent their top staff take part in 'control', in principle much as do senior business executives; and staff below or ancillary to them mix 'control' with 'coordination' in much the same manner as their private sector equivalents. But there are many other central government agencies with no such clear-cut role *vis-à-vis* global capital. Health, education and social security services mix support for capital purposes with coordination of the sort needed whatever the overall thrust of the economic system, and in turn with a degree of provision of real benefits for labour. If they help to 'reproduce labour' and 'maintain legitimacy', their activities have also grown under popular pressure and to some genuine though limited redistributive effect. So the staff of these services have significantly more chequered 'functions' *vis-à-vis* capital than do central government staff – say in economic policy agencies – whose work is more or less fully in line with capital's interests.

Yet at each particular level of the administrative hierarchy, civil service pay, conditions and prospects are much the same whatever the 'functions' of the department; and from about midway up they also show in common a lack of the special perks and privileges of equivalent private sector employment. Though there are qualifications, government employment is on these scores enough of a world to itself to resist ready assimilation to a model of the class structure which takes location in it to be set only by productive function *vis-à-vis* capital purposes. Mobility of staff between offices with different mixes of function adds further weight to the point. All in all, by the test of interest formation, it makes sense to describe the class situation of civil servants in posts of authority, let alone of welfare professionals, at least as much by reference to the career circumstances they have in common as by reference to the differences between them in the functions of their particular offices. They might also be ascribed some special common stake in maintenance, even advancement, of the public sector from which they draw their livelihood.

Re-focusing on exploitation

The work of Eric Olin Wright – my third example – has made a formidable contribution to the debate about class boundaries. His opening shot (1976) was followed by a series of influential books (1978, 1979, 1985) and papers; and his ideas there have shown a notable and explicit shift: from once overriding concern with control and subordination in production, to a later focus on relations of exploitation. But this shift still did not take him all the way to allowing distribution the place it warrants in all analysis of class.

Wright set out this change of stance in detail in *Classes* (1985). Before that he had underlined interest formation as the ultimate concern for class analysis. He had highlighted ambivalences of class position as the distinctive common feature of the 'middle classes', and coined the term 'contradictory locations' for them. He had elaborated new classifications of class to incorporate such 'structural ambiguities' (to use the more or less parallel term coined by Crompton and Gubbay), and tried these out first in application to American data. All this and more, however, had still turned on the limiting assumption that, for analysis of class 'in itself,' people's places in the structure must be defined by their roles in the system of production and its chain of command. What they get will, by and large, follow from what they do in these senses; and whether it does follow is one test of such a class typology. But it is still role in production – by way of control, subordination or some internally contradictory mixture – that is the key to defining class. In retrospect by 1985, Wright described this assumption as over-concerned with 'dominance'. The upshot of his doubts was a distinct shift of attention to 'exploitation'. Wright now distinguished four types of asset, unequal possession of which makes for class exploitation. Unequal ownership of labour power was the key to feudal exploitation of serfs by lords; unequal ownership of capital in the means of production is the pivotal mode of exploitation in capitalist economies; occupation of controlling office in powerful formal organizations is the prime form of exploitation in 'statist' societies, such as the Soviet Union as it was then; possession of credentials – recognized skills in specialist work – would remain a source of some privilege even in an alternative 'socialist' society that fell short of full egalitarian 'communism'. Each type of asset, however, is not unique to the mode of production it typifies. Modern capitalism thus puts capital ownership first among the means of exploitation; but it allows exploitation also through the third and fourth types of asset, organization (for short) and credentials.

It follows that a schema to map class locations in a modern capitalist economy must recognize three dimensions of exploitation: ownership of productive capital; but also organizational office, and work expertise or credentials. And, Wright now concluded, with allowance for degrees of marginality in the possession or non-possession of these assets twelve categories were needed for adequate classification. These ran from the bourgeoisie proper, as distinct from small employers and the petite bourgeoisie employing virtually no hired labour; through various mixes of 'contradictory location' among employees; to 'proletarian' wage-earners – whether blue-collar or white-collar – who have not even minor supervisory authority or a modicum of recognized skills to part-offset their lack of capital owner-ship.

Wright's tests of this exploitation-centred model, against survey data for the working population of the United States in 1980, showed a better fit with both income distribution and political opinion than did classifications based either on Poulantzas's prescriptions or on the conventional distinction between manual and non-manual labour. And, complemented by Swedish data, the schema also seemed to undermine a common assumption that the 'working class' is a mi-nority of fast-diminishing significance. As against a bourgeoisie and petty bourgeoisie of at most 15 per cent all told, some half or more of all people in paid work could be classified as 'proletarian' if 'semi-credentialled' workers without supervisory authority were added in. Still, at least a third of the working population in either country was assigned to some sort of 'contradictory location', rather more if house-holds were counted instead of individuals. Ambiguity of class posi-tion is a prominent feature of modern capitalism's socio-economic structure; and Wright later found grounds to stress precisely the steady growth of 'non-proletarian locations' (Wright and Martin, 1987).

Careers, jobs and exclusion from jobs

The practical serviceability of the schema has been sharply challenged (for example, Marshall et al., 1988); and Wright himself has added some second thoughts (1989). My concern, however, is with the basic rationale of his 1985 model as an example of the preoccupation with places in production which still held sway then over Marxist ap-proaches to class, even with exploitation readmitted centre-stage. Subsidiary points apart, I see two shortcomings to the logic of Wright's paradigm shift.

One is that it focussed only on the various sources or means of exploitation; not, for purposes of typology, on the outcomes of exploitation. True, income distribution was used to test the schema; yet its patterns were not examined in their own right, for possible feedback effect to modify that schema. Had they been so examined, they would almost certainly have shown a significant line of distinc-tion among employees, overlying their classification by 'organization' and 'credentials'. This is the distinction between 'jobs' and 'careers'. It takes typical courses of life experience in and from work into account. And it marks off employees in mundane work which, whether ma-nual or non-manual, offers at best small prospects of advancement, of pay incrementation and of pension security, from employees who by contrast can count on some sustained personal progress during much of their working lives and on relatively good protection in retirement.

I try to look at how the distinction between jobs and careers applies in Britain later in this book (chapter 10). If this division is indeed prominent in the unequal distribution of economic life circumstances, it must have considerable bearing on the way people to either side of it manage or cope with their lives; can or cannot effectively plan for the future; are likely to see the world around them; and so also are likely to form political views and allegiances. Means to chart this line then need to have a place in the tools of class cartography. The outcome may be to show a line between jobs and careers more blurred than schematic typification suggests. It may be, in any case, to show rough coincidence between that line and the initial exploitation-centred model's division between working-class jobs and more or less indisputably 'contradictory locations'. It is also a distinction open to manipulation by employers, as large Japanese corporations' provision for 'lifetime employment' well down the occupational scale indicates. But it can be mapped only through direct attention to distributive inequalities of condition in life.

Not that conventional classifications of class are better designed to pinpoint the division between jobs and careers than Wright's 1985 typology; and he, indeed, explicitly regretted his inability at the time to pursue analysis of employees' 'trajectories' over their working lives (a line of inquiry he has since begun to explore: Wright and Shin, 1988). Yet full mapping of the differences between jobs and careers requires not only that direct account be taken of patterns of income, security and mobility during people's working lives – in itself a widening of focus from sources of exploitation; but also that their economic experiences be followed up in their lives out of work, in retirement and ill health, unemployment and non-employment.

Here is a second main shortcoming to Wright's exploitation- centred model. When he paradoxically excluded non-working *rentiers* from his survey coverage, this was no doubt largely because practicalities prevented collection of information on ownership of capital. But when he also excluded all others not in paid work, this seems to have been on grounds of logic. Exploitation takes place only in work: people outside work cannot be exploited, because they produce nothing for others to appropriate. So an exclusive focus on exploitation, like an exclusive focus on production and its chain of command, leaves the front door of class analysis closed to large numbers of people who are out of paid work, severely deprived though many of them are.

There are back doors which can let them in. I have noted two already. One door may admit 'housewives', as engaged in 'maintenance and reproduction' of members of the active labour force. The other may admit a 'reserve army of labour' on the fringes of the employment market. Both categories can be said to have a 'function' for the productive system. They may even be regarded as 'exploited', because they get little or nothing for performing that function. But neither back door can be used to admit all those people who will stay outside the world of paid work because they are retired or chronically ill, or because modern capitalist economies may be moving towards a permanent excess of labour supply over demand. Most such people can still be assigned places in the map of class by other conceptual devices. One is relevant if they worked before: they may be placed according to the work they did then. Another device is relevant if they are 'dependent' members of households with one or more active earners: they, like children, may then be assigned to the class location indicated by the earners' work.

Use of both devices is, of course, common practice and hangs on an assumption that the circumstances of non-earners are likely to reflect the nature and rewards of the work which either they did themselves when earning, or those other earners do on whom they depend. That is a sound enough assumption. But the trouble about it for production- or exploitation-centred analysis is that it would allow, into the definition of class locations, a relevance to circumstances of living which this sort of analysis is not in principle willing to concede. Alternatively, production-and exploitation-centred analysis might resort to a different assumption, if only to use the first device. It could argue that former earners are likely to carry with them, into retirement, unemployment or non-employment, those inclinations of socio-political interest which were suggested by their class locations when they were at work. Such an assumption, however, implies a greater concern with individual movement in life, and the ways in which it is experienced, than fits with a rigorously production-centred focus on work roles alone.

In any case, those who want and need paid work but cannot find it have a claim to representation in class maps in respect of their condition as it is; not merely by reference to such work as they may have done in the past, or as dependents of other household members who may be employed. They are short of an asset that did not figure in Wright's 1985 list: access to regular employment. And that is a crucial asset in an economy where, for the majority of the population without income from property, livelihood above a low level of state support depends on regular employment.

Class interests and economic life chances

Capitalism then is not just a system of command and subordination, exploitation and subjection to exploitation, in the processes of production. It is also a system of distribution, the distinctive inequalities of which spread from the world of work, employment earnings and market profits to affect the livelihood, security and opportunities of all – those outside that world, or on its fringes, as well as those within it. Maps of the class structure therefore have to cover all, and to take account of distributive inequality both in and outside work. They need to do so in all class analysis, because the structural inequalities of distribution set very different terms of life for different groups of people. Class mapping in Marxist analysis needs to take direct account of distribution for yet another reason: because long-term collective interests for and against change of the economic system and its socio-political framework are bound to be charged by considerations of welfare and ill-fare, privilege and deprivation – by people's contrasting experiences in the order of distribution.

It is pertinent then to ask: if distribution really does matter so much for class analysis, why did a good many Marxists from the 1970s turn a near-blind eye to it? The answer, I think, is not to be found mainly in the convolutions of abstraction, and the distaste for empirical inquiry, with which I charged some then leading neo-Marxist schools in my Introduction. At least, such charges would be grossly unfair applied either to Crompton and Gubbay or to Wright. The answer is rather to be found in a concern to retain, intact and unsullied, more of what seemed central in Marxist theory than was either necessary or compatible with fruitful present-day development of the theory.

Widening the scope of class mapping to take in distribution fully alongside production could be seen as contaminating Marxism with Weberianism; and it was so seen, for instance, by Crompton and Gubbay in 1977 in very explicit terms. They were in my view right, like other Marxists, to insist that the main chain of causation runs from power over production to benefit from distribution. But if the further logic of Marxist analysis nevertheless requires direct attention to the latter as much as to the former – to people's economic life chances as much as to their economic roles by way of command or subordination – then for my part it makes no odds that the term 'life chances' was Weber's. It may be a moot point just how far Marx, while not coining the term, still gave weight to its substance. But that is a point of more interest for scholastic exegesis than for understanding of the world as it now is, and may become. If Marxism can draw on 'bourgeois' theory to amplify its force, this should count as gain rather than contamination. Even should the outcome be a hybrid compound of theory in which Marxist strands intertwine with others to the frustration of textbook schematics, this will be gain provided only that it stands up to the tests which must be set to all theory: of consonance with reality and of insight for explanation and conjecture about the future. Purity or impurity of conceptual origin is of no matter in itself.

2 Corporatism as a New Economic Order?

Framework planning and labour discipline

The preceding argument may have been rather abstract. But in turning now to discussion of the shifting parameters of economic policy over the past half-century, I aim also to illustrate more concretely the general point that distributive inequality must figure centrally in class analysis. Those fifty years or so have seen the rise and decline of 'tripartite corporatism'. This was the set of extended relationships between government, business and trade unions which evolved for macro-economic management in many western countries during the post-war boom, in Britain reaching their height in the 1960s and 1970s; and matters of share-out between classes were very visible on corporatist agendas.

The development of tripartism raised questions about the larger nature of the changes in economic organization involved. One view, vigorously if somewhat idiosyncratically asserted for a time, held that corporatism was close to constituting a wholly new order, equally distinct from capitalism and socialism. I focus on that thesis in this chapter because, so I suggest, the test of the general character of any economic system turns on its dominant criteria for resource allocation, among which the criteria for distribution of wealth and welfare are ultimately decisive. By a test of that sort, corporatism involved no displacement of capitalism or of a capitalist mode of class structure.

This conclusion repeats an argument from an earlier paper of mine (Westergaard, 1977). But, as I go on to discuss in chapter 3, tripartite corporatism has of course since been the target of fierce political challenge, in Britain not least from 1979: this on a reigning assumption that it involved a move, not to an economic order of its own separate kind, but into socialism. That assumption had some obstensible plausibility only in one case, that of Sweden; and even there an abortive social-democratic move towards public control of the commanding economic heights was in fact a quite explicit attempt to breach the policy constraints of corporatism-within-capitalism, rather than any evolutionary development of corporatism itself. Tripartism's vulnerability to political challenge from the right came, not because it harboured radical socialist substance, but in large part because it highlighted tensions from distributive inequality which it could not resolve. Yet the old laissez-faire regime with which the 'new' right have sought to replace it may prove no less unstable, on grounds no less connected with class inequalities of distribution.

The sorts of arrangement for the governance of economic affairs which have been called corporatist, prominent in many western countries from the 1950s onwards, involved a still further extension of state economic intervention, above and beyond those measures which, a decade or two earlier, had been prompted by interwar recession, wartime mobilization and post-war reconstruction. To take the British case, the package of reforms adopted in the 1940s for 'social reconstruction' had in no way been intended to take the country's economy out of a capitalist framework. The purpose was certainly to reduce economic insecurity, for labour as well as for business; but also to ensure the future viability of property, profit and markets. That was to remain the case even with the subsequent further enlargement of the role of government. Though once perhaps familiar enough, in the present era of marketeering the story of state growth from the 1940s to the 1970s has taken on a character of public mythology, where right-inclined demonology vies with left-inclined nostalgia. So the story needs summary retelling here, to set old bare facts against new favoured fictions.

The main ingredients of the 1940s settlement – 'full employment', promotion of economic growth, comprehensive welfare provision – were endorsed in principle by both major political parties; and though only completed by the post-war Labour government, measures to implement them were set in train already by the wartime coalition government. The prime economic objectives were assumed to be achievable largely through budgetary management of aggregate demand, without government planning in more directive forms; wartime controls were steadily diminished even before the Conservative party took office again in 1951; and if at first seen by the left as a step towards socialism, Labour's nationalization programme was broadly confined to industries over which some form of public regulation was then widely thought necessary, in the interests of economic growth and business development at large. A few other policies of the late 1940s had more radical overtones – the establishment of a free and universal National Health Service; an attempt to transfer future 'development value' in land to the public purse; concentration of the provision of new housing in the hands of local and other government authorities. But the latter two features of policy were progressively abandoned during and after the 1950s; and the main social security provisions were explicitly intended to keep rates of benefit well below wage levels, so out of competition with labour market 'incentives'.

The general thrust of 'big government' was thus still scrupulously limited in purpose to fit with the economic imperatives of a capitalist economy. The process of state growth, however, did not stop there. From around 1960 in Great Britain, first Conservatives and then Labour in office moved to the adoption of a series of measures to extend public control and guidance of the national economy. These were essentially of two kinds.

One kind went towards steerage and support of capital investment: an enhanced mix of controls, grants, loans, infrastructural provision and pilot projects to promote industrial 'restructuring' and 'modernization'; even a short-lived national economic plan in emulation of the 'indicative planning' which was then widely believed to have brought the French economy from the early into the late twentieth century over just a few years.

The other kind comprised measures to restrain wage demands and maintain labour discipline. 'Incomes policies' were here the centrepiece. But since prime emphasis was put as yet on achieving labour discipline in cooperation with the trade unions, such policies were extended in name and form to embrace salaries as well as wages; and, on occasion, to include some provision for supervision of prices and profits. They also at times involved government promises of a more tangible quid pro quo for labour: of relatively better real wages for the lowest-paid; of positive redistribution through tax or benefit reform; or of enhanced union recognition. Such promises were in Britain most explicit in the Labour government's 'social contract' with the trade unions from 1974, and similar in broad purpose to the policy of 'wage solidarity' which had become a feature of Swedish corporatist measures for regulation of the labour market. They were intended as inducements for labour to acquiesce in the industrial discipline that was the overriding aim. In turn, labour acquiescence in discipline was one of the inducements held out to business for its cooperation; support for investment, aid in business adversity, greater market predictability, were others.

Government resort to measures of these two kinds was a response to similarly dual pressures. On the one hand, the economic boom had been carried at first by expansion along previously established lines: by reconversion of industry to peacetime production; by raising output from existing capital resources nearer to full capacity; by ploughing back profit into further investment in much the same types of production, this well before the information technology 'revolution'; and by drawing on 'reserves' of labour, married women and immigrants in particular. By the 1960s, however, continued expansion along these lines had already begun to look uncertain. Profits showed incipient signs of slippage; international trading competition was sharper; and production from new competitors in the world market was putting the industrial dominance of the North Atlantic metropolitan core at risk. Intricately tied into the international economy, long characterized by slower growth rates than most of its rivals, and with a steadily falling share of world trade, Britain seemed especially vulnerable.

These pressures towards public economic planning, restructuring and modernization also helped to give another set of pressures a full head of steam: they were to curb what increasingly came to be seen as labour indiscipline. Boom had put organized labour in a seller's market. By the 1960s workers, through their unions and on the shopfloors, had begun to pull muscle more than for several decades before. Wage claims were pitched more ambitiously. Pay settlements could be reached locally that allowed 'wages drift' above the norms set in 'framework agreements' at national level. The incidence of strikes was rising: first and always foremost in 'unofficial' and localized disputes; but by the end of the 1960s also through industry-wide action with central union sponsorship. The lead in militancy, moreover, no longer came from old historically strike-prone yet declining industries; but, ominously, from some of the growing sectors hitherto regarded as relatively immune from overt strife – from engineering, car manufacture in particular, and later from some public services.

None of this gave workers or trade unions any self-evident power to command, for all the comment which so asserted. More aggressive wage claims might for a time disturb the detail of pay differentials between occupational groups and industrial sectors. But when settlements exceeded productivity gains, wage increases could generally be passed on in – or were themselves triggered by – higher prices. They led to no substantial redistribution of real income in favour of wage-earners at large. The shop stewards and conveners who ran the now greatly expanded sub-union network of shopfloor organization were far more engaged in preventing than in fomenting active conflict; and their role was, in general, correspondingly appreciated by management close to production, if not by top executives and board members. Strike action remained the exception in everyday working life, not the rule; and it never put Britain so high in international league tables as was implied by the conventional wisdom that labour unrest was 'the British disease'. (I have drawn for this compressed summary largely on Westergaard and Resler, 1975, and on the sources cited there.)

Nevertheless, labour indiscipline was on the increase. The pressure of wage claims could be seen as inflationary, and it was commonly so seen, before the spread of a 'monetarist' economic theory which put the blame more on the 'softness' of governments in allowing the supply of money to grow out of control, in response to a clamour of generally 'rising expectations'. In turn, rising inflation was seen to accentuate Britain's weakness in world trading competition; to put the City of London's distinctive role in international finance at risk; and to augment market uncertainties. Perhaps above all, growing labour assertiveness – especially the spread of shopfloor organization outside the ambit of centralized bargaining between national trade unions and employers' organizations – appeared to herald 'anarchy'. Enhanced shopfloor self-confidence also put inhibitions in the way of managerial discretion to 'restructure'. For all these reasons control of labour became the prime purpose of corporatist policies: more persistently pursued than economic 'planning'; and in Britain especially so, where the international vulnerability of the national economy helped to raise political, business and media criticism of labour indiscipline to campaign proportions.

Elaboration of tripartite liaison between government, business and unions was not the only way in which resolution might have been sought. An alternative set of policy prescriptions would be to crack down directly on unions and shopfloor organization, and to seek more leeway for market forces to discipline ailing business as well as obstreperous workers. Advocacy of this line of approach grew from the mid-1960s. But though foreshadowed in some features of policy from then onwards, notably during the first year or two of the 1970–4 Conservative government under Mr Heath, a combination of free-market liberalism with authoritarianism became the ruling formula only from 1979. Until then corporatist prescriptions were usually in leading place. They were nearest to hand. They required no overt breach of the 1940s political settlement. And they sought support from trade union leaders, when the alternative of head-on confrontation with organized labour was still risky in the eyes of government and many employers because economic boom had not yet definitely turned down into recession.

Corporatism *sui generis*?

'Corporatism' is a tag sometimes applied to widely varying pheno-
mena: including even Fascist and Nazi suppression of independent
trade unions and their replacement by purportedly common organizations of employers and employees; including also a whole range of
relationships between government and other large organizations
under which ostensibly private bodies are given public accreditation
as consultants on, and agents of, government policy (see especially
Schmitter, 1974; cf. also Cawson, 1986). In the main, however, the term
has had more specific application to the most significant triad of such
relationships: those between government, business and unions for
macro-economic management. There is now a considerable literature
on such tripartism, from which I need list only a few key examples
(Crouch, 1977; Middlemas, 1979; Panitch, 1980, 1981; McEachern,
1990) besides the distinctive thesis which I take up next.

This was one argued forcefully by Jack Winkler (1975, 1976, 1977).
One point in it was a prognosis which subsequent events have signally refuted: that by the 1980s Britain would, in all likelihood, be
fully immersed in corporatist arrangements for economic steerage.
True, Winkler toyed briefly with an alternative scenario directed to
'freeing' market play. But he put his own bet plainly on extended
corporatism. The failure of this prophecy, however, is far less an
adverse commentary on his analysis than just one illustration of the
widespread failure of professional social commentary to foresee the
sea-change which the Thatcher electoral victory in 1979 was to mark.
And while the potential instability of corporatism which that change
underlined escaped Winkler's attention, the core of his thesis still
deserves careful examination. This was that, taken to full-blown form,
corporatist arrangements would constitute an economic system *sui
generis*, qualitatively different from both capitalism and socialism. The
argument can be summarized in three points. First, the state had
acquired and could be expected further to acquire effective powers of
control over business policy which went far beyond earlier measures
of support, guidance and occasional selective intervention. These
powers included, crucially, control over profits, prices and investment
as well as wages and salaries: in short, over the key variables hitherto
determined by business policy and market forces. This was control
capable of direction at will to individual businesses and particular
sectors of the economy; not just to modifying an overall climate in
which decisions were still made and their criteria determined by
private enterprise. Legal ownership of business remained

predominantly in private hands, however. The privileges of property no longer included the capacity to take those crucial decisions about resource allocation formerly regarded as prerogatives of private ownership; even the right to extract profit was now hedged with restrictions. But state appropriation of these powers would continue to leave an elaborate facade of private property in being; by the same token also of managerial responsibility for the implementation of state-determined policy and managerial authority over labour. It was that conjunction of state control with private legal ownership and private exercise of everyday management which first signalled the emergence of a new corporatist economic system. In Winkler's summary, the qualitative range of state control marks corporatism off from capitalism. Retention of the legal framework and managerial machinery of private property – coupled with policy assumptions that 'distinct class and functional interests' will remain but 'must be made to collaborate' – marks it off from socialism.

Second, state control in its new forms was steered by four principles, which together gave corporatism its distinctive stamp. One was unity, a sanctification of cooperation in place of competition. Another was order, the application of discipline and collective self-restraint in place of both market anarchy and industrial conflict. The third was nationalism: corporatism sought prosperity for the nation as an entity, over the particular interests of particular groups or the freedom of individuals to make their own ways to success or failure; and it involved mercantilist assertion of a common national interest *vis-à-vis* other nations and economic operations controlled from abroad. The fourth was success, a commitment to results with scant concern for means: corporatist policy was prepared to ride roughshod over the rule of law to realize its objectives.

The principle of 'success' loomed sufficiently large to merit elaboration as the third main feature in this picture of the emerging corporatist system. State control was exercised in large measure behind the scenes: by discretionary use of financial force, bargaining strength and elastically defined authority, in ways which would shield decision-making from effective public scrutiny. If legislation was needed, the model was the enabling act, which confers large and loosely bounded powers on government and its agents. The crucial decisions on resource allocation would be made in negotiations between state and private enterprise; but with the state in a position generally to ensure business compliance in its policy and in the principles of 'unity', 'order', 'nationalism' and 'success'. Parliament delegated policy-making to government; government delegated policy implementation and managerial authority to business; the trade unions, too, were recruited as agents in so far as they could be reliably co-opted. But the power to prevail in the processes of bargaining in Whitehall, corporation and union headquarters where investment, expansion and contraction were determined, prices, profits and wage levels set – that power was with the state.

Both the growth of state activity and a progressive separation of control from ownership were familiar threads in familiar arguments that capitalism was in process of erosion. But the valuation which went with this version of old themes was hostile. There was to Winkler's argument none of the complacency which had marked earlier theses proclaiming the 'civilization' of market forces through managerial supremacy or 'mixed economy' welfare policies. On the contrary, the vision here – like Burnham's long before (Burnham, 1945) – was that of a new, insidious usurpation of bureaucratic power. While corporatism would leave the formal shells of liberal democracy and legal procedure intact, it was embedding irresponsible economic control in processes hidden from sight. Even so, Winkler did not pin his designation of corporatism as a distinctive economic order to his description of the machinery of government. The keystone of the argument was the postulate of state direction, whatever its forms, and of its conjunction with a continuing framework of private property and private managerial authority.

It should be obvious that this reading of a funeral sermon over capitalism could not be dismissed merely by a counter-assertion that capitalism remains so long as private ownership remains. That would be to retreat into semantics. Nor would it be sufficient in rebuttal to pick out features in the ideology schematically attributed to corporatist policy which have a long history in uncontestably capitalist economic systems. Conservative and even free-market liberal appeals for 'order' have been a perennial refrain in education and exhortation directed especially at labour. Successful capitalist enterprise has long sought – and often managed to get – state aid to consolidate its success by eliminating insecurity from market competition: 'unity' in that sense was no new aspiration. 'Nationalist' protection of domestic private enterprise had been the rule rather than the exception in capitalist economies. Nevertheless, these well-worn features, so the logic of Winkler's argument appeared to be, had acquired new significance when they came together as the bearing ideas in a new context. It is the shift of context which is the issue: the postulated subordination of economic decisions on key matters to state direction.

So any critique must focus on just that contention; and it must test it, I suggest, by asking three closely related questions. First, in what sense can a corporatist state be said to direct: where in fact are the sources of control over economic affairs? Next, wherever the sources of control, what are the criteria by which it is exercised? What yard-sticks and operating assumptions are used to allocate resources in a corporatist set-up? What finally, and crucially, is the distributional outcome: to whose benefit does corporatism work, by what principles of interest and justice?

Sources of control: the state

These are the issues central to any characterization of an economic system, any attempt to demarcate one mode of production from others. Winkler's analysis, however, was addressed in the main only to the first question; and even in his answers to this there were noticeable gaps.

One gap concerned the conception of the state. Concede, for the sake of argument, that the state had acquired the decisive means of economic control attributed to it. The question then looms large: what was the nature of this state, on the face of things capable of directing privately owned business this way or that? Winkler briefly recognized the question, and translated it from 'what is the state?' to 'what does the state do?' The translation was reasonable enough. But to ask what the state does must be, in large part, to ask what concrete interests the state serves by its actions. Yet there was no answer even, as I shall argue later, from the four guiding principles of state policy. The state, for all the powers attributed to it, was left a paradoxically unknown quantity.

At some points the argument implied that state policy was shaped by a variety of 'outside' pressures: popular pressures, for example, to trim monopoly profits. But the nature and direction of such influences upon state policy, above all their relative impact on the outcome if and when they pulled different ways, were issues barely even identified. In turn, that neglect of the balance among prevailing winds suggests an alternative assumption that there were no prevailing winds which mattered very much. *Either*, then, the corporatist state was in some absolute sense an autonomous entity: a creature with will and interest of its own – of some or all of its office holders in this or that combination of predominant influence – to infuse into state use of the means of economic control. But if that was the assumption, this 'state will' remained unexplained. Its sources, formation and direction were not described. *Or perhaps* state will could not effectively be distinguished from the wills of significant 'outside' interests, because state policy objectives largely coincided with the policy objectives accepted by other interests: interests co-opted, cajoled, pressed into service as agents of the state. But if the state then is assigned a dominant role, its dominance must mean that there is at least a logical divergence between its interest and those of other significant groups: at least an initial, maybe a perennially latent, divergence of interests, though this in practice is resolved or suppressed by the state's postulated capacity to bring about 'outside' endorsement of its policy objectives. So in this version too the corporatist state must be an entity in its own right, with interests for the direction of economic management somehow peculiar to itself. Yet the argument evaded this conclusion.

If the state thus figured in a curiously disembodied form, so its ability to put its powers to uses of its own was only asserted, not demonstrated. If a 'pluralist' methodological prescription were adopted to assess the hypothesis that the state must prevail in corporatist bargaining and manipulation, these processes themselves would need systematic observation. The 'inputs' from the various contending parties would have to be compared with the outcome, to establish the locus or loci of power. Winkler did not attempt to clinch his case in this manner. A pluralist procedure would in any case be insufficient for the purpose, because it would leave out of consideration the ways in which areas for reciprocal bargaining and pressure are usually confined by prior assumptions on the part of the contending parties about the limits to their potential influence and the bounds of practicable policy 'in the world as it is'. Winkler indeed suggested just some such prior confinement of areas of dispute to a narrow range, when he referred to business and union endorsement of objectives which he ascribed to government. But he neither showed, nor set out criteria by which to show, that this concordance marked a predominance of state over business and unions – rather than, say, of business over state and unions. Yet that is just the point at issue.

Purposes of control: production

To tackle it one must look at the purposes of the measures of state direction said to define corporatism. More particularly, one must look at the criteria for resource allocation which govern such economic decisions as a corporatist government takes or underwrites. In short, an answer to the first test question, concerning sources of control, requires now an answer to the second: by what yardsticks and operational assumptions are key decisions for production and investment made? Were corporatism truly a mode of production categorically distinct from capitalism, these yardsticks and assumptions must be

correspondingly distinct from those which determine resource allocation in a capitalist system. There was, however, little in Winkler's
analysis to confirm that new economic criteria were at work. The four
guiding 'principles' of corporatist policy set no prescriptions for
allocation of resources. They were empty vessels into which this, that
or another formula for investment and production might be poured.
Corporatist concerns for 'unity' and 'order', 'nation' and 'success'
need in no significant way clash with the general use of profit yardsticks.

Market competition may indeed be curtailed, and the need for
'unity' invoked in justification. But the ascendance of oligopoly and
monopoly has been a long trend; it does not by itself signify any
displacement of profit optimization from its role in economic decisions. Injunctions for 'order' – especially when directed to labour, but
in other forms too – similarly carry no definite prescriptions for resource allocation alternative to the profit criterion. 'Nationalist' protection against foreign economic penetration may be perverse
according to classical doctrine. But it makes as good sense to threatened domestic business, concerned with its own profitability, as does
state-supported restraint of domestic market competition to firms
thereby enabled to mark up safer returns to their capital. Corporatist
policy may very well put 'success' before adherence to liberal-demo-
cratic conceptions of due legal process and parliamentary scrutiny.
But that need point to no substitution of new ways to measure success
for the old ways of reference to profit.

In fact, the new measures of government intervention in the 1960s
and into the 1970s had one overriding economic purpose. This was to
restore, on a secure long-term basis, that business profitability which
looked under threat – under threat especially from labour indiscipline; but also from obsolete enterprise organization, inadequate
adaptation to new challenges and mounting competition from foreign
capital. True, spin-offs for everybody were assumed from enhanced
business profitability. It had been a constant premise of public policy
from the 1940s that continuous economic growth would boost popular levels of living as well as returns to capital, and so – importantly –
help to keep distributive conflict off the agenda of politics and industrial relations. Growing militancy from the 1960s seemed to put a
question mark against this assumption. But by then the prospect of
continued even economic growth had itself begun to look shaky. All
the more reason therefore to extend the policy armoury for promotion
of growth. But that still meant promotion of business profitability. Nor
were corporatist measures all of equal weight. Wage restraint had
been a recurrent element in the catalogue of government regulation

since the Second World War. It now acquired pre-eminence. And it was joined by other means to tighten labour discipline, though corporatist policy favoured persuasion over confrontation – to tame shopfloor organization, for example, through its assimilation into the regular machinery of collective bargaining. Selective support and subsidization of capital investment, together with aid to vulnerable key businesses, had been another recurrent feature of public economic policy; and it was now taken further. By contrast, measures which might have suggested some displacement of the profit yardstick figured only marginally.

Price codes, supervision of profits and restrictions on dividend distribution were thus operated only intermittently, and widely recognized as public relations exercises to elicit trade union support for wage restraint. When, for example, a Conservative government-established Price Commission in 1973 found business complaints that profits had suffered groundless, even *The Times* backed it by editorially describing such complaints as 'the tears . . . of an exceptionally brazen crocodile' (17 October 1973). Again, though seen by Winkler as prototypical of corporatist state power over business, the 'planning agreements' envisaged under Labour's Industry Act 1975 were aimed only to set a consultative framework for investment and restructuring. Barely ever implemented anyway, their purpose was, like that of French 'indicative planning', to bring longer-term rationality to profit-making; not to supersede it.

While Winkler acknowledged the trend and prospect of falling profits as one main cause of ascendant corporatism, he failed to explain how and why then a search to secure returns for capital should result in a dispossession of capital. An argument that corporatism was a response to unacceptable tendencies towards monopoly looked equally lame, if the result was indeed something like state monopoly. The question would in any case remain: 'unacceptable' to whom? Business as a whole has no unified interest either for or against monopoly. Where the interests of particular enterprises, conglomerates and sectors lie on the issue depends on their market circumstances. Even the anti-monopoly invective of the laissez-faire regime which succeeded corporatism from the late 1970s has, in effect, been directed far more against trade union and some professional monopolies.

Whence then came the pressures implied to curb monopoly profit by means of corporatist power? If they were 'popular' pressures, exerted in whole or part through labour organizations as the third leg of tripartism, the new corporatism should show a popular and trade union imprint at odds both with reality and the logic of the *'sui generis'* thesis.

Purposes of control: distribution

Let me play along with the thesis nonetheless. For corporatism to have displaced capitalism, the latter's mode of productive resource allocation by reference to profit maximization must have been displaced by some alternative mode. But by what? The last of my three test questions now comes into play: to whose benefit? For if state policy determines production and investment by criteria other than profitability, those alternatives must reflect some conception of 'public interest', of the 'national good'. And that conception must rest on stated or unstated principles of justice – principles of distributive allocation – distinct from those which characterize capitalism.

Yet neither in Winkler's characterization nor in observable fact was there any distinctive code of distribution to mark off corporatism from capitalism. True, one could perhaps read into concern with 'nation' and 'national achievement' a concern with economic growth at large, 'for its own sake'. But there is no key there to the criteria behind most economic decisions. If growth *per se* were the prime objective of policy, alternatives between investment in one line of production and in another would still have to be weighed against each other. If the yardstick were not now profit, it could be only some conception of 'general good for the nation'. This might be nebulously defined, and in practice to coincide nicely with the good of those who shaped policy. But any such conception would have to include answers, if only implicit in decisions made, to the question who is to benefit. Otherwise no allocation of resources among alternative uses could take place: none apart from expenditure on national defence, security, order on 'prestige'.

It seems, however, that corporatist prescriptions for distribution in this model would merely echo those at work in a capitalist system. The new order harboured, so Winkler underlined, 'no principle favouring redistribution or equality . . . corporatism is in principle hierarchical.' Power and authority would, by imperative of corporatist morality, be unequally distributed. Material rewards might not be, by reference to principle alone; but in practice they were almost bound to follow the hierarchical pattern of power and authority. The mere presence of marked inequality, however, does not make my case. Capitalism is not defined by the fact that inequality is inherent in its social being: so it has been in all complex societies hitherto. What does make my case is the character of corporatist inequality: the sources of privilege and deprivation, the rules which govern their allocation. For in Winkler's model and reality alike, these were the same sources and the same rules by which class inequality is set within capitalism.

Distribution in a modern capitalist economy follows certain working rules rather than any deliberately reflected principles of justice. The first rule is that private ownership constitutes, of itself, a claim on resources for livelihood. No test of either contribution or need is imposed on an owner, who may have acquired the assets by positive personal effort but equally well by speculative enterprise or by inheritance, gift or windfall gain. But concentration of private property makes substantial income-yielding ownership the privilege of a small minority. For the great majority, therefore, one or other of two alternative rules applies to set their places in the distributive order.

The second rule of distribution in a capitalist economy has precedence over the third. It commands the propertyless to hire out their labour; or to find private support from others, usually members of their households, who so hire out their labour. The terms on which labour is hired out differ widely: they include special favour for people whose work involves authority of organizational office, requires recognized credentials and/or allows them some control over their own corner of the labour market by 'closure' (see especially Wright, 1985; Parkin, 1979). But labour markets acquire much of their inequality of outcome from their gearing to profit for capital; and even in the public sector, wage and salary differentials follow generally the patterns set in the private sector, though often below or behind the latter in response to policies of government. This second rule, then, makes for distribution according to 'contribution'; but contribution is valued according to the pressures and vagaries of labour markets ultimately directed to profit.

The third rule follows directly. People who have neither substantial property nor income from paid work can now in most western countries rely on a degree of state support in cash and kind. But cash support is generally set in intended principle below the bottom floor of the labour market as a whole, or below the particular bottom floor of the labour market for this or that particular category of the labour force. The rule takes account of 'need'. But applied in a context where monetary incentives are given overriding priority for labour markets to function, the rule defines need by reference to the workings of those markets. So it keeps the range of distributive inequality extended well downwards.

Nothing in British corporatist policies of the 1960s and 1970s suggested any departure from these rules for distribution. The enticements offered to labour for cooperation in tripartism neither transformed the general pattern of real income inequality nor breached the rules of thumb which dictated it. The squeeze on public welfare entitlements and the regressive shifts of taxation which came at the hands of government after 1979 were associated with a dismantling of tripartism and a general sharpening of inequalities under all three rules. But they involved a less generous interpretation of the third rule; not its abolition, as if that the rule had been peculiar to the corporatism of the previous two decades. By this final test too, then, corporatism could not be described as a new economic order on its way to displacing capitalism.

The purpose of my argument is not just to drive home that conclusion, but to show that capitalism as an economic order must be defined by its mode of distribution as much as by its mode of productive organization. The three test questions I have applied to the hypothesis that corporatism is a distinct economic system hang together in a significant sequence. From the question about sources of control, because the locus of power cannot be established only by simple observation of decision-making behaviour, we are led to ask about the criteria of resource allocation for production and investment. From that question in turn, because those criteria inescapably imply criteria for distribution, we are led to ask about the notions of fair reward which inform allocation for life and livelihood. Class inequality takes its shape in line with just such notions.

3   From Tripartism to Free Marketeering

Scenarios for labour ascendancy: the case of Sweden

Few of the many other commentators on corporatism followed Winkler through to the conclusion that it heralded a quite distinct mode of economic organization, neither capitalist nor socialist. Yet some went part of the same way, in assigning to the elaboration of tripartite relations between state, business and labour a potential for a significant transformation of capitalism. I leave aside for the moment the new right's caricature of tripartism as a socialist project to subvert market enterprise. But one careful line of analysis saw 'bargained corporatism' as giving organized labour a new means of leverage for reform in its own interests, though within parameters that remained essentially capitalist (see especially Crouch, 1977 and 1979). Another added to this a surmise that even those parameters might be eased aside in particular circumstances. Where organized labour was well embedded in public policy-making, and where this was coupled with wide cross-class acceptance of government dedication to Keynesian prescriptions for macro-economic management, the situational logic could lead to state acquisition of effective powers over otherwise private investment and production: this to keep business active overall and employment truly 'full' in a now more adverse economic climate (Martin, 1979). This was suggested as a plausible scenario for Sweden; and it chimed in with a number of other analyses which presented that country as a possible model for an evolutionary transition from capitalism through corporatism to eventual socialism.

Whatever the future they saw ahead, diagnoses of this kind shared a far more positive emphasis on the role of labour than figured in

Winkler's analysis. If policy-makers' first concern had been to recruit trade unions as co-agents for discipline against the 'industrial relations crisis' (Crouch, 1977), nevertheless the outcome for labour according to this line of argument was by no means the self-frustrating compliance in subordination to capital interests which opposing commentators (for instance, especially Panitch, 1976, 1980, 1981) asserted. Labour had acquired bargaining leeway for change in its own interests of just the sort to match, or even go beyond, its leaders' hopes from participation in tripartism. The unions now had extensive representation in councils for management of economy and polity. The labour movement could press effectively there, and from its organized strength in employment markets, for policies to keep markets buoyant even against incipient recession. And the further rewards it could exact, for the price of industrial discipline, were no less tangible: still firmer union negotiation or consultation rights; and measures for fairer shares, whether as adjuncts to pay-restraint or by way of tax-benefit system reforms.

This argument, however, did not prove easy to sustain by reference to actual labour achievements. True, union representation in policy formulation and management was very evident. But representation is not by itself power, when the unspoken limits to policy and policy change set in advance tell against this. So in Britain in fact no significant narrowing of real income inequalities took place in the 1960s and 1970s (see chapter 7). Phases when incomes policy sought some relative improvement of low *vis-à-vis* higher pay rates alternated with phases when it sought to restore differentials, with the long-run outcome at best quite modest compression. Profits and high executive incomes were in any case effectively out of reach of incomes policy. The government promises of redistributive tax and benefit reform which accompanied the 'social contract' of the years 1974–9 remained unfulfilled, with only child benefit a late and limited exception. It can be well argued in retrospect that tripartism helped to stave off the accentuation of inequality which an alternative freed-market regime woud bring. But, by way of positive gains, the labour movement had little more to show in return for its 'incorporation' than some legislative enhancement of union bargaining rights. Even this was countered by a rise in unemployment which gathered pace even before 1979. Tripartite corporatism in Britain did not prove the defence against 'stagflation' on which hopes for it had come to be pinned.

Tripartism did, however, seem to prove such a defence in some other countries, most notably in Sweden where firm commitments to 'full employment' continued to hold sway until around 1990. Correspondingly, scenarios of corporatist development favourable to labour prospects drew strong support from the Swedish case; and a new school of analysts came to see Sweden as pointing the way towards a steady conversion of welfare-tamed capitalism into socialist control of the commanding economic heights (especially Korpi, 1978; Stephens, 1979; Himmelstrand et al., 1981). The definitive step was supposed to be the establishment of 'employee investment funds' which, financed by an annual levy on business profits and controlled by trade unions and government, would accumulate shares in the larger companies and so, over some decades, build up popularly responsible command of key production and investment. This strategy had been formulated first in a report (Meidner, 1976) accepted in principle by the LO, the main Swedish counterpart of Britain's TUC; was incorporated with some modifications in the programme of the social-democratic Workers' Party for the general election of 1982; and, when the party had won that election, was in fact enacted with further modifications.

A triumphant demonstration of the transformative potential which radical-labour analysts ascribed to tripartite corporatism – and a vindication of business mistrust of corporatism on just the same score? It is easy enough to dismiss such interpretations with the hindsight of the early 1990s, when Sweden has a free-market-sympathetic bourgeois coalition in government, unemployment there has soared, and the Meidner Plan even before that had proved virtually a dead letter. But the projections for which that plan was the kingpin, and the analyses of labour strength-through-corporatism which lay behind them, were open to question from the outset.

In their favour, without doubt, was the fact that Swedish labour came better equipped to tripartism than British labour. It showed firmer institutional unity, from early centralization of union organization and in close links between the industrial arm of the movement and its political arm, in government already from the 1930s. The Workers' Party drew more solid electoral support from its main constituency of industrial workers than did its British counterpart, and wider-spread additional support from other groups. Concomitantly, if less tangibly, labour sympathies and egalitarian values seemed to have a larger presence in everyday culture (see especially Scase, 1977). All this could suggest a strong base for the movement to give corporatism a 'labour shape': in particular to squeeze down class inequality for the benefit of ordinary wage-earners, active and retired.

That did happen to a degree. By the 1970s to 1980s at least, general income inequality after tax was comparatively moderate in Sweden by western standards (for example, O'Higgins et al., 1990); and so was inequality of individual opportunity by reference to social mobility from one generation to the next (Erikson and Goldthorpe, 1992). Yet these achievements came late. They were hardly, as adherents of socialism-by-evolution usually claimed, evidence of a power for change which labour had built up over long years before the high elaboration of corporatist institutions and processes from around 1960 onwards. Welfare reform had not substantially dented class inequality in Sweden up to the 1960s, beyond the effects of the full employment still common then across most western countries, though buttressed in Sweden by an 'active labour market' policy. And 'wage solidarity' policy for reduction of earnings differentials in association with restraint on pay claims acquired no bite until the late 1960s. Nor was the claim plausible, on the part of analysts who saw a steady evolution from the 'politics of distribution' to the 'politics of production', that eventual socialization of the commanding heights of the economy had long been inscribed on the agenda of Swedish social democracy. This contention was one prop of the argument that the labour movement in Sweden had brought special strength from the past into high corporatism; but it was a contention hard to square with the history of class compromise, ideological as well as tactical, through which the Workers' Party had maintained its leading place in government from the 1930s into the 1970s. (For a cogent analysis in support of all these points, see Fulcher, 1987; also *idem*, 1991.)

It was in breach with the past, rather than continuity with it, that the movement began to set its sights beyond class compromise from around 1970. Giving wage solidarity policy some teeth then began to challenge the second rule of thumb for distribution by bearing down on employment market inequalities of pay, professional salaries as well as wages. But far more significantly, adoption of the Meidner Plan in 1976 signalled an intention over time to seek large public powers of direct economic control: not only in order to steer investment towards sustained growth and full employment; but also, and not least, to bring private profit and capital gains out of their immunity from redistribution through wage solidarity policy and welfare reform by themselves. This would challenge the first rule of thumb, and from the proceeds allow still more generous interpretation of the third. But these indeed remarkable shifts of aim are hard to see as the outcome of some immanent logic of Swedish labour history and corporatism hitherto. They came rather out of conflict and distributive discontent: conflict within the movement; discontent on the part of rank-and-file workers, especially the lower-paid, which had taken increasingly militant form in the course of the 1960s (see again especially Fulcher, 1987 and 1991). Such discontent arose precisely, so it seems, from the clash between the rhetoric of fairer shares intended to hold labour to tripartism and the tight limits to fairer shares set by tripartism as it actually worked.

Conflict within the movement and class compromise beyond it continued, however. Pressures in the Workers' Party to tone down the Meidner Plan vied with pressures to keep its radical purpose firm; and the former won out, if in part because the ideology of moderation was strong in the party still, then also because tactical considerations were taken so to dictate. Out of office for six years, the party seemed to need to make its electoral programme for 1982 acceptable at least to many of those in the political centre, and among the growing ranks of salaried and professional people, on some form of alliance with whom labour's past place in government had come to depend. Alliances of that sort had long helped to blur party leaders' concern with radical redistribution: notably so, for example, in controversies around 1960 over pensions policy, the outcome of which was an earnings-related scheme nicely graded to build privilege from higher pay during working life into public provision for retirement. Now, in the early 1980s, the tactics of compromise worked to similar effect. As proposed in the programme for the 1982 election, the Meidner Plan had been softened. As enacted in 1983/84, it had lost the potential to wrest power over production and investment from capital.

It may be doubted anyway whether it could have survived with such potential even if it had been enacted in earlier radical form. Business opposed it strenuously throughout, and responded to the passing of the statute with a clamorous publicity campaign against it: 'away with the funds'. In any case business would for long, in the gradualist programme Meidner envisaged, have retained the economic power to withhold cooperation (see, for instance, Pontusson, 1984). Such power may have been somewhat less in Sweden then than, for example, in Britain or even Sweden's neighbour, Denmark, with their close tie-ups between domestic and international capital. But the threat of non-cooperation is always a potent one in defence of business interests. Just that seems a main reason why, whatever its sometime gains from participation, labour has stayed effectively the junior partner in corporatist set-ups of triangular shape; and why any fairer shares that followed have not overturned the principal capitalist rules for distribution.

The free-market alternative

For all this, the notion became well-entrenched that corporatism both accorded real power to organized labour and hamstrung capitalist economic processes. The idea has, of course, been prominent in the campaign for 'free markets' of British Conservative governments since 1979; and their policies have dismantled much of the machinery of tripartism. Formal incomes policies have been abandoned, though cash limits on public expenditure – introduced already during the Labour regime of 1974–9 – and related devices have been elaborated to hold back pay rises in areas of public employment not singled out for special favour. Maintenance or restoration of industrial discipline has remained a pre-eminent goal. But in place of persuasion in top-level consultation, the prime means to that end have been legislative restriction of trade union powers, especially to call and picket strikes; encouragement of employer resistance and police harassment when strikes have erupted, even on occasion provocation of strikes for causes lost in advance; erosion of statutory protection in low reaches of the labour market; by-passing or rejigging of former arrangements for resolution of disputes involving public employees; and, overall, reliance on the 'natural' discipline of employment markets whose terms have been turned distinctly against rank-and-file labour by two bouts of protracted recession, by substantial unemployment even during boom, and by shifts of economic activity from fields of high to fields of low trade union density.

Restructuring and modernization of the economy are still key stated aims. To a degree, too, state financial support for private business remains one means to their achievement, though this takes a less direct form than earlier and has worn a neatly cut free-enterprise dress when involving the sale of nationalized industries at bargain prices. But the prime emphasis post-1979 has been on freeing markets to do most of the long-term growth trick. There has been parallel stress on reducing direct taxation, and shifting its incidence in a regressive direction, in order to raise incentives for business initiative; on trimming social services with a view both to enhancing individual opportunity for choice backed by cash and to limiting state activity; finally, also, first on gearing education more closely to presumed market demands, then on widening access to post-school training or learning of such generally more vocational cast.

Yet sweeping as all this has been, its 'anti-corporatist' thrust is of a qualified sort. It has been directed mainly against the part played by organized labour in corporatism as it was before. Its target has been 'tripartism', rather than close liaison between state and accredited outside interests at large. There have been government challenges to some professional power blocs as well as to labour, though to significant marginalising effect only *vis-à-vis* teachers. But business remains firmly accredited: its top circles and financial powerhouses more closely enmeshed in consultation with the state given the absence of counter-accreditation; its junior representatives well ensconced too in the governance of education and training. Both the logic and the practice of neo-liberalism in economic affairs have been to entrust more of the execution of public policy to private enterprise. Corporatism lives on in a sense, as a much truncated form of liaison between state and business.

'Privatization' of course has been applied extensively: to a range of once public industries, utilities and even some penal services; in 'inner city regeneration' by urban development corporations and property consortia little trammelled by planning controls; through pressure on municipalities and hospitals to farm out ancillary work to profit-making contractors; in a variety of measures for housing. The claim that privatization in such fields will restore competition among suppliers and widen choice for consumers is highly contestable. Yet valid or not, this claim of 'general benefit' signals that the services privatized are still formally defined as concerns of public policy, even though private business is entrusted with their delivery. The curious claim, too, that utilities can be more rigorously subjected to public regulation if privately than if publicly owned is a signal to the same effect. In similar fashion, public subsidization still of private enterprise or provision – directly or indirectly, by grant, cheap loan, or often tax relief as for private purchase of housing – shows a continuity between past 'corporatist' and present 'free-market' practice. It helps, of course, to nurture profits, property values and privileged incomes, as it did before. But, as before too, its proclaimed justification is that it serves the general good. This again is a declaration that the service so promoted is, in name at least, a concern of public policy: to be implemented in 'partnership' between state and private enterprise, with the latter as prime 'agent' in ostensible principle if also as substantial beneficiary in real fact.

Moreover the state, in the British dispensation post-1979, is a state with teeth. Dismantling the former machinery of tripartism and allowing market forces more free rein has made for government which, while it is to be smaller, is also to be strong (see especially Gamble, 1979, 1981 and 1988). To harness local authorities and educational services to its own purposes; to curb trade union activity; to cope with the risks of popular unrest; to trim and restructure welfare provision; to re-educate a public still widely if ambiguously committed to post-war-settlement views of public responsibility – all these have required government to assert authority and centralize control – even to proliferate quangos – on a well-nigh unprecedented scale by peacetime standards. Conservative government has added, moreover, an extra dose of autocracy reflecting more traditional right-wing concerns with maintenance of social order, assertion of nationhood, preservation of secrecy in government despite counter-gestures, and discouragement of dissent.

Neo-liberal policy thus at least formally acknowledges that many privatized areas of economic activity remain legitimate concerns of public policy. But since it also firmly maintains that such concerns are best met through private management, there is recurrent tension between this acknowledgement and a balder thesis: that public policy has no place in economic affairs, except to encourage and support an institutional framework within which property and markets can work unfettered. In so far as this thesis prevails in practice, the new prescriptions certainly mark a distinct departure from corporatism, over and above the amputation of the latter's labour leg.

The change, however, involves no 'reversion' to use of market profitability as the yardstick of resource allocation. This was always the yardstick: corporatism was certainly never socialist, as new-right demonology likes to describe it. What the change does involve is a marked diminution of collective mobilization for profitability 'in the long run' and on the part of British capital 'as a whole'. The corporatist state of the 1960s and 1970s worked in good part as a kind of broker between separate business interests, to the long-term advantage of the more predominant among them. The organized labour movement was a party to corporatist arrangements. But it was always in economic logic the junior partner: rather reluctantly and dividedly enrolled for the prime purpose of exercising discipline *vis-à-vis* its own constituency; yet acquiescent in its enrolment because the alternative of direct restriction from above seemed worse, because labour as well as business had an interest in continued economic growth, and because it hoped to be able to extract this and that quid pro quo as its price for cooperation. The key relationship even in tripartite corporatism was between business and government. And reluctant as business too might be to maintain the relationship, it made some good sense overall for it to do so, at least in economic circumstances as they were till the 1970s.

The spin-off for business, if corporatist measures achieved their ends, was in part more labour discipline without head-on confrontation. It was also greater predictability of markets for the future; a framework of forecasting for the planning of investment, with some of the anarchy of uncoordinated decisions by individual enterprises removed; aid to investment and rationalization, and sometimes support in market adversity. There was no single or united business interest in all this. There would be losers as well as winners. Nor was the balance of gains and losses ever easy to estimate. But if it worked, more of private business at large – and more of big business especially – would gain rather than lose in long-term profitability.

It is this role of the corporatist state in coordination and support of otherwise separate and mutually divided business enterprises which 'free market' policy has much diminished. In some one-time Marxist theory (see, for example, Holloway and Picciotto, 1978) corporatist enlargement of the state had been regarded as an inevitable development within modern capitalism, emerging as if of functional necessity. Events since then plainly go against so stark a thesis. The contention in any case was faulty on several grounds. It made too little of the inhibitions and costs which central coordination imposes on separate profit-making by business enterprises that remain mutually divided. It postulated, even within any single country, too uniform a predominant long-run interest among business to be credible. It assumed too great a capacity on the part of somebody – a core capitalist elite or government or whoever – to identify this interest unambiguously and to deploy the means to pursue it consistently. On these scores it rode roughshod over the intricacies and cross-currents of conflict, outside as well as within business, which enter into practical politics and policy-making. And in failing to specify causal mechanisms, it implied some teleological process by which, as 'functions', effects become causes. Nevertheless, twentieth-century enlargement of the western state has not, in either purpose or practice broken the bounds of capitalism. It has, on the contrary, served predominant business interests pretty well in the long run. So, too, in respect of the special twists to state enlargement marked by corporatism. If so, how can the new ascendancy of 'free-market' prescriptions in Britain be explained?

Instabilities of corporatism

Explanation seems to require answers to two fairly distinct questions. One is how a Conservative Party dominated by the radical right has been able to win sufficient popular support, in four successive elections, to sustain a parliamentary majority. There are still no clear answers to that puzzle, though I shall try to add a little to the continuing debate around it later (chapter 11). The second question is why bearing ideas and assumptions in policy-forming circles, even beyond the Conservative Party, began to swing in favour of 'free markets' during the 1970s. That swing became a challenge to much of the political settlement of the 1940s: to the premise that 'full employment' must be maintained; and to the notion of 'citizenship for all' which was, though nebulously, inscribed in the programme of post-war social reconstruction. The immediate impetus to the swing came, however, from an inherent instability of the corporatist system which had grown out of the 1940s class compromise. Both business and labour pay a price for their participation in tripartite corporatism: the system is then liable to collapse if either or both find the price too high and withdraw. When this happened in Britain, the door was open for the alternative of a free-market policy.

Business stands to gain from corporatism in ways I have indicated. But the price includes concerted effort to liaise across enterprise and sectoral divisions; and a degree of regulation which has financial costs and requires adaptation to keep the regulation more nominal than real. New devices to evade the impact which incomes policies might otherwise have on distribution of profits and executive pay are a prime example. None of this need make the price to be paid very heavy; but the returns from participation in corporatism are not too certain either. Aid for investment and rationalization is a clear bonus for the companies that get it. But some will suffer from others' rationalization; some can manage well without aid, and will win out if their weaker rivals go to the wall. And while there remains a broadly common interest in having a known framework for coordination of investment, to avoid too risky duplication in competition, this is a long-run benefit not always easily seen here and now. Market dominance through individual corporation growth, company mergers and cartel formation is an alternative, if less comprehensive, means to the same end. Interests are liable to be divided over the issue of labour discipline not least, the central target of corporatist policies. It matters much more for labour-intensive industries than others; and then mainly if labour resistance to management direction is strongly based. Transnational corporations are in general no doubt relatively well placed to cope for themselves; and they have been growing. Service activity too, including especially financial enterprise – which has a key role in British capital – is likely to gain a good deal less directly from tripartite corporatism than traditional heavy industry; and the latter has been in long decline.

Organized labour's participation is at least as liable to disruption. Trade unions pay the price of turning themselves into agents of discipline against the employees whom it is their job to represent. That duality of role is hard to sustain. It becomes even harder if the gains supposed to come from it prove elusive: if economic growth still seems to falter despite corporatist efforts to promote it; if there is little redistribution in labour's favour at large; and if such redistribution as there is merely sets this category of wage earners at odds with that. The latter is a particular likelihood where organized labour's main strength is on shopfloors and in unions fairly distinctly separated by craft, trade and sector. This has been traditionally so in Britain where the old central union body, the TUC, acquired a measure of influence *vis-à-vis* its constituents on the whole only in the process of incorporation into tripartism, rather than (as in Sweden) bringing previously forged unity to its participation in corporatism. When such circumstances all come together, there is little to hold labour to corporatist commitments.

In Britain labour openly pulled out of those commitments on two occasions during the corporatist era: towards the end of the 1960s, when the unions decided formally to hold back future participation in incomes policies in the absence of specific agreement with government on a quid pro quo package; and again in effect when a wave of strikes during the 'winter of discontent' in 1978/9 finally buried just such an agreement. On both occasions the government in office was Labour, and a general election soon afterwards put a Conservative government into office freshly committed to replacing tripartite corporatism by free-market prescriptions. True, the Heath government's experiment with the latter from 1970 did not last long; but its Industrial Relations Act 1971, designed to impose drastic curbs on unions and shopfloor organization, obstructed the same government's subsequent attempts to bring back corporatist cooperation with labour involvement. Tripartism then still seemed worth another try. When the next try collapsed – at the hands of a Labour government 1974–9 – recession was visible. As it became deeper under the first Thatcher government, it weakened union muscle. But with union resilience vulnerable from mounting unemployment already before then, much of the purpose of tripartism had in any case become very dubious.

It was organized labour's withdrawal in 'the winter of discontent' which signalled the failure of tripartite corporatism in Britain. But just as this reflected the short change which unions and workers got from their involvement, so too for business the balance had tipped to disadvantage as time went on. Tripartism had not guaranteed industrial discipline; and with union disavowal of incomes policies, there was little point to it any longer on that score in many business eyes. The spread of recession now promised to do better in taming labour than corporatism had ever done. Recession would ease the way, too, for restriction of union powers in law because, in contrast to 1971, collective resistance would be crippled. Events in the 1960s and 1970s, moreover, had exposed larger social risks from corporatism and all that went before it. Full employment, economic growth, ostensibly comprehensive welfare provision, seemed not to have dulled or even merely 'privatized' popular aspirations, nor to have written conflicts over distribution off the agenda of political and industrial affairs; but,

on the contrary, to have driven 'ordinary people's' expectations steadily upwards and to have spread distributive discontent, collective
militancy and creeping distrust of authority in the process (see for
example Goldthorpe, 1978; Hirsch, 1977). The rhetoric of tripartism
added more fuel to this fire, because it appeared to promise unions
and workers rewards for their cooperation; and because, in making
incomes policies its centrepiece, it seemed to claim for governments a
will and a power to shape – and so perhaps change – the distribution
of real income to a degree not previously asserted. All the more reason
then, as corporatism was collapsing anyway, for establishment eyes to
turn hopefully to alternative formulae which saw market forces as a
means, among other things, so to 're-educate' people that they would
no longer expect 'more and more for less and less' (cf. for instance
Brittan, 1978).

On these issues of distribution, as on other scores, tripartism involved a precarious balancing act. The trick needed here was to keep
plausible the promises of fairer shares made to labour in order to hold
unions and workers to continued cooperation; yet also to leave those
promises in the air – because, pitched too firmly, they neither would
nor could be kept, they might raise popular expectations to militant
flashpoint, and they would frighten off business cooperation. With
the failure of this balancing act, three-cornered corporatism in Britain
gave way to a philosophy of policy which instead, more simply, has
sought to declare distribution largely out of bounds as a matter for
government action.

Instabilities of laissez-faire

True, the three rules of thumb for distribution remain the same in
broad principle. But their interpretation now accords the first two –
for rewards by property-right first, and by the play of market forces
on employment earnings second – both enhanced sanctity and greater
force for inequality. Concomitantly, the essentially residual nature of
the third rule – for below-market-level reward by reference to need –
has acquired new emphasis: in practice, through realignment of the
tax–benefit system in a sharply regressive direction; and, by way of
intended re-education, through castigation of benefit-receipt as 'dependence' and of taxation – on high incomes especially – as bordering
on robbery. Beyond provision of a low minimum still, so the ascendant policy creed runs, the state has no business to seek 'fairer' income
shares: the very notion of fairness here is out of place. Nor indeed can
the state realistically do this, so a subscript adds with a nice touch of

irony: not very much, after all, came of the fairer shares promised in the 1960s and 1970s.

Quite so: just that proved a key source of corporatist instability. But declaration of distribution as largely out of bounds for public policy remains a statement of hope. It does not seem a plausible forecast. 'Fairer shares' has already rejoined the agenda of political debate with the second post-war 'rediscovery of poverty' in the 1980s; and this with the more alarm because the poverty so rediscovered has now patently been growing, rather than emerging as merely persistent despite earlier faith in its banishment. That may not by itself be enough to give distributive discontent full political clout, in so far as the poorest – those outside the world of work or only insecurely within it – are a minority of ostensibly mixed make-up and frail organizational power, and as their sympathizers may have weightier interests of their own to pursue. But there are other sources of discontent to keep contest over shares in the economic cake well in place on policy agendas: and popular subscription to notions of greater social justice have proved remarkably resistant to radical-right re-education (see chapter 11).

These pressures may come more to the fore again when growth picks up once more – be it still precarious, on a still narrowing front, and still with a large tail of un-, under- and non-employment. Collective demands from those now more secure again in employment are then likely to be pressed with greater vigour: not, in high probability, to egalitarian effect; nor even much to militant fervour in 1960–70s style; but mainly in the form just of backstage group contests for higher pay levels. The first outcome may be little different from what it was in the short-lived boom of the later 1980s. Then, in freed-market circumstances, the competition unleashed by resumption of growth gave the trend to new inequality a distinctly sharper twist, with still wider pay differentials and with soaring profits to boost the pattern (see, for example, Jenkins, 1991). It also helped to stoke renewed high inflation. So, supposedly vanquished, the old bugbear reappeared in full strength; once more, as around 1980, deflationary measures were applied in full strength; and once more recession followed, the harder-set as consumer debts accumulated during the preceding burst now added to the downward spiral of demand. But that repetition of economic waste has proved so protracted and devastating – for business widespread as well as for employees who have lost work, the latter this time from a wider range of the occupational hierarchy than before – that the economic orthodoxies of the 1980s are at plain risk of losing credibility even among once stalwart supporters. So the door could swing back again to allow, the next time round, some sort of return to corporatist measures in new-old effort to combine growth with low inflation: this never mind how such measures may be dressed up, or what may be the colour of the government which adopts them.

The next time round. . . . But the pressures merely to get growth going firmly could have similar effect. Two bouts of recessionary attenuation of Britain's economic base over less than a decade and a half have bleakly exposed laissez-faire policy's vulnerability as a means to sustained capital growth: its neglect of collective infrastructure; its lack of concern to provide a framework of common knowledge to guide business investment; the priority it encourages for short-term and single enterprise-by-enterprise calculation of profit, without reference to longer-run cost-benefit balance sheets across capital more broadly. With the vacuum on these scores more visible in retrospect in the early 1990s than it was in prospect in the later 1970s, corporatist coordination may be on the verge of regaining respectability. Its likely spin-offs would, as ever, be unequally spread among business; and, as inter-business coordination under government promotion (somewhat in Japanese style), it might not seem to need re-establishment of tripartism with the now weakened union movement also recruited to its ends. But maintaining growth after slump would entail a high risk of renewed inflationary pressures, with part-collective, part-anarchic pay claims significant among their sources. Hence in turn the case could re-emerge for some sort of concordat with labour: the more so since, whether half- or fuller-hearted, the country's larger involvement in a moderately tripartite-corporatist European union looks inescapable. And any attempt at concordat with labour would put distributive contests openly on the agenda of policy again.

For that reason not least, new tripartism would have instability built into it no less than did old tripartism. But the free-market alternative would itself have proved – arguably, has already proved – devoid of the stability it promised, because devoid also of the steady and inflation-free growth it promised. Growth, after all, remains the holy grail of economic policy: despite 'green' warnings on the one hand; despite recurrent official obsessions, on the other, with control of inflation to growth-stifling effects. And when growth retains its pride of place among long-run aims of policy, that again is in good part because distributive concerns remain central. Now as before, growth – more cake for most people, or for enough of them to keep political trouble away – is seen as a smoother solvent of social discontent than fair shares in the cake that is.

Part II
Public Policy and Distributive Inequality

4 The Welfare State and Capitalist Distributive Logic

Welfare state limits in centrist perspective

I argued in the two preceding chapters that neither corporatism nor, by implication, the welfare state in the forms out of which tripartism grew, set new rules for distribution to supersede those which can be read off from capitalist economic practice. The aim now of this chapter and the two following is to examine that proposition more closely, and in the process to explore the issue of 'welfare state limits'. By this I mean the question how far reform through public welfare provision can go, by itself, to change patterns of distributive inequality. That it makes for some change is evident. But how, specifically, can a set of points be defined beyond which state welfare meassures might be said no longer to complement, but instead to supplant the distributive rationale of capitalism?

Answers offered to this question from the right and the left have one feature in common: both flanks assume that such limits can be categorically defined. The radical right in particular implies a tight definition of limits, when it asserts that public welfare provision has long put property and market mechanisms in jeopardy. Left-wing opinion which abides by Marxist convention has set the limits much wider, when it has claimed that ostensible state altruism serves in essence to conserve capitalism; but this claim also implies a categorical notion of limits, whose hypothetical breach would 'de-capitalize' the economy. Both arguments need further comment. But it is worth noting first that, by contrast, 'centrist' opinion has taken a more gingerly approach to the issue.

This verges on a circular statement since I have in mind here crude definitions of right, left and centre which hang chiefly on varying conceptions of the welfare state. I take the 'centre' as exemplified in practice by that still large middle ground of opinion and policy which held general sway for several decades from around the 1940s; came to political expression in Britain as 'Butskellism'; and promoted a combination of Keynesian prescriptions for macro-economic management with a range of new welfare measures. The point that this central bloc takes a rather gingerly approach to the issue of welfare state limits follows not just from the fact that its politics of compromise tend to the gingerly. It reflects also a particular internal tension to its aims. On the one hand, social-liberal and social-democratic opinion has sided with the right in principled limitation of welfare reform to measures consonant with capitalist economic institutions. True, it takes public intervention to be necessary on a scale which the right views with distaste. But a prime purpose is to remove friction from the workings of property and market mechanisms, not to put them out of action. On the other hand, this cautious goal has often been coupled with a social ambition hard to square with it: hence a temptation to cover up.

That ambition looks to a society of common 'citizenship', to use a now classical formulation (T. Marshall, 1950). It has set an ideal where collective provision to counter individual adversity, and to promote parity of opportunity irrespective of personal background, should ensure that nobody lacks the basic means for participation in the 'community'; and where universal subscription and entitlement to collective provision would symbolize that common participation. Property and market forces would still work to stretch out disparities of individual livelihood quite widely. But disparities would be just that: no longer the divisions of a class-fractured society. Shaved at its bottom end, and transcended by the shared status of all as participating citizens, economic inequality would have lost its social power to divide.

This ideal is certainly at odds with the celebration of privileged 'active citizenship', by way of autonomous charity on the part of successful individuals and corporations, which the radical right revived in the 1980s. But incongruence just with the latter brand of 'Victorian values' is not incongruence with the basic imperatives of a modern capitalist economy. True, a generous vision of shared citizenship draws on an ethic of 'fraternity' (Halsey, 1978; Dennis and Halsey, 1988). But the emphasis is on that rather than 'equality'. Moreover, while proponents of social citizenship acknowledge that the welfare state necessarily imposes some limits on still functioning markets, they have generally shied away from the question of just what limits (as noted by Roche, 1987, 1992). Hopes have been loosely pinned on some 'middle way' to join to the incentives of property and markets a pervasive spirit of cooperative involvement. Yet for such a sense of common participation to take hold, it must surely have material substance to sustain it; and there lies a sore tension with capitalist prescriptions. For these require, first, a tangible separation of market-gained livelihood from, and above, collectively guaranteed livelihood; second, a no less tangible diversity of outcomes in market-gained livelihood: on both scores, a range of inequality which seems to go against the grain of a conjectured community of citizens.

There are critics who, even from within the broad tradition of Fabian reform, have come to see the circle as unsquareable. Thus the foremost present-day British analyst of 'poverty' has defined that condition, precisely, as deprivation of the means to participate in common styles of life; and in his *magnum opus* he advocated measures for the abolition of so-defined poverty, which would implicitly involve considerable demotion of property and market mechanisms for distribution (Townsend, 1979). He has not been alone (see, for instance Walker, 1984). But it has been far more usual for endorsement of shared citizenship to stop short of close concern with the issue of welfare state limits. Labels like 'the mixed economy' generally begged the questions of how 'mixed' precisely, and to what priorities. Even so eminent and radical a social policy analyst as Richard Titmuss (for example, 1958, 1968, 1973, 1974) was open to the regretful charge from an intellectual biographer that 'he never specified the ideal balance between public and private sectors' (Reisman, 1977, 164). And the typical middle-ground assumption seemed for long to be that a way to larger collective altruism could be found which might at no point have to bring the divergent interests behind alternative conceptions of distribution into frontal conflict: this through a process perhaps of prudent, incremental and pluralistically adaptable manoeuvre in a spirit of 'mercantile collectivism' (Pinker, 1979).

Government by the 'new' right in Britain has since done much to disturb confidence of that sort. Even so, broad centre and hard right continue to share one significant article of faith: that economic growth can keep discontent about distribution at bay. In laissez-faire right-wing diagnosis, sharper market-driven inequality is both ethically justified because, with that spur to economic advance, much increased wealth at the top may spread down to improve the lot even of the poorest in absolute terms; and it makes political sense, if majority public opinion can be brought to accept that only absolute terms matter. Though committed to a far more generous vision of shared citizenship, centrist thinking has often also seen steady economic growth as the key to social consensus: as the national cake gets larger, the thin slices so far cut for the poorer-off may be made disproportionately thicker without trimming the handsome portions of the better-off (for instance, Crosland, 1973). This hope clashed with some of the realities of economic growth after the Second World War. Inequalities in fact stayed cast in broad relative terms within the newer mould set for them during the 1940s. Rising average 'affluence' intensified competition for 'positional goods', whose enjoyment by some people by very definition required exclusion for most people. Both growing 'affluence' and the quasi-egalitarian rhetoric of public policy seemed to accelerate rather than satisfy popular expectations. Especially set against the first, the second and the third points put distributive conflict more squarely on the agenda (see chapter 3); and some advocates for the radical right proved sharp in drawing a lesson to bolster their cause: 'Why bother with so much public provision, when it doesn't shift shares much anyway, and only increases strife?'

For all this, the hope of some time using economic growth to give consensual leeway for progressive redistribution stayed a keynote to midstream political faith. That has a part in explaining centrist opinion's neglect of the issue of welfare state limits: if growth will do the trick, the issue need never arise.

Views from right and left

By contrast the laissez-faire right has been vehement in its postulate that post-war public provision for welfare went well beyond proper limits: to the effects of undermining market incentives, stifling initiative and spreading a culture of dependency. True, the new governments in Britain from 1979 were slow to match such action to words, *Ad hoc* revision of social security and a major Act of 1986 trimmed help for the poorer-off in a spirit far from 'fraternal'; yet this fell well short of fundamental deconstruction of the system. With a third successive electoral victory in 1987, a mood of triumph was brought to bear on recasting provision for education and housing; but in ways as much concerned to take strips off local government and centralize control as to encourage market forces. The Cabinet had earlier toyed with the idea of reducing public provision for health to a minimum basis, topped up by private insurance; but it aborted that exercise. When the government moved again to review the National Health Service, the proposals (in 1989) included tax relief for private health insurance on behalf of elderly people and measures to develop 'internal markets' within the service; yet this came with assurances that general medical care would remain open to all, free 'at the point of delivery'. Such hesitation over dismantling the structure of public welfare, however, showed sensitivity to political risks rather than principled suspension of the view that state provision had grown well beyond its proper bounds.

Even so, this is a view which its proponents have done little to back up by specifying at just what points acceptable public help for the 'genuinely needy' turns into intolerable subversion of market mechanisms. There would be no difficulty for them on this score if they went to the extreme of requiring all welfare responsibility to be left to self-help and private charity. But once the point is conceded that some minimum state provision is justifiable, the need for specification comes into play. It may seem more a problem of practice than of principle then to specify who 'genuinely' deserves such support. But it becomes very much a problem of principle, still only diffusely addressed from the radical right, to specify what constitutes the 'minimum' to which their support should be limited. Must it be sufficient only to allow bare existence? But what then is 'bare existence', in circumstances that differ from one economy to another and change over time? If more, how far should allowance go to take account of varying, and usually rising, overall 'societal standards'? Again, just where and how would any specific resolution of these questions – familiar from long-standing debates about 'poverty' – begin to clash with the express priority assigned in laissez-faire policy to free-turning property and market enterprise?

Contrasting arguments from the left that public welfare provision serves to prop up capitalism has often, too, relied more on assertion than specification. This was true especially of neo-Marxist diagnosis in the manner of 'state derivation' theory (see, for example, Holloway and Picciotto, 1978); and of Poulantzas in critique of Miliband (Poulantzas, 1969; Miliband, 1970; also Poulantzas, 1973 and Miliband, 1969). The theme of accommodation between public policy and dominant private interests certainly warranted the close attention which it began to receive at Marxist hands from the 1960s onwards. But when some theorists gave short shrift to either factually informed inquiry or direct engagement with 'bourgeois' interpretations, their work lost in force what it gained in abstraction. A conclusion then that, short of a socialist transformation, the thrust of public policy must always be in close affinity with overall long-run capital needs, was more subtle than a vulgar dogma describing the state merely as the 'agent' of a unitary capitalist class. Yet it was ultimately unconvincing. I have already suggested some reasons why (chapter 3). A few others are worth brief note.

For one thing, neo-Marxist state analysis in this functionalist style made too little in practice of a distinction it underscored in principle: between particular interests within business and the larger 'systemic' interests of capital. The range of potent sectional interests in mutual rivalry goes beyond the familiar examples of finance versus manufacture, big versus smaller business, transnational versus national enterprise, this sector of production versus that. There are also significant features of public policy which help to serve privileged *distributive* interests far more than they promote long-term efficacy in production and profit-making. Entrenched reluctance to dismantle institutional and reduce cultural barriers to 'equal opportunity' – barriers, therefore, to free mobility of individual talent – is one example; regressively skewed tax relief for mortgages is another. In either case, the spin-off for vested privilege is patent, and constitutes much of the political driving force. By contrast, the cost-benefit sheet for 'capital at large' certainly includes 'dysfunctions'. Here are instances where the class inequalities endemic to a capitalist order in turn generate social power to some negative effect for 'the system'.

The notion of dysfunction, to widen this point, is of course no stranger to Marxist theory. And as dysfunctions by another name, neither of the two prime contradictions said to be built into capitalism– a profit-driven tendency for profit to decline, and equally unintended nourishment of a soil liable to promote the growth of class opposition – could be readily squared with a version of Marxism which read overriding functional harmony between capital and public policy into analysis of the state. The dilemma became acute for neo-Marxist 'capital logicians' when, reasonably enough in itself, they gave space for class struggle as one potent influence on state activity. For the thesis of functional alignment between public policy and capital needs could then be sustained only on an assumption that the outcome of such struggle never significantly transgresses capital needs. So, ostensibly labour-friendly measures must either be devoid of all but trivial labour-friendly substance; or they must work more to perpetuate the system in good order than to inhibit its operation. It is not enough to argue that one or other of these points applies often, in good part – that for example, public welfare provision involves far more horizontal than vertical redistribution, and cuts little into capital profit; or that policies for full employment at one time, or for widening education more continuously, have been geared to coupling popular benefits with business gains in growth and efficacy. A thesis of functional congruence between state activity and capital requirements must argue that something of this sort is always and wholly the case. The loophole used for that purpose in theory of the 'capital logic' type was not a new concept; but it had to carry a heavy load. It was the notion of 'concessions' which, despite some labour-friendly substance, would serve overall to bolster the capitalist order's 'legitimacy'.

The trouble with this is that it tends to defy proof or disproof. 'Maintenance of legitimacy' becomes a ragbag category, into which any feature of public policy which serves no more specific function for capital must be stuffed. Take the case of public provision for health, if its purpose goes any way beyond 'reproducing labour power'. The extra element must then be explained as conducive to the capitalist system's legitimacy. But how demonstrate this? How prove that the postulated political benefits for stability of the order outweigh the total costs? How do so, not least, when the costs will include new vested employee interests in the furtherance of state activity; and when they may include unintended encouragement of wider popular expectations, which could become progressively hard to contain within the system? Neo-Marxist theory of functionalist persuasion answered such questions, in the end, only by doctional fiat: a capitalist state must strike the balance within the limits set by the imperatives of its capitalist economy.

There were Marxists, even in the heyday of left-wing structural-functionalism, who were explicit in finding the thesis of functional consonance inadequate to explain the 'welfare state' (for example, Gough, 1979; Offe, 1984). Their emphases not least on the inertial dynamics of provision once set in motion, and on unintended consequences, acknowledged more latitude and indeterminacy to the character of the state in capitalist economies than 'capital logic' allowed. Yet for many others a trail was left which still seems to take purity of Marxist theory to require an assertion that the welfare state is wholly circumscribed by its functions for capital viability and 'legitimacy'.

Capitalism's distributive amorality

So the issue of welfare state limits usually evokes postulate from hard left and hard right alike, fudge from the soft centre. To get closer to answers of substance we must look, in quite specific terms, to welfare state norms for distribution; and assess how far these either clash with, or stay within, the allocatory rules of a capitalist economy. In trying to do this, I shall build on an earlier sketch (Westergaard, 1978) but take account also of the shift of policy climate since then.

The very first point to note, however, is that capitalist allocatory prescriptions are just rules of thumb, not principles reflecting some distinctive philosophy of distributive justice. Capitalism entails inequality, but this is not an end in itself; and the logic of capitalism ascribes no inherent virtue to any particular degree or incidence of inequality. Instrumental considerations may suggest adjustment of the pattern which happens to prevail in given circumstances. But the test of such measures will be their efficacy for the system – as incentives for enterprise and labour effort, in encouraging individual self-reliance, in reducing friction, in taming or dispersing resistance – not their conformity to a canon of social justice. The point is not that capitalism, either as an economic model or as an associated set of philosophical ideas, lacks all ethic. It aspires, in stated principle, to aggregate growth of wealth, of individual opportunity and of personal choice. But the emphasis is on the aggregate: any distinct distributive dimension is absent.

Qualifications may sometimes be added. Advance of aggregate wealth, opportunity and choice can properly, when productively, involve diminution of the relative shares of those previously worst-off; but it ought not, so it may be acknowledged, involve diminution of their absolute shares. Leave aside conceptual problems to this concession; leave aside also the artistry of governments which adopt the concession in their rhetoric but pay no heed to it in their practice. The concession still comes with no general ethic of distributive justice to back it. So, too, when laissez-faire liberalism proclaims the virtues of private charity. The proclamation may reflect moral as well as pragmatic misgivings about distributive outcomes in a 'free economy'. But the morality is devoid of any distributive code to guide the discretion of donors of charity.

This ethical vacuum is not always easy to see. It is obscured, for example, because capital interests are commonly represented by parties and pressure groups which mix market liberalism with traditional conservatism. The latter does offer some notion of distributive justice: an ideal of hierarchically ordered community, in which inequalities would be differences of rank rather than divisions of class; distinctions firm and even sharp, but tempered by common acceptance of disparate obligations and rights. The vacuum has been veiled also by the emergence of a broad centrist alliance concerned to civilize capitalism by spreading citizenship. Diverse influences have come together here: classical liberal emphasis on individual dignity as well as market choice; traditional conservative emphasis on 'community' across and above inequalities; emphasis from an alternative popular tradition of 'fraternal community'. And the distributive ethic associated with the goal of common citizenship, within trimmed but continuing capitalist economic parameters, is hard to pin down; but proponents certainly claim to have one. Not so, however, those market liberals who are most consistent about their doctrine. They denounce the very notion of social justice as delusive and improper (for instance, Hayek, 1973), and so rule considerations of fairness wholly out of court in application to inequalities of economic outcome.

Even so, the point may be contested on two grounds. First, it can be argued that liberal capitalism has a code of distributive justice unique to itself: an ethic of equal individual opportunity. Whatever the obstacles to its fulfilment, this aspiration may appear to provide a yardstick for moral judgement in matters of distribution. That argument, however, is double-flawed. For one thing capitalism allows, in ideology as well as practice, the ownership of property acquired by inheritance, gift or windfall gain. This flies straight in the face of any principle of equal opportunity. If it is defended nevertheless on the ground that free disposal of private property constitutes an essential incentive to capitalist enterprise, the defence, because wholly instrumental, strips the goal of equal opportunity of the independent moral status claimed for it. If it is defended on the ground that transmission of property between kinsfolk is natural and good in maintaining family ties, the same applies; and the defence then draws on a traditional conservative philosophy of society at odds with the liberal celebration of individualism.

For another thing, the ideal of equal opportunity by itself says nothing about opportunity for what: about the equity of the range of unequal outcomes that follow. Allow (very implausibly) that only the most talented get the plum positions, and only the least talented end up at the bottom. Never mind, moreover, who judges talent, and how. The question still stands: should the plum positions give life circumstances, say, twice as good as the poorest ones; or twenty times as good; or two hundred times? On its own, the principle of equal opportunity has nothing to say here. And liberal capitalist principle at large gives again only instrumental answers: market forces will find the balance that works best for the economy; or if they don't quite, then push a bit here or trim a bit there. Behind these answers lies another: the 'should' in the question must have to do only with what works; not with what is good in itself. Indeed, it is hard to conceive any canon of justice that declares it 'good in itself' that, when full-time manual work yielded average gross incomes of barely £6,500 a year for women and around £10,000 for men, the chief executive of one large multinational corporation based in Britain notched up at least an annual £10 million (over £1 million in salary, the rest in share

dividends from his own company: *The Independent*, 26 May 1989).
Notions of intrinsic equity plainly cannot come into this.

So appeal to 'equal opportunity' does not make up for capitalism's
distinctive lack of an ethic of distributive justice. But a second argument may be brought into play that market rewards are fair because
they represent valuations aggregated from individual consumer
choices. At least this will be so, the argument continues, if market
imperfections can be eliminated: a legitimate concern for the state.
Leave aside what the latter concession may imply, when market imperfections are themselves market-generated. The argument is still
flawed. It is circular, because markets aggregate choices unequally.
The rich, individually and corporately, have many more market votes
than the poor. Market outcomes then can be described as fair only
if that inequality of votes is in some sense fair to start with. To determine this requires just such an ethic of distributive justice as liberal
capitalism does not offer: we are back to square one.

Capitalist rules of thumb: the property rule

For all this, a capitalist economy does have distinctive operational
rules for distribution. I have already outlined these (chapter 2). But
they need some further comment. Under the first rule, ownership of
productive property constitutes of itself a recognized claim to share in
resource output. It also often, though far from always, gives owners a
formal claim to take part in resource management, if only by way of
vote-carrying shareholders' right to a voice on limited occasions. That
is relevant here in respect of two points. First, it bears on the purported rationale of the property rule: the right of owners to an income
is justified because it gives them incentive to put their property to
profitable but potentially risky use. This is a flimsy defence of the
property rule: it assumes that no other distribution of property than
what prevails could offer as good results in productive risk-taking.
But it underlines the centrality of the rule: it is the search for optimal
returns to property that drives the wheels of the economy. Second,
vote-carrying shareholders' 'managerial' rights illustrate a general
feature of the rule. Just as shareholders' votes are counted by size of
holding, so with owners' claims to ownership-income: the more they
happen to have, the more by and large they will get from it.

All this may seem obvious. But not to restate it is to risk forgetting
some curious corollaries. One is that the right of owners to a part in
societal income stands with no questions asked about their 'contribution', let alone their 'need'. They are required to make no other

contribution than to place their assets in the market; and that is a 'contribution' they happen to be able to make only because they happen to have assets, never mind how they came by them within the law. For all others, legal receipt of income requires either a work-contribution, or somehow certified proof of need. Provided that their ownership is substantial enough, property owners are exempt from both these restrictions; and their exemption strikes a high note of paradox in economies whose credo otherwise preaches the virtues of commitment in work and parsimony out of it.

Another corollary stems from the structure of modern capitalist economies: ownership of productive property is heavily concentrated, though not so heavily as is control. The minority who own enough to live from the proceeds therefore include some with so much as to live extraordinarily well; and they take between them a sizeable slice of the total cake: the high peak of inequality comes from capital possession. Where personal ownership of company shares has spread, this has made for little qualification of the point: the large majority of people are still not involved; and most individual shareholders hold only small packages. Some 1980s growth of petty business enterprise also makes little odds: the great bulk of the economically active population still depend essentially on employment by others for their livelihood. The spread of home-ownership has entailed a more significant diffusion of property-holding. True, owner-occupancy is not possession of 'productive property', and does not yield steady income directly. But it contributes to real income when it leads to effective reduction of personal housing costs over time. It has also spread the means to windfall gains from property, and to the pot luck of inheritance. One result is new lines of stratification – between owners in different sectors of an erratic housing market, as well as between owners, tenants and homeless: inequalities little less devoid of reference to 'contribution' or 'need' than other property divisions.They come into play well down the socio-economic hierarchy. Yet they do not supplant the major cleavage generated by the property rule. In a society like Britain that cleavage still distinguishes a very few, whose extreme privilege turns on large capital ownership, from the rest.

I have noted a third corollary earlier. Property rights invariably include the right of owners to pass on their assets by inheritance or gift. Certain limits are often set to this right: in some countries, to restrict a testator's discretion over who should inherit; commonly, to tax assets on their transmission, though this is notoriously susceptible to avoidance by the very rich. But such limits do not dent the principle. One implication is to underline the unconditional nature of the property rule: heirs inherit irrespective of contribution or need. Another is flagrant denial of 'equal opportunity'. Principled resistance to equal opportunity is inscribed in the law which allows inheritance of property: a matter remarkably overlooked by those sociologists who have proclaimed 'achievement', by contrast to 'ascription', the institutionalized determinant of individual destinies in a 'modern' social order.

Capitalist rules: labour earnings and welfare restraint

The second working rule applies, by contrast with the first, to most people for much of their lives. This requires those without sufficient income-yielding property to rely first on the labour market for their livelihood: to hire out their own labour; to depend on others who do so; or to draw on savings or pension claims accumulated from earlier employment. Income here is a return for a 'contribution'. But directly or indirectly returns are measured by market worth, not by reference to any independent canon of distributive justice; and their wide-ranging variability turns in the end on the drive for optimal capital profit encapsulated in the first rule.

Neither point is invalidated by trade union pressures or 'market imperfections' generally. Unions have often appealed to the notion of a 'fair wage', an appeal historically so conceived as to imply exclusion of women from significant engagement in the labour market. But conception and enforcement of a fair wage have alike been contingent on market circumstances of time and place. Where unions dig themselves well in, they may bring the wages of their more vulnerable members closer to the wages of others, by imposing on employers average labour costs approaching marginal costs; and this and that union may acquire some control over recruitment and job-definition in its own corner, if less firm control than that of high-status occupational groups commanding an officially credentialled professional mystery. But even the latter source of premium earnings entails no assertion of any ethic of distribution for general application. When intent on keeping up 'differentials', however, union and professional organization plays a supporting part in making earnings under the labour rule distinctly unequal; and the multiple inequalities of distribution under that rule engender multiple tensions of interest which obscure the dichotomy of principle between acquisition from ownership and receipt according to labour market contribution. That dichotomy can be still harder to see because incomes at the business top often draw on *de jure* capital ownership, *de facto* capital control, and ostensible labour earnings as hired management, in a mixture which defies disentanglement. An effect in turn is to veil the monstrosity of the clash in doctrine between the two rules: one rule has inculcated the many with an 'ethic of work', at least enough for them usually to see paid work as some safeguard of personal dignity; the other allows the few, when they wish, to lead lives which for the rest would be condemned as 'scrounging'.

Two points need to be added. First, both rules entail that incentives are institutionalized in monetary form. There are other institutionalized incentives: officially awarded 'honours' and more diffuse distinctions of general social status. But by and large, quirks near the top aside, certified and uncertified honour goes in step with monetary advantage. Second, even apart from 'welfare state' interventions, money incomes from property and the labour market are not the sole determinants of consumption power. Access to the means of livelihood is influenced also by the workings of consumer markets and by differential ability to obtain credit. But here again disparities generally favour the wealthy and hamstring the poor: their effect is to reinforce initial inequalities of money income, not to counter them.

The primacy of the rules of property and labour logically requires addition of a third rule: to keep government activity in its proper place. The growth of the state has made for a new complex of influences on shares in real income: direct benefits in cash and kind; government support for private welfare provision; taxation in greatly extended forms; state intervention in labour and other markets; public and quasi-public employment of substantial though minority proportions of the economically active population. Along with all this, considerations of 'need' – or of 'social desert' to denote citizenship – have come to constitute some ground for shares in distribution. For the economic system still to remain capitalist implies then a requirement that the complex of state influences should work with and within the first and second rules; not against them. The question is how far this is in fact the case. I turn to that matter in the next two chapters.

5 Market-Tied Welfare Aims

To find answers to the question how far state activity works with or against the grain of capitalist prescriptions for distribution one has, I suggest, to identify the aims of principle which underlie public provision for welfare in late twentieth-century western countries. As I see them, there are five broad sets of such aims. The first four involve no substantive breach of the distributive rationale of a capitalist economy, though they work towards moderating class inequality to variable degrees. These, which I discuss in the present chapter, are establishment of a minimum level of living guaranteed to all; provision for individually graduated risk reduction above that level; aspirations for equality of opportunity; and concerns for progressive redistribution, only loosely conceived. But a fifth aim does in principle transgress the boundaries which full adherence to capitalist distributive logic would set to welfare state provision. This involves ambitions for equality of condition, though only in selected areas of life. I reserve discussion of that for chapter 6.

Minimum guarantee

Some formal guarantee of minimum livelihood for every citizen is now common in western countries. Often, as in Britain, it comes in two forms. In the first, certain categories of life contingency that cut out earnings from work – retirement after a specified age, illness or disability, 'involuntary' unemployment – give entitlement irrespective of income from other sources. In the second form, entitlement requires proof of lack of alternative means. The latter may have been conceived originally as residual provision but in fact continues to play a large, even a growing, part. The reasons include, arguably, an inherent insensitivity of entitlement by 'category' to individual variations of circumstance; a normal dependence of category entitlement on past employment records; and, at some times in some countries, government determination to limit expenditure and target it on the 'genuinely needy'.

Policies to the latter effect can appeal to everyday notions of equity; and, in principle, means-tested provision could be more progressively redistributive than universal payment of minimum pensions, sick benefits or dole without regard to other income. Tax-credit systems have been advocated as a way to more effective redistribution which, while incorporating test by need, could avoid the stigmatization and discouragement of 'take-up' commonly associated with support dispensed only in response to specific application on individual initiative. In practice, however, such schemes for 'negative income tax' have often been proposed primarily to confine cash help only to the very worst-off, and to allow more free rein for market forces to determine incomes above the cut-off level. The tax-credit programme proposed by Mr Heath's Conservative government in 1972, though never implemented, was a British case in point. If negative income tax is nevertheless conceivable in more generous versions, provision for means-tested support in more familiar form has proved largely counter-productive for both 'targeting' and progressive redistribution.

One trouble is that it adds nothing to the incomes of people who cannot pass the stringent, often confusing and sometimes discretionary tests of need, however close they may be to circumstances that do pass the tests. But also, it adds nothing for people who are eligible yet do not apply; and these are many. Popular knowledge of entitlements is usually patchy. The benefits obtainable may be marginal relative to the hassle and indignity involved in obtaining them. The tests commonly take inquisitorial form, and may incorporate an official premise that claimants should prove innocence of intent to defraud. The latter feature expresses a spirit of animosity to dependence on public 'charity' which, spread wide through popular allegiance to an ethic of work, potential claimants are likely to share themselves or to suspect their family, friends and acquaintances of sharing.

Such impediments to take-up are not entirely confined to means-tested provision. For example, unemployment benefit for a period after redundancy is not subject to tests of financial need. But it is subject to tests of willingness to take work when available; and where unemployment has risen high, the tests have grown sharper. Notably at the hands of recent British governments, they have increasingly demanded hard proof af active continuing search for work; and they have been reinforced by official nurture of a climate of opinion equating unemployment with personal shiftlessness. One intended result is to force more unemployed people to look for support instead under the alternative system of test by means. Shortening the period of unqualified benefit entitlement after redundancy, or lengthening the period of previous consecutive employment required before entitlement, has the same effect. In general, the large part played by claims submitted on individual initiative, for inquisition into personal circumstances, is the most potent reason why actual provision for minimum livelihood falls short of the provision promised in welfare state principle.

Advocates of 'citizenship' have a sound case, then, when they prefer entitlement by category over entitlement by means-tested claim. The argument for 'universalism' in this sense does not rest just on the symbolism that all are potential recipients of public support; or on a fear that it could be hard otherwise to persuade the better-off to contribute to funding. It rests also on the fact that conventional means-testing is relatively ineffective. Yet the two forms of provision share a feature which marks a significant break with the past. Both in principle declare life at some basic level of real income a right of citizenship: no longer a condition contingent on the vagaries of markets, private fortune and misfortune; on charity and distinctions in charitable dispensation between the deserving and the undeserving.

While it is hard to make that right stick when the instrument is means-testing of individual claims, measures can be taken to reduce the obstacles: to publicize entitlements; to notify rules for award which limit the discretion of awarding officials; even, as in Sweden, to impose on official agencies an obligation to search out eligible non-recipients. But there are times and places where the broad impetus from authority is to the contrary.

Thus, British government policy in the 1980s–90s has sought to trim instead. Despite exercises to publicize entitlements, it has generally discouraged claims through increased stigmatization of claimants and aggressive invigilation for fraud. It has cash-limited the total fund available for supplementary discretionary awards. It has converted such awards from grants to short-term loans. And it has substantially disentitled single adolescents and young adults if they have parents on whom they might conceivably depend. The latter three measures represent a significant curtailment of rights to minimum livelihood. The last in good part removed its victims from the status of social citizenship; and young unmarried mothers have since been rather similarly threatened. Even so, the right of others to some means of basic living has remained; and its wholesale abrogation does not seem to be on the political agenda.

Important as it has been, however, institution of this right does not breach the logic of capitalist rules for distribution. It has been accommodated within the rules by tying the right to labour market requirements. This is evident, first, from the fact that most entitlement by category depends on past employment. Thus in Britain, receipt of a full base-rate pension from the state requires a record of national insurance contributions paid, up to a specified level, while in work; for a widow unentitled in her own right to receive a pension, her late husband must have had a similar record to his credit. Sickness and unemployment benefit similarly in the main require demonstration of a previous regular work record. The fact that proof of the work record comes from past payment of contributions has no linked significance for funding. Benefits are paid from other government revenue as well as the national insurance fund; their levels are set and altered at government will. Contributions constitute in effect just one form of taxation among others. Their significance is that they mark a steady history of individual effort in the labour market. Their effect, therefore, is also to diminish entitlement by 'category' for those whose employment records are irregular, slim or nil: in particular, married women are liable to a status of only part-or proxy-citizenship under such arrangements.

Those so debarred are still eligible for state benefit to bring their level of living up to minimum standards: this chiefly through the alternative means-tested system. But both systems are tied to the labour market in another way: the minimum standard guaranteed is set in principle below the lowest general wages levels. The guarantee is intended to meet need unmet by market forces. But no autonomous definition of 'need' is involved: the definition comes from the working of market forces themselves, and is designed to avoid conflict with them.

The standard will often be allowed to rise in real value over time as and if national output grows: this perhaps through index-linking to average wages. Index-linking to retail prices – as in Britain from the 1980s – will by contrast at best only keep the minimum steady in real terms, and so leave the officially designated poor to fall cumulatively behind as others' real incomes generally grow. In either case the rule pertains that the current floor of labour market earnings ought to be above the basic level of livelihood guaranteed in public policy. How much above varies. Scandinavian policy tolerates a much smaller gap between state-guaranteed minimum and wages floor than in Britain. But a gap there still is, and has to be in any economy that sets labour contribution as a prime condition for allocation of income. For how otherwise induce enough people who can work in fact to do so?

It can still be hard to maintain the gap consistently. For one thing there is no single practical definition of the wages floor. For another the conception of 'need' built into minimum welfare provision has to take account of household circumstances in ways that market pay does not. Dependants – including children, and 'housewives' so long as tenacious convention assigns married women a less proper place in paid work than men – have needs that must find some recognition, once a general right to subsistence is acknowledged. Some households will then be able to claim more by way of state-benefit income alone than they would get from low-wage employment: take the case of many mothers now alone-with-children. This is a prime source of charges that the welfare state encourages 'dependency' and 'scrounging'. But standard defence against such charges itself underlines the labour market orientation implicit in policy. The defence argues that it usually takes dire circumstances to persuade adults to choose resort to state benefit over the dignity of paid work. It concludes that provision for dependants irrespective of earned income – such as child benefit in Britain – should be extended to diminish disincentives to employment. This is a sound case in its own terms. But it is sound just because those terms include the premise that public provision ought not to put labour market workings at risk.

Personal benefits from public funds are the major means to implement a guarantee of basic income but they may be complemented by government influences on the workings of the labour market itself. Minimum-wage legislation, other measures to protect the most vulnerable employees, encouragement of collective bargaining, macroeconomic policy to keep demand and growth buoyant – these will all, if effective on their own terms, both help to reduce the numbers forced to resort to state benefit; and exert an upward pressure on the floor of labour market earnings, which may make space to up-rate the baseline itself. Conversely, policies to deflate the economy, to inhibit union activity, to erode protection and 'casualize' employment in the lower reaches of the labour market, will both increase the numbers dependent on direct state relief and depress the wages floor. The logic of that in turn – as very visible in British government measures from the 1980s – is to set more stringent limits to guaranteed basic provision: in order to keep public expenditure in check, and to preserve the gap between the lowest level of general wage earnings and the 'poverty' baseline beneath it.

Government labour market policies, then, help to provide significant leeway for variations in application of the minimum guarantee.

But in practice the leeway here has come foremost from scene-setting macro-economic measures to boost or deflate market demand. And even where these have come in larger progressively directed programmes to combine overall boost with more specific measures for wage-earner protection – as in Sweden until recently – the concern has been maintained to hold the guarantee of minimum livelihood free of substantial conflict with labour market requirements. No conception of 'need' independent of lower-end market workings has been asserted.

Individually graduated risk reduction

A minimum guarantee thus keeps individual benefit low. But policy in western countries has turned also to provision of benefits above that level, graded by reference to past incomes. This involves a different objective: to seek, not basic parity among citizens in adversity, but instead some continuity of circumstances for individuals between times of regular employment and times when they are 'involuntarily' out of work. Pensions are then graduated in some way according to previous earnings; and basic unemployment benefit may, as in Britain for a time until the 1980s, attract a supplement that takes account of past wages above the general floor.

The rationale is to allow more flexibility than does flat-rate provision: to prevent extreme drops in levels of living; so to counter some of the common risks of dependence on the labour market, but at rates which bear an individually graduated relation to pickings in that market. The rates of 'compensation' provided vary greatly: from levels generally well below past regular earnings in Britain and Germany, for example; to short-term benefit rates of up to 80 or even 90 per cent of the individually lowest wages, under reforms instituted around 1970 in Sweden and Denmark. There the argument that seemed to clinch the case at the time gave priority to 'rehabilitation': sharp loss of earned income was otherwise liable to pitch victims into such personal crisis as would inhibit their return to employment. Labour market considerations ruled the roost here too, though to generous effect; and they rule the roost in all graduated provision. Whatever the rates of compensation for lost earnings, the principle remains that there should be some gap between earnings in work and benefits out of it.

That principle is applied even where it might not seem necessary to apply it: to people permanently out of the labour market. It could thus pose no direct threat to employment incentives if pensioners were guaranteed incomes unrelated either to their individual past earnings or to the general floor of wages: say a 'citizen's pension' at a level corresponding to national average pay. That happens nowhere, even in Scandinavia; and the possibility seems so remote that a case against it has rarely been articulated. Were such a case to be put, it would no doubt reflect market considerations. To detach pension provision so wholly from employment earnings would require a tax burden liable to debilitate market incentives at large. It would, to continue this devil's advocacy, undermine 'private thrift' to boost public base provision for old age. And it would challenge an axiom which, unreflected though it usually is, again bears an imprint of labour market priorities. This is the assumption that it is proper, even 'natural', for most people – *rentiers* excepted – to suffer a decline in livelihood when they are past work for pay.

Individually graduated provision may make for reduction of class inequality all the same. It can allow many rank-and-file wage-earners some part of that security from unpredictable risk which salaried career employees have long typically enjoyed. One aim of Scandinavian reforms towards enhancement of graduated provision was precisely this; and there are parallels in such changes of labour law – in many countries, including Britain before the 1980s – as have been designed to give wage-earners some of the insurance against dismissal or redundancy previously limited by employers' discretion to 'staff'. Employers' discretion is in any case exercised variably. Thus large Japanese corporations generally draw the line between 'staff' and insecure labour quite far down the employee hierarchy. Whether through selective business practice as there, or by means of more widely applied public policy as in many western countries, the effect has been in varying degrees to diminish that unpredictabiity of livelihood which was classically characteristic of the 'proletarian condition.'

Some provision may also be built into graduated schemes for rates of 'compensation' for lost earnings to be proportionately highest at low levels of previous work-income. Public pension schemes in Scandinavia are again a main case in point. But effective leeway for a redistributive element depends further on how previous earnings are defined. The greater the emphasis on past regularity of work, and on recent earnings, the shorter will be the straws drawn by people from wage-earning jobs, especially if unskilled; and the longer the straws drawn by those from careers with incremental pay scales and continuing promotion. So too with redundancy payments which, whether statutory or private, are commonly also graduated by reference to both earnings and stable duration of employment before redundancy: by and large, they give the smallest sums to the work-losers hardest hit and most in need.

Scope for progressive redistribution turns not least on the interaction built into scheme management between public and private agency. Take the case of recent pensions policy in Britain, where a scheme laboriously agreed in the 1970s mixed graduated supplement of basic pensions from public funds with provision for 'opting out' into more advantageous employer-sponsored arrangements. Already this enshrined a tiered structure to underscore inequality, since opting out was of disproportionate benefit to the better paid. Even more so from the 1980s, when the scheme was changed to limit direct public provision and promote yet greater resort to private insurance. The declared aim was to reduce prospective government expenditure, in the face of rising numbers of old people. The effect will be to reinforce inequalities: directly, by extended tiering of the system and reduction of leeway for higher-rate 'compensation' at low levels of past earnings; indirectly, through tax concessions to encourage private pension provision. This latter feature in turn takes substantially away from the advantage to government funds supposed to justify the policy shift. It also confirms the artificiality of the conventional distinction between 'public' and 'private' responsibility for welfare (cf. Titmuss, 1958, chapter 2; and 1962). Private agency often both depends on public sponsorship and cuts into public funds; its hallmark is accentuation of inequality.

There is room, then, for significant variety in the detailed incidence of graduated provision. But its essential character is to 'shadow' market inequality. To seek to avoid extreme discontinuity of individual circumstances between times in work and times out of work involves some notion of equity. But it is a notion necessarily at odds with equality, when the world of work that sets the pace is very unequal. When, to boot, its demand for monetary incentives requires income out of work still only to shadow income from work but not to equal it, the subordination of graduated provision to market imperatives is plain. Indeed, graduating benefits according to past employment earnings comes close to putting a stamp of approval on market inequalities. Public policy in this form consciously sets out to maintain the distributive rules of capitalism beyond employment. The road to any autonomous conception of economic justice is firmly closed here.

Equality of opportunity

Another cornerstone of present-day social policy is purported provision for 'equal opportunity', or at least for substantial reduction of inequalities of opportunity. Measures to guarantee minimum livelihood pick out the 'what' in the question 'who gets what?' and decree that, however else shaped by market workings and property ownership, incomes should never fall below some given threshold. By contrast, measures towards equal opportunity translate the question into 'who goes where?' and they imply a principle that, however unequal the rewards attached to different positions in economy and society, only personal merit or demerit – coupled with choice – should determine who goes where. The notion *pre*scribes open access for individuals, according to talent and aptitude, in markets of all kinds. It *pro*scribes in principle the barriers to such mobility set by circumstances of birth and upbringing; by direct and indirect discrimination on grounds of gender, ethnicity or creed; by socio-geographic distance and by obstacles to information.

Barriers in the routes into labour markets have been an outstanding target of reform, especially since educational qualifications have become increasingly institutionalized as a means to occupational achievement. There is a long history to the ideal of equal educational opportunity in the United States – where indeed popular ideology has tended to conceive equality in any positive sense as limited to equality of opportunity, yet has all the more vociferously asserted its centrality to the 'American way of life'. But in Europe too, the twentieth century has seen a proliferation of measures to promote equal opportunity in education. In Britain, for example, the ostensible aims of the 1944 Education Act took a significant step in conception beyond earlier policies to widen access. The goal previously had been to set a ladder upwards 'from the gutter to the university'; yet not a system of selection which might also carry traffic downwards, of untalented children from privileged families towards 'the gutter'. Blithely though it left the loophole of private education alone, the 1944 Act now declared the public sector of education, by intention, just such a system: a multi-way filter in which pupils were to be sorted, and set on appropriate routes to diverse destinies in adult life, according only to their individual potential regardless of origin. The logic implied downward mobility as much as upward mobility; and so the logic of other reforms has implied – for example of still contested measures, across Europe, to temper social selection through 'comprehensive' secondary schooling and 'mixed ability' teaching.

Mitigation of inequalities of opportunity is the target of a variety of other state activity. Thus the 'poverty programmes' launched in the United States in the 1960s aimed to release poor young people from the trap of debilitating circumstances they were deemed to have inherited. A similar emphasis was evident in British 'priority area' policies of much the same time, when these were presented as means to break a 'cycle of deprivation'. Modest provision for mobility allowances in Britain in the 1960s to help victims of redundancy look for new work, later British work-training schemes, and more notably the 'active labour market' policies of Swedish governments, again exemplify concerns to reduce barriers to individual mobility. In more recent years, the most conspicuous examples of policy for equality of opportunity have been aimed against disadvantage from gender and ethnic origin. Indeed, the very phrase 'equal opportunities' is now often taken to carry the connotation 'for women along with men, and for blacks along with whites', to the neglect of those disparities of opportunity by class which once figured first on agendas and still have good reason to figure prominently.

Of course the case for equality of women with men, and of blacks and browns with whites, rests on a demand for equality, not just of opportunity but of full human respect, dignity and autonomy. And the case for open access to education has sometimes also incorporated goals well beyond the instrumentalities of effective and equitable deployment of occupational talent. There have been, for example, arguments for 'comprehensive' provision and organization at all levels of education which aim towards a higher quality of life for everyone; towards realization of personal potential outside work still more than in it; even towards a 'common culture.' More modest in aspiration, there are reformers who have seen reduction of barriers to educational opportunity as a means to reduction also in inequalities of condition: enlarging the supply of qualified labour should diminish pay differentials engendered by demand for scarce skills.

Such aims express a more generous social vision than is commonly attributed to the ethos of a capitalist economy. But they are not, as usually formulated, in principled conflict with its prime distributive rules. In practice, moreover, it is the notion of equal opportunity *tout court* which has given policy-making in these fields most head of steam. Much of the rationale has been utilitarian. Concern to draw into economic use otherwise 'wasted' human resources has played a major and explicit part in reforms to widen educational provision; a significant part too, if more tangled, in policies towards parity of women with men. But the appeal to equity has also been influential: ready to be joined with arguments for efficiency, because the ideal of equal individual opportunity is as old as capitalism itself. Far from breaking capitalist distributive rules, the call for 'careers open to talent' is one expression of the spirit of capitalist rationality, and of the iconoclasm which capitalism historically brought to bear against the order which it displaced. It is a twentieth-century phenomenon, by and large, for the state to take major initiatives in response to that call; but the call itself is neither new nor at odds with capitalist principle.

So it seems at least if the contradictions within capitalist principle are ignored, and the case for equal opportunity is not pressed too hard. The reality of social divisions substantially impedes its implementation: the reality of division by class inherent in a capitalist economy; of divisions also by gender and by ethnicity which, though neither inherent nor peculiar to capitalist economies, are widespread and stubborn. Class inequality poses the dilemma at its sharpest, just because it is inherent in capitalism. The prime distributive rules dictate sharp disparities of condition as an inescapable corollary of property and market means to goals of aggregate economic growth and choice. When both long-standing capitalist principle and twentieth-century state policy proclaim a goal also of equal individual opportunity, a circle is set that cannot be squared. It cannot be squared because, even apart from *de jure* inheritance of property, class advantage and disadvantage tend *de facto* to be transmitted from parents to children. The pattern of transmission is far from rigid; but it is the more resistant to change because cultural transmission tends to reinforce material transmission. True, even the privileged will not, nowadays, usually oppose the aim of equal opportuniy expressed as an ideal. The rhetoric of 'careers open to talent' has become too entrenched for that; and just because the pattern of transmission is not rigid, quite a number of today's privileged are people themselves who have 'made it up the ladder'. But their views thereafter, when it comes to the prospects for their own offspring, resemble those of the educational reformers who wanted to lift talent 'from the gutter to the university': the ladder is good for traffic up, but not to be trusted for traffic down.

So the privileged constitute a lobby – or a cluster of lobbies at different levels of privilege – to see that policies for equal opportunity are not taken too far. If not activist in group pressure, they are generally active in deploying their prosperity, contacts and know-how to protect their own young from the full blast of a doctrine of equal opportunity. In so far as they succeed, the doctrine in practice will be implemented asymmetrically: to make more for upward than for downward mobility. There is pragmatic viability to this, if the trend of economic change makes for fewer low-ranking jobs and more employment with the advantages of career-life. That precisely has been the case: most clearly in respect of men's work; more ambiguously so in respect of women's work, since the kinds of non-manual employment which now recruit many women often mix routine-job with minor-career features. In the case of men at least, then, the trend has been able to accommodate an aggregate growth of upward mobility –

an overall expansion of occupational 'opportunity' – without a corresponding growth of downward mobility. Equal opportunity, however, remains almost as far from achievement as it was several decades before (Goldthorpe, 1987; Erikson and Goldthorpe, 1992).

True, there is no watertight test of social reality's conformity with the ideal of equal opportunity. The ideal prescribes only mobility enough to make personal aptitude, and free choice with it, the sole determinants of individual destiny in life. When research shows continuing but not rigid links between (in the main) fathers' fates in the world of work and their sons', this *might* be the result only of genetically inherited differences of personal aptitude and/or of differences in predilection for free choice somehow naturally passed on from one generation to the next. More colloquially, middle-class children still do better than working-class children; but, so the sanguine argument runs, this is no sign of unequal opportunity: it is just that working-class children are born less able; or that they and their parents are less concerned to do well. For all its limitations the balance of evidence on measured 'intelligence', however, tells against the first proposition, and points still to a large 'pool of talent' wasted by social impediments to open opportunity (for example, Halsey et al., 1980). The second proposition is naive in allowing that predilections for choice may be transmitted from generation to generation, while yet discounting the influence of economic circumstances on the formation of the attitudes transmitted. When classes tend to acquire the features of partly distinct subcultures, they do not acquire them out of the blue. Lives circumscribed by dependence on mere jobs, for example, are likely to give rise to different – and in significant respects restricted – orientations and expectations by comparison with lives centred on incremental careers.

The two propositions alike, moreover, are out of key both with the sheer magnitude of the relative disparities of opportunity demonstrated in research on social mobility; and with signs that such disparities can, nevertheless, be reduced through sustained measures of policy. Recent experience in Sweden looks a case in point (Goldthorpe, 1987, chapter 11). By contrast, some of the educational measures first mooted by the British government in the late 1980s seem set to widen inequalities of opportunity. New provision for publicly funded schools outside local authority jurisdiction will probably boost socially selective recruitment. In higher education, increased concentration of research funding is likely to accentuate academic-cum-social hierarchy of provision in teaching; and gradual displacement of student grants by loans may aggravate impediments to access 'from below', at odds with fast overall expansion.

The lesson then is not that state intervention for – or against – 'equal opportunity' is bound to be abortive. But the odds against substantial progress through reform are tough. These are odds set by the inertia of inequalities of condition and of vested interests in privilege. Disparity of opportunity is not functionally necessary for capitalism as an economic system, but on the contrary under-uses human resources. Just so the ideal of equal opportunity poses no challenge of principle to prevailing rules for distribution. But because it poses a severe challenge in practice, it is rarely pressed anywhere near its limits.

Diffuse redistribution

Each of the three objectives I have so far tried to disentangle from the knot of contemporary social policies has a well-definable character. I turn now to a range of policies – or ingredients of policy – whose character and focus are less clear-cut. These are measures geared to some mitigation of inequality; but in a manner that leaves the extent, purpose and boundaries of the redistribution intended at best very loosely defined.

A 'diffuse redistributive' aim of this sort is often one tacked onto provisions in large part directed to other ends. Direct taxation is the most obvious example. The incidence of direct taxation by itself is generally progressive: so graded as to take proportionately more money off high than off low incomes. This is true to a degree even where steps have been taken significantly to reduce the element of progression: as in both the USA and Britain during the 1980s, by compression of income-tax bands to a narrow range. Yet there are evident ambiguities of purpose to such progressive redistribution as direct taxation involves. For one thing, tax scales may be set and modified with a wholly overriding view to aims quite distinct from welfare-distributive effects – balancing treasury books, boosting or slowing growth, controlling inflation. Moreover, failure to adjust the scales over time may surreptitiously alter the real incidence: in regressive direction, so long as rising money incomes bring more low-aid people into a tax net whose bottom threshold is kept constant meanwhile in nominal terms. Second, 'equality' sought under the tax system in one respect may be at odds with it in another. Taxation of married women separately from their husbands thus seems a legitimate step in principle towards sexual equality; but unless tempered by a new and gender-blind form of 'household-partnership' taxation, it is liable to favour prosperous households at the expense of poor ones: so to lessen gender inequality at a price of more class inequality.

Third, the rationale of progression in direct taxation is often inexplicit: is its purpose only to place the heavier burdens on the stronger shoulders; or, more actively, also to change patterns of real income? Finally, even when the latter is the case – as commonly in Scandinavian social-democratic policy – there is no model proclaimed or even implied for the ultimate pattern of real income aimed at. An active and sustained progressive tax regime does constitute a declaration that, left only to market and property forces, the distribution of real income is unfair; and it seeks to make it fairer. But it does not say what, in the end, a fair distribution would look like.

There could be some radical-left potential to such open-endedness. But in practice, so long as private enterprise is the main engine of the economy, the effective incidence of taxation has to be tuned to allow business and markets a loose enough rein to function. Rates of personal tax for 'top people', and of corporate taxation, may be set at high levels. But actual payments are then notoriously amenable to institutionalized abatement: through ever more ingenious accounting devices, through continous elaboration of tax-free perks, and through negotiation between business and authorities. High rates of direct tax are also ever subject to attack as 'penal', and so are politically hard to sustain over periods long enough to allow substantial redistributive effect. Even so seemingly well entrenched a social-democratic regime as that of Sweden has now proved vulnerable on this front; and there is commonly a vicious circle to the electoral politics of taxation. With tax avoidance pursued most effectively by people at the top of the income tree, and by petty enterprise in or bordering the 'black economy', much of the weight of progressive taxation falls on salaried employees whose privileges are limited but voting numbers considerable; much too on larger numbers of plain wage-earners. Regressive tax proposals dressed up as initiatives just to 'cut taxes' may then have quite widespread electoral appeal, even when majority opinion continues to assert ideal preference for tax-funded policies towards fairer shares (see chapter 11).

There is a source of further political confusion in the fact that direct taxes do not make up all taxation. Indirect taxes – on goods, services and transactions – constitute always a considerable proportion of the total; and they have two features crucial here. First, they are less visible than most direct taxes, even if trade unions and consumers are more conscious of their impact now than before. Second, their incidence is generally either neutral or regressive in proportion to incomes. So progressive redistribution by way of direct taxation is in good part offset by indirect taxation. But the fact that this is not readily seen gives large scope again for electoral artistry. It has thus allowed recent governments in Britain to claim illusory achievements for their 'anti-tax' policies. What in fact they did over their first-decade or so in office was to reduce income tax (from a third to only a quarter of all tax proceeds) and compress its gradations; but to increase less visible taxes roughly apace; and on both counts to shift the weight from high to lower and low incomes (see especially Hills, 1989). Yet above this the banner of 'cutting taxes' was confidently unfurled.

Progression of tax incidence is not the only instance of policy in a 'diffuse redistributive' mode. Provision for some redistribution to boost low incomes may be built into otherwise labour market shadowing schemes for earnings-related pensions. Subsidies to public or 'social' housing tend to lift lower-end living standards, yet are then often countered by regressively pitched tax concessions to promote private home ownership. Regional aid and employment promotion programmes are primarily directed to putting wasted resources to use and enhancing individual opportunity, but can also work towards changing the balance of labour demand and supply with some consequent progressive effects on the distribution of real income. Corporatist incomes policies have varyingly joined with overall wage restraint some provision to favour the lower-paid, if perhaps in a later cycle to restore differentials. All these cases share with direct taxation the twin features, first that no clear target is set for the redistribution of real income to be achieved; and second that, as part only of a mixed policy package, the redistributive component may be neutered by others.

This is not to say that no such packages can ever make headway for fairer shares. Where left-of-centre parties backed by organized labour have been long in office and influence – in Sweden notably, and in Finland at least also from the mid-1960s – recent evidence suggests an eventual compression of inequalities in disposable income (for example, Uusitalo, 1989). Fairly consistently pursued wages-solidarity policy may have played some part in that, progression in the tax system more clearly so. But both of these have in turn been coupled to a larger regime of social security couched in generous terms by comparative international standards. It takes persistence in implementation of a comprehensive programme to make much of a dent. Britain's record, though different, suggests similar conclusions. Here the 1940s saw some real diminution of economic inequalities: the combined effect of wartime mobilization, extensive welfare reform and full employment. Over the next three decades however, and under both Conservative and Labour governments which prioritized objectives other than redistribution, class disparities changed little further in relative terms. Yet this still left Britain closer to the 'Scandinavian model' of income distribution than, by way of notable example, the

USA (see again Uusitalo, 1989). Since around 1980 by contrast, under a government dedicated to reversal of the 1940s settlement, inequalities have distinctly sharpened (see chapter 8). State intervention does matter, whether to ameliorate or accentuate class division.

Yet amelioration of inequalities is one thing, conceptual breach of capitalism's rules for distribution another. Policies of 'diffuse redistribution' declare no such breach, even when embedded in larger policy packages of egalitarian orientation. Take Sweden again. It was the very restrictions inherent in working 'with the grain' of the current economic order – the immunity of profit from wages-solidarity policy, and the autonomy of private corporations in respect of investment – that led the labour movement there for a few years to adopt a programme which might over time have broken with capitalist rules. But that would have required, precisely, a durable transformation of the 'politics of distribution' into the 'politics of production': welfare state measures would not do the trick on their own (see chapter 3).

Even so, policies of 'diffuse redistribution' can seem to pose a latent threat to capitalism's economic prescriptions. Just because they are diffuse, they may look at risk of being taken further than everyday practice intends. Provisions for minimum guarantee, graduated risk reduction and greater parity of opportunity imply only quite limited questions about the equity of the distributive order: about poverty at the bottom end of that order, about disruptions of personal livelihood when people are compelled to give up paid work, about arbitrary impediments to individual advancement or demotion on the rungs of the ladder of inequality. But provisions for diffuse redistribution tend to hint at questions about the equity of the distributive system as a whole: questions without firmly pre-set limits. Just such questions hove into sight when many western governments resorted to elaborate corporatist management of their domestic economies. Government claims then to control over market incomes began to pose awkward issues about the social justice of distribution; and that almost certainly helped to raise already rising popular expectations. In Britain, it is true, the effects by the 1970s proved a shambles. In the face of 'stagflation' there came just a competitive scramble among unions and shopfloor workers; and a reopening of doors for policies of 'discipline' by free-market forces (chapter 3). In Sweden, however, wages-solidarity policy probably both reflected and further encouraged popular expectations in a tone more egalitarian than in Britain; and one consequence was to put the issue of control over the economy as a whole onto the active political agenda.

Though the issue has since slipped well off the agenda there again, the story is a reminder of the point that measures of progressive redistribution need not be mere palliatives. They can have unintended political consequences. They may, in some circumstances, carry an ideological impetus towards targets beyond the limits of usual practice; they can raise questions about the economic order which policymakers did not have it in mind to raise. Some such subversive potential is latent in policies for diffuse redistribution because they imply unfairness as things otherwise are, but leave open what fairness would look like. Yet by itself, of course, this is no material breach of capitalism's distributive prescriptions.

6 Welfare Aims beyond the Market

Selective equality of condition

The four sets of aims considered so far account between them for the larger part of welfare state activity. Measures associated with them can significantly moderate class inequality, and have done so to varying extent in most western countries this century, while their curtailment over the past decade or more has worked to substantial inequality-hardening effect. They necessarily impose some restraints on market workings; and they require tax loads that readily become political footballs, yet prove hard to reduce even at the hands of harshly cost-cutting governments when, as in recent recessions, needs for base-level relief from poverty grow steeply while economic stagnation holds back pro rata tax yields. Demand for provision in any case tends to acquire some momentum of its own, if in part through demographic shift – the long past and prospective further 'ageing' of the population – in good part also through rising popular and welfare-professional expectations. Yet for all this, no measures under the four headings set out in the previous chapter have involved any breach of principle with the distributive logic of capitalism, have subverted the overall gearing of economic activity to property and labour market imperatives, or have put some autonomous conception of distributive justice in the place where the philosophy of market enterprise has a moral vacuum.

One type of public welfare provision, however, does constitute such a breach, though more clearly in conceptual outline than in sustained practice. What this involves is a policy declaration to immunize distribution in a particular field from private property and market forces.

Access to welfare in the designated field is then to be open to all citizens on an equal basis regardless of means: varying only, if the notion is appropriate at all, according to 'need'; and at standards of provision as high as the economy at large is thought able to afford. Though vague, the latter condition is central, not least if scope be still allowed for private purchase of services alongside their free public delivery. For following such a policy declaration, private means must be unable to buy any more than frills or 'social cachet' irrelevant to substantive welfare in those matters of life so taken out of the market. The ultimate aim, then, is equality of condition within a prescribed sphere; and on an assumption that something like equality of condition can be achieved there.

The closest approximation to this model comes in comprehensive public health services, where these are provided largely free of charge to users. Present-day public services for education may also seem to qualify in so far as they seek equality of access irrespective of means. But they generally fall short of the model, on scores more significant than does health care in the form exemplified by the British National Health Service at its conception. Even apart from the large loophole of private provision, the effective goal of public policy for education is equality of opportunity rather than of outcome. Formal selection of individuals for the best educational outcomes within the public system may be deferred till fairly late in schooling; and the selection involved, by aptitude, may resemble selection for medical care according to medically assessed need. But in practice educational selection – and self-selection – is a good deal more liable to 'social contamination' than is assessment for health care. Moreover, the goal of education appropriate to aptitude, defined with more concern for labour market requirements than for individual fulfilment in life, is primarily instrumental. By contrast the vision which inspired the originators of the British National Health Service was eventual equality of health itself, rather than just equality of access to the means of health care.

There is more than parochialism to these references to the NHS in Britain. When set up in 1948, this scheme was internationally unique. Provision in some Scandinavian countries at least has since moved close to the NHS model; and the USA may now be exceptional within the West in offering even limited public guarantee of medical care only to the designated poor and the old. But few countries have yet adopted quite so radical an approach as did Britain just after the Second World War. The concept here was full public provision across the board, with free entitlement to use for all according to medical need. True, the accompanying aim of equality of health was never plausible, so long as most other conditions in life remained significantly unequal; and class disparities of mortality, for example, have proved remarkably stubborn in relative terms. Yet the idea behind the British NHS is probably the plainest specimen of this sort of qualified yet distinct breach of capitalist distributive prescriptions.

There were precedents of a kind. Right across the western world, public provision for 'external sanitation' – water supply, drainage, sewerage, street cleansing and rubbish disposal – were in large part measures of preventive medicine, if in part also of public order. They preceded comprehensive measures for direct medical care; and they often came to involve (more or less) equal provision free of direct charge. No doubt the breach here with commercial guidelines for distribution was largely pragmatic. Reformers managed to make extensive sanitary provision a recognized 'public good' because this was a straightforward way of meeting high general costs, aimed to cut back disease whose effects spread readily across class boundaries. The alternative of individual charges sufficient to yield direct profit hardly seemed feasible. Moreover, the main services in question were 'natural monopolies', over which even market rules justify in principle some public control: public ownership is again a straightforward device to that end. Similar considerations played a prime part in tax-funded provision of some other services – toll-free roads for example – which, like institutions for law, order and national defence, are central components of economic or societal infrastructure though hard to classify as welfare measures designed for equal spread of benefit.

Some notion of welfare and at least wide spread of benefit figure openly, however, when central and local governments define a range of recreational facilities as public goods: museums, galleries and libraries; playgrounds, commons, parks, rights of way in countryside and on beaches. Policy motives have been mixed: privileged-class self-interests in high culture and property conservation have variously intertwined with ambitions for popular enlightenment and with wider-spread campaign pressures. Such public services have not, of course, sought universal free access to all or most recreational land, or to anything like the entirety of 'culture heritage'; only, at most, to significant fractions. Yet the larger the fractions, and the more effectively dispersed, the closer then public provision here comes to the model of exemption from monetary rationing of access. Medical and recreational services, moreover, share a significant feature when provided as public goods. Their charge-free status cannot be ascribed to economic rationale of the sort which goes far to explain public provision of basic sanitary facilities or primary road networks. They do not offer incontestable infrastructural benefits for business and the economy at large, from a service necessarily monopolistic and involving costs hard to meet through user-charges. While no doubt some baseline public provision for medical care is in modern capital's material interest, the rest could still be left to private enterprise without obvious net detriment to business. It is in large part so left in the United States, never mind the detriment to much of the population.

It takes, in other words, a long stretch of the imagination to argue that capital interests today positively require universal entitlement to full medical care, more or less free of charge. It takes no shorter a stretch of the imagination to argue that free admission to the shelves of local libraries, say – or to the National Gallery, the Victoria and Albert Museum, the beaches at Brighton, Bridlington and Bognor – helps to keep the wheels of private business turning smoothly. No doubt it gives the prevailing order a better image. But that matters only because such provision has come to be a popular expectation; and it entails some counterweighing cost, displacement and so 'dysfunctionality' for private enterprise. Immunization from markets here is then indeed a tangible breach of capitalist guidelines. But as just such, its range is short, patchy and well open to political challenge.

It can be open to challenge from leftward perspectives as well as from the right. Charge-free universal services benefit rich as well as poor. So does general subsidy of any common service in kind, even when the subsidy – in a spirit often of 'diffuse redistribution' – goes just to reducing charges. All such services may therefore have a regressive impact on real income distribution, contrary to their usual declared intentions (see, for instance, Le Grand, 1982). True, this argument generally applies the less if benefits are measured in proportion to original incomes than in absolute terms. Yet it has indisputable substance by either measure, when the rich and the comfortably off make much more real use than others of an ostensibly common service. The routine realities of an unequal society make this quite a frequent phenomenon.

Take two examples: art galleries probably draw more of their visitors, head for head, from among upper- and middle-class people than from among workers and their families; full course 'academic' streams in state schools, and universities including former polytechnics, certainly draw many more of their students from upper- and middle-class homes than from working-class ones. So, when actual use stays distinctly class-skew despite free access, why not make admission charges the norm? Many or most current users – if students, then in practice often their parents or corporate private sponsors – could afford to pay the costs of their privileged benefits. Would not the public money now spent on letting them in free be more fairly spent to relieve just the more needy of entry fees, and otherwise to boost service resources? Reasoning of this sort plays a good part in recent suggestions, in Britain, for entrance fees to museums and galleries hitherto charge-free, and especially for full-cost or top-up fees in higher education.

It is a serious argument, sometimes made to genuinely progressive intent. Yet centre-left advocates would do well to take a dose of scepticism to it. It is much easier to introduce charges than to devise effective ways to abate them for 'the needy'. Abatement in the relatively minor case of admission fees to museums and galleries can go only by blue-stamped category: say for certified pensioners, the registered unemployed, card-carrying students, children visibly under age. This is a familiar practice already; it even makes commercial sense if it boosts demand in circumstances of under-use. But it is no great shakes for targeting 'need' overall. And the recipe is liable to deploy some money still to holding charges down, while yet deterring popular use through fees that may reinforce cultural estrangement between classes. Public subsidization of opera is a notorious instance of this little dilemma.

The dilemmas would be more critical in the case of full-cost fees for higher education: certainly if fees were levied on entry, and not as later conditional charges required only according to income in postgraduate employment. Abatement of admission fees would take the ostensibly finer-tuned form of means-tested bursaries. But it is very hard to conceive of so fine a tuning of means tests that they would not, at several income thresholds, discourage significant numbers of potential students: both among the sorts who do now enter universities, and among those who do not. For the latter especially, the odds in decisions whether or not to work towards admission might easily tip still further against entry through new uncertainty about getting a bursary. Means-testing plainly deters take-up in other fields of welfare provision: surely here too? But the problems go beyond this. Once in place for students without bursaries, 'commercial' fees would constitute a temptingly expandable source of revenue for some institutions: for those whose prestige, academic-cum-social, would allow them to recruit moneyed students, with an eye to the extra fees they would bring in; these as well as gifted students, with an eye to their talents. The clientele of prestigious places would then, once again, tend to divide into two kinds: 'scholars' and 'gentlefolk', the latter including nominees of corporate sponsors as well as students from prosperous homes. Gradations of both esteem and resources among universities would incrementally sharpen. Because these must generally translate into gradations of academic calibre and range, hierarchy in quality of provision would incrementally intensify, however blandly disguised as just 'diversity'. Even if access did expand more overall, it would be access to learning of very different formats: this with socio-cultural selection for the different formats now openly augmented by monetary selection. Equality of opportunity would no longer be even an aspiration far short of achievement. It would be off the agenda altogether.

This remedy, then, looks worse than the defect. But the defect is real enough, and poses a familiar quandary for reform policy to progressive intent. The wholesale inequalities of a distinctly unequal society set formidable obstacles – material and cultural – to efforts aimed at a fairer spread of conditions in just one or other corner of life by itself. Only very substantial and enduring compression of inequalities across the board would offer a full way, leftwards, out of the dilemma; and there is no sign of this on the current horizon. Yet there are ways to moderate the quandary without such drastic foreshortening of aims as reversion to fee-charging in higher education would exemplify. Coherent recasting of taxes could do much more to claw back what the rich gain from free public goods. And though class divisions do bring cultural divisions with them, these are not wholly unbridgeable and static. Free public libraries thus have a fair historical record of 'social spread' to their credit. Free secondary schooling in comprehensive style has helped to open educational opportunity somewhat in Scotland (McPherson and Willms, 1987) as in Sweden. Moves towards something like comprehensive post-school education might similarly help to build bridges, where full-cost fees by contrast would widen gaps. When a field of service deemed essential to the quality of life is taken out of the market, that declaration of immunity makes a small but principled breach in distribution of welfare by the purse. If too few people then slip through the breach, must the answer be to close it up again? To conclude so is unwarrantedly to give up hope of working to open the breach wider.

Provision for health care in NHS style remains far and away the main breach of this kind so far. Effective access is still socially skew, when measured against tenaciously persistent class differences in need. But since use has spread nonetheless widely across classes, no good case can be made here for wholesale fee- charging with selective abatement as a means to more progressive distribution. Yet this has in no way made the health service secure: either from trimming and attrition over time; or, more recently, from political challenges setting its very aims in doubt.

There were obstacles to the goal of universal provision built in from the start. NHS consultants were allowed leeway for private practice on the side, with all the risks of resource-diversion which that entails. Professional autonomy in control, and the hierarchical tiering of professions in the medical world, are ever liable to set distances between staff and patients that tend to widen down the patient class scale. Top-tier preoccupations with curative technology have held back development of preventive measures and long-term care; socio-geographical disparities in provision have proved hard to overcome; and keeping growth of overall resources in step with growth of demands has posed perennial political problems. Money charges, moreover, were reintroduced early on: at rates first described as nominal, with relief anyway for scheduled categories of patient; and for matters deemed only on the 'fringe' – in respect of teeth, eyes, prescriptions for medicine. But so to marginalize these services was itself at odds with 1948 intentions. And charges have been successively increased: whether the stated aim was just to bring in extra money; or if it was also to discourage 'abuse' (a plea hard to square with continuing evidence of consultation too little and too late) and, with similarly disciplinary overtones, to symbolize that 'nothing comes free'. Under governments dedicated to the latter propositions, prescription charges rose from 20p per item in 1979 to £4.25 in 1993 – a twenty-one fold increase, many times the rate of general inflation. Dentists and opticians' charges have been raised so high for non-exempted patients as to take these services, in effect, more than halfway outside the NHS.

The Thatcher governments, it is true, shied away from wholesale replacement of the service by some system combining public provision only at base-level with higher-level market provision through private insurance. They held back although proposals of the sort were in vogue among marketeers; and although private health insurance had been growing, to a point where substantial further growth would require enrolment of older people and/or wage-earners at higher risk of illness and so at higher cost. But the government's eventual 1989 measures did go part-way to helping medical insurance companies out of the latter dilemma. People over sixty, even relatives subscribing on their behalf, were offered tax discounts for enrolment in private health insurance. Such use of public money to encourage two-tier provision was a blatant disavowal of 1948 principles. Other new measures were not. Their proclaimed aim was to promote better use of resources and more choice for patients, while maintaining the principle of 'primary care' free of charge. Yet some of the means chosen may well further stratify provision. Encouragement for the more efficient hospitals to opt into self-governing status could leave others to face a downward cycle of decline. 'Contract shopping' by general practitioners, working within enforcable budget limits, is

liable to disadvantage costlier hence needier, so also disproportionately poorer patients; it could also prove a source of concealed public
subsidy to private health contractors.

Strenuously organized opposition to the proposals from doctors no
doubt in part reflected fears of loss of professional autonomy; but
fears also of evertightening restrictions on public funds, and so perhaps of new unevenness to the distribution of rewards and influence
within the profession if provision for patients became more unevenly
spread. Wide popular fears that even basic universality of the service
was now at risk fed anyway on more than the medical campaign
against the 1989 White Paper. They were prompted by perceptions of
the proposals as a deliberate alternative to more generous funding; by
the government's evident haste to impose 'internal marketing' with
little advance trial; and by the larger policy package of which these
measures were part. 'Fringe service' charges had already been drastically increased. The principle of no tax relief for privileged private care
was now to be flouted. And, in a parallel move widely distrusted on
newer green as well as older pink grounds, the government had
determined to privatize even the elementary public good of water
supply. Its claim that health provision would be 'safe in our hands'
plainly evoked much popular scepticism.

Still uncertain of outcome, the story points up two lessons: one that
a clear breach with market-distributive rules is hard to sustain in a
profit-driven economy; the other that, nonetheless, such a breach can
win many friends. Creation of the National Health Service was the
most radical of the measures for 'social reconstruction' taken in Britain after the Second World War; but it has also proved by far the most
popular. Successive public opinion polls testify that high-level support spreads well across classes (see chapter 11). It was surely recognition of this that held the 'new-right' regime back from any
comprehensive demolition exercise in the 1980s. But just that popu-
larity also helps to explain why, by more devious means, the service
has been subject to recurrent trimming from its edges inwards. For
with such solid endorsement by the electorate, there might come
pressure to follow the example of the NHS into one or two further
fields; if so, at enhanced risk to the general sway of market rules for
distribution.

Hence trimming instead, and no other comparable breaches with
market rules. Public provision of personal social services, for example,
is not a comparable case. These services have inherited concerns with
social control while adding concerns with advice and protection, even
advocacy, for the poor. Public social work may aspire to status as a
universal service for 'social therapy'. Even so, constraints of funding

and policy conception keep its role largely to one of damage limitation *vis-à-vis* inequality, and its clientele largely drawn from among the economically most vulnerable. No doubt health was the obvious candidate for 'market immunization', if there was to be a candidate at all. Once socio-economic disparities in health are no longer taken for granted as if they were natural, it becomes hard to find arguments for their toleration. Yet other fields might conceivably also have been picked for some significant insulation from market demand.

Take housing: not an implausible candidate when the general notion of a 'decent home for all' has wide appeal. True, the case for consumer choice in housing has a salience for which there is no parallel in health care; and latitude for choice would be very hard to safeguard against gravitation of irresponsible power to the managers and professional experts of any comprehensive 'national housing service'. Yet this need not preclude a more limited application of market immunization measures to housing. One key measure would be unqualified guarantee of a home for every household: at low price (or even conceivably no price) for a rising level of good quality. Another would be public appropriation either of all land or at least (as in Britain for a short span of years after 1947) of all development values and rights in land. The purpose of this would be to secure for the community the windfall gains from land appreciation which now accrue arbitrarily to private owners; and thus also progressively to neutralize one key element in housing costs. Neither measure would dictate uniformity of provision or suppression of consumer choice. Stock could be provided by a diversity of agencies and contractors: private, cooperative and public. Security of tenure and latitude of use and disposal could be offered in the form of long public leaseholds of up to lifetime duration: owner-occupation in effect, but without rights of fortuitous profit and transmission to heirs. Households would be left free to use purse to acquire homes of higher quality than the guaranteed standard: full equality of condition would not be the goal. But the range of inequality could be much compressed; speculative private gains and arbitrary losses in the property market eliminated; and a 'decent home' made a firm reality for all.

A hare-brained sketch? Not obviously so, from a 'social reconstructionist' perspective of 1940s vintage. Of course a scheme of this sort is enormously much harder to imagine floated in the 1990s, when unconditional owner-occupation of homes-with-land has become the prime preferred form of tenure; and when public or 'social' housing has tended concomitantly to revert to a residual and stigmatized role in countries where it earlier had some potential to spearhead a comprehensive guarantee of good housing for all. My purpose here, however, has been only to suggest that a significant adaptation of market immunization ideas to the case of housing need not have been beyond the wit of reform zeal for social 'citizenship' in the fairly recent past. Yet no project of this order seems ever to have gained a real foothold on any western political agenda.

In the event, then, the case of health is unique. Even modified extension of the notion of insulation from market demand to other significant fields would not just cost public funds more than goes well with profit yardsticks for economic enterprise and with protection of vested privileges. It would also magnify the question marks implied against the whole remaining order of distribution. Even were the hypothetical policy objective to buttress capitalism's 'legitimacy', the result more likely would be to throw more doubt upon it. High-quality free provision of health care is, where it has been accepted as a worthy goal, the thin end of a wedge inscribed to say that fairness means equality of condition: a notion quite out of line with the prevailing general rules for distribution. Small wonder, then, that prudent policy has been concerned to squeeze the wedge back rather than to toy with extravagant ideas for widening it.

Socialist equality of condition: vision and yardstick

Back now, in summary, to the general question of welfare state limits (chapter 4). A capitalist economy sets two primary rules for distribution: the rules of property and of labour market earnings. Public policies modify the impact of the two rules. The question is how far they break with them, or may be brought to do so. Of the five objectives which I suggest can be identified within present-day western policy packages three, despite progressive purposes and effects, involve no significant disjunction with capitalism's working rules. Provisions for minimum livelihood in adversity, and for further income-graduated reduction of personal risks, are explicitly intended to avoid a clash with profit and employment incentives. Measures towards equality of individual opportunity echo an aspiration as old as liberal capitalism, which the latter's internal contradictions and everyday social realities continue to impede. None of these three asserts any norm of distributive justice which might fill the moral vacuum of an economy geared to private enterprise (chapter 5). Nor does the fourth set of policies; and redistribution of a diffuse character has not in practice been taken so far as to block business activity or shred its basic prescriptions for unequal access to the good things in life. Yet just because policies of this sort set no target for the greater fairness they seek, they carry a hint that they might be taken further. Measures in the fifth mode, however, go beyond a hint into tangible breach of the primary rules. But only health care qualifies in effect so far for near-full inclusion in this category of direction to 'selective equality of condition'; and then only at risk from pressures for retraction.

In overview, this can be read two ways: with emphasis on the latter breach of rules, and the hint of potential breach from other measures that currently stop short of it; or with emphasis on the narrow front of that breach, and the force of constraints which have held most public welfare provision within capitalist bounds. But the two emphases are complementary rather than alternatives; and, so taken together, they go against each of the copy-book formulae for assessment of the welfare state discussed in the early sections of chapter 4.

The first reading finally undermines neo-Marxist theorizing of the functionalist sort which postulated inherent consonance between state activities and general capital needs. But the second reading tells as strongly both against neo-liberal dogma that the welfare state has subverted free enterprise; and against surviving broad-centre hopes that the boundaries for reform towards comprehensive social citizenship may still prove elastic enough to pose no necessity of serious conflict between business and popular interests. Certainly, says the first reading, those boundaries are not rigid and impermeable. But, says the second, they are plainly hard to break through; and durable widening of any breach looks very unlikely through reform directed mainly to distribution, without extensive public control also of production.

There is nothing in that conclusion to satisfy those who hanker after some neat theoretical fix to encapsulate a social reality which shows structure but no simple determinacy; and nothing to enthuse those who want a much fairer society but see no political prospect or practicality to socialist prescriptions for economic management. Yet it is worth adding a few comments about the conception of equality which has lurked backstage in my argument: as an implicit left-radical yardstick of welfare reform so far, and even as a potential aim of policy beyond welfare reform some time.

That conception looks to general equality of condition. By this I mean a state of affairs in which the quality of life circumstances and opportunities would be much the same for all, so far as measures to that end could be practically found; and where avoidable deviations would be justified only to the extent that they were necessary for the achievement of other ends explicitly awarded higher priority. Inequalities would not be ruled out. But initial presumptions would be against them; and above all against cumulative inequality, as distinct from discrete and particular inequalities.

Maybe Marx had something like this in mind with his prescription, 'to each according to need'. But if so, he still left unsettled the relationship of this prescription to his anterior injunction 'from each according to ability'. Should some people not contribute according to ability, would they then lose entitlement according to need? And if so, would the grounds properly involve moral disapproval (with intentional stigma in consequence) or be only utilitarian (to encourage compliance)? These may seem rarefied questions to ask of a dead guru; and I shall not try to pursue them by way of exegesis. But they underline the provisos attached to my own crude first formulation: equality of condition in so far as practicable and compatible with other explicit objectives. There are three main points to make here.

First, some obstacles to parity in quality of life will remain insurmountable. Even the most assiduous compensatory treatment is unlikely ever to make up for the stultification of human potential associated with mental or physical handicap. More generally, individual dispositions and temperaments will continue to vary widely in ways that have nothing to do with pressures from socio-economic inequality. In so far as some such features of personality can impede individual self-fulfilment, they may be open to therapy; and an egalitarian society must ensure that therapy is commonly available. But it has no business generally to enforce use of it, and none ever to seek individual uniformity or conformity. On the contrary, the larger point of reducing material inequality to the minimum is to allow everyone, as nearly as possible, the same means to quality of life: all in their own ways. Each phrase here would be trite, were it not for the conventional conservative wisdom that caricatures egalitarian ambition as both oblivious to individuality and yet intent upon destroying it. But a practical corollary follows. When the end is to couple expansion of choice with its equalization there must, still, be markets in which expenditure of money can express choices effectively. There would be services wholly or partly outside the market: infrastructural facilities of a necessarily collective kind; and such services as health and education whose positive use requires more knowledge than most users can reasonably be expected to have. But the case for consumer subsidies to mitigate inequality would dwindle as and when money incomes became markedly more even.

Second, however, much current diversity of personal disposition and preference that appears individual is in fact conditioned by socio-economic inequality. Differences of class position, gender and ethnic status make for differences of subculture which set privileged vantage points and high personal expectations against restrictions of individual aspiration, horizon and effective opportunity. The purpose of real-income equalization would not be to rule subcultural variety out of bounds: far from it. But it would be to level out those material disparities which at present feed opposed charges – negative versus positive – into such variety. There is again a practical corollary. In a complex modern economy, functional specialization will continue: this even if labour effort in aggregate will be less; and if change, complexity and equality alike will make for growing emphasis on widespread general knowledge and adaptability of skills. Functional specialization in turn will continue to produce a range of specialist milieux whose occupants will assert claims of special need to match their special functions. Policy in an egalitarian spirit will have to be wary of the risks that, once acknowledged, such claims may generate privileges enlarged and perpetuated beyond the utilitarian purposes of their acknowledgement. Premium earnings to promote work recruitment or performance, for example, need not automatically attract also premium pensions as now. Again, especially if privileged by professional autonomy as well as by premium earnings, specialist subgroups are likely to find scope both to influence policy in line with their own perceptions and interests, and to secure transmission of advantage to their children. Resistance to the latter may require measures of 'positive discrimination', to back a comprehensive pattern of education aimed at parity of outcome over and above equality of opportunity. Pressures towards renewal of inequality will not disappear, nor will recurrent conflicts of interest. Capitalism is not the only barrier to equality, as critics of socialism never tire of pointing out.

Critics are likely to charge equality of condition with injustice as well as impracticability. They may perhaps concede that rewards in hierarchically organized enterprise could be more fairly shared out than now. But surely only blind dogma can deny that individuals or genuinely voluntary cooperatives deserve to enjoy the full fruits of initiative that is solely their own, provided only that this does not diminish the total otherwise available to others? The product of independent enterprise is then wholly a top-up: good luck to its makers; and a good example may they be for us all. Proponents of this argument can find distinguished philosophical support for it. Thus even the ostensibly egalitarian thesis that inequality should never leave the poorest- or the poorer-off in worse circumstances than otherwise (as I read Rawls, 1972) would allow self-contained enterprise its own full reward on the condition stated. Yet appealing though it is in abstract, the contention should cut little ice in practical application to a modern economy and society. For virtually no enterprise now is self-contained. Even the smallest of one-person outfits rarely produces anything marketable, or even unmarketable, without use of a complex collective infrastructure and of supplies from outside; and to that network of infrastructure and supply unnumbered others contribute: superiors and subordinates, privileged and poorly-off. The interdependence of practically all economic enterprise today leaves the point-in-justice of this critique with nowhere to go. There remains, however, a point-in-utility to it. A polity committed to parity of outcomes in principle would need to be alert to the risks of escalation from petty initiative to larger enterprise, and thence to cumulative privilege and power. But it could not seek to ban all small enterprise without despotic control, stifling of initiative, and so ultimate destruction of its ambition towards a greater common freedom.

Incentives come in here; and my third point concerns the objection that the project is bound to founder on this rock. Encouragement of economic virtue requires incentives; and inequality is a necessary corollary. True enough: some inequality. But it follows neither that incentives need be primarily monetary; nor that they be allowed to line up in cumulative fashion. Even a capitalist economy relies on much commitment that finds little or only modest reward in cash. Rewards by way of self-esteem, others' esteem and varying degrees of work satisfaction make some way up for that, over and above sheer habit or necessity. But tension and resentment growl nonetheless, because high earnings and still higher profits go to yet others whose commitment is not visibly greater. More money is then demanded, because money is the prime institutionalized form of incentive. And when monetary inequality ranges wide, monetary incentives increase cumulatively up the scale. Well rewarded already, top managers and prestigious professionals have learned to sniff at anything but prize premiums for extra effort – if extra indeed it is. By contrast, once established, egalitarian policy would need to choose cash prompts only when they would do the trick better than incentives of esteem, work satisfaction or custom. All the latter might prove to go quite a way for much work that currently gives high pay; and with generous standards of common education, it could be rather the dullest jobs that needed extra cash inducements. The initial baseline of equality, moreover, should help to keep pay differentials within bounds a good deal tighter than we have become used to.

Money would continue to matter, especially as the key marker of consumer choices. Would this then constitute the Achilles' heel of the project? Retention of consumer markets must require retention of some mechanism of profits and losses in order to signal demand back to suppliers and producers. The point, however, is fatal to an egalitarian scenario only on one assumption: that profits and losses cannot work as signalling devices, unless suppliers and producers are motivated to respond by permission to appropriate most of the profit, or bear most of the loss, for themselves. Capitalist economies provide no test of the assumption because money-profit incentive for enterprise, like pay-incentive for employment, is their very grain. Nor does the dismal experience of Soviet-style economies, never mind the laissez-faire sermons read out of the tides of change in eastern Europe since the late 1980s. Command management with little use of markets has plainly proved abortive. But even pre-collapse experiments there with profit-and loss-accountancy as signalling devices can offer few lessons, when their context included political oppression and tension from divisions of socio-economic inequality denied public acknowledgement. The hope that market accountancy to signal demand might in good part be uncoupled from entrepreneurial appropriation of profit, and carriage of loss, could be fully tested only in its proper context: that of a democratic socialist economy committed to pursuing equality of condition.

The test might tell against the speculation; indeed the speculation may never be put to test. Democracy itself would ensure this, if no durable majority can be persuaded to endorse an egalitarian move well beyond welfare reform. But bleak though it may look, the future is not so settled as to make all conjecture about a possible shape for socialism wasted effort. In any case, even only as a means to assess the achievements and shortcomings of welfare-modified capitalism, the notion of equality of condition gives longer measure than those yardsticks which stay close to conventional wisdom: the pragmatically constrained notions of safety nets below market level; of more equality of individual opportunity for individual outcomes still arbitrarily unequal; or of a vague parity of 'respect' unmatched by tangible conditions that would make respect stick to those who do not now get it.

Part III
Is Class Now Dead – Again?

7 Class Beclouded

Counter-class theses

The definitive demise of class has been widely proclaimed since around 1980. Standard commentary in Britain now takes it for granted that class divisions have lost most of the political clout they once had; and that behind this lies an erosion of class inequalities and their social significance which leaves, at worst, only a new 'underclass' cut off in deprivation or depravity from an increasingly 'classless' mass majority in secure prosperity. Professional social scientists have, on the whole, been more cautious in diagnosis than media pundits and politicians. But some number even of these have climbed onto the bandwagon, by postulating recent decisive shifts of economic structure and cultural climate which, they say, are draining class of its once familiar social salience.

My purpose in this part of the book is to contest assumptions of that fashionable sort. They are not, however, new assumptions. Commentary to much the same effect was the vogue in the 1950s and well into the 1960s, until growing 'working-class affluence' proved to lead then less to complacent embourgeoisement than to an escalation of material expectations, popular 'desubordination' and industrial militancy (cf., for example, Goldthorpe, Lockwood, et al., 1968/9; Miliband, 1978). Denial of class is indeed long-standing conservative stock-in-trade; and there may be a cycle to its varying recurrence in wider conventional wisdom, in some sort of tune with the long wave of economic development (cf. Tylecote, 1992). But its recent revival is remarkable for at least two features. Significant strands to the thesis of class eclipse have found favour with some on the left (for instance, Hobsbawm, 1981): this even before eastern Europe's pretensions to socialism were finally shattered. More strikingly, class has now been re-declared dead or dying in all social significance, at a time now when its economic configuration has become even sharper.

The main immediate stimulus to class-eclipse conjecture, however, was the same in the 1980s–90s as in the 1950s–60s: the trend of electoral politics. Influential opinion had taken the Conservative victories in Britain of 1951, 1955 and 1959 as more or less certain evidence for erosion of Labour's class base. So now the successive Conservative triumphs of 1979, 1983, 1987 and 1992 have convinced all but a handful of public commentators that class, and popular commitment even to mildly leftish reform, are things irrevocably of the past. Such reasoning involves a curious adaptation of vulgar Marxist determinism. The latter traditionally held that socialist revolution *must* follow from the contradictions and tensions of capitalist class structure; stock assessment now holds that electoral collapse of the socialist project *must* testify to a dissolution of class structure; both inferences imply a simplistic equation of class 'in itself' with class 'for itself', of which Marx himself was wary when he made just that distinction. But current commentators' conviction about their inference is all the stronger because the string of recent parliamentary victories has gone to a Conservative Party in radical-right hands, and in times when unemployment has soared high. A spread of economic insecurity has plainly not polarized politics in leftward favour (as I for one had earlier thought it might: Westergaard, 1970). One ready deduction, tempting to journalists and eagerly embraced by government supporters, is that few people have suffered long and hard from economic change; while most have gained prodigiously enough now, at length, to lock embourgeoisement firmly into place.

Analyses of more substance have been added to flesh out the initial inference. One has thus claimed evidence, from opinion poll data, of a general trend towards dissolution of class-based voting allegiances altogether (especially Crewe et al., 1977; Crewe, 1984 and 1986): extrapolate from electoral inclinations to popular ideology, and class would then no longer have any such political weight as it once did. Moreover, the literature of the past decade or so has advanced an array of reasons why, precisely, one might expect increasing divisions of economic interest and socio-political outlook among those whom the labour movement has historically sought to represent. One set concerns changes in those circumstances of and around work that had hitherto done much to make for a sense of collectivity among wage-earners. Not only is blue-collar work increasingly displaced by white-collar and white-blouse work: by employment of kinds which may either offer employees enough to engage their loyalty to things as they are or practically obstruct collective organization and resistance. But blue-collar work itself is changing character. Where conveyor-belt manufacture once brought large numbers of workers together in visibly common subordination to work routines, new technology and process-organization in tactically shrewd managerial hands make now more for small-team and even isolated-individual work. That trend to workplace fragmentation of the labour force is one of several strands to an elastic description of today's world as 'post-Fordist', which has taken hold especially among those on the left who have seen in 'Thatcher's Britain' the signs of a structureless flux to societies at the turn from the twentieth to the twenty-first century. 'Post-Fordism' here becomes an ingredient of 'postmodernity'.

Conclusions to similar but wider effect have been drawn from changes seen, beyond workplaces, in the character of markets. 'Fordist' mass production for mass consumption is said to be giving way to flexible and specialist production to meet more variegated demand (see, for instance, Sabel, 1982; Piore and Sabel, 1984; Atkinson, 1986). In turn employers need greater flexibility to the terms on which they employ labour: longer and more secure terms for some, shorter and less secure terms for others. The result deduced is widening disjuncture between a primary labour market and one or more secondary markets. (For just two examples from an extensive literature, see Edwards, 1979; Craig et al., 1985.) Employment in the former is relatively well paid, secure and usually backed by firmly established union or professional organization. As in large Japanese corporations, it offers 'staff status' increasingly to a steadily engaged core labour force of manual workers too, if at the price of a new-style company-focused unionism. By contrast, such readings of the trends claim, employment outside the primary labour market has become distinctly less secure; much of it part-time or casual, perhaps under subcontracting devices that offer only intermittent work; with diminished protection, if any, by either unions or public regulation. Moreover, effective exclusion from any labour-market at all has spread, with unemployment high even between peaks.

Into such signs of labour market polarization a number of commentators have read the coming of a new and crucial line of societal division. What could once be seen as one working class is being cleft into two increasingly separate and distinct groups. Above the new line are 'core employees' who, whether blue-collar or white-collar, have a solid stake in things as they are, and fair individual prospects in life from them. Below the line are a growing number, yet permanently a minority, whose livelihood from paid work is at best poor and infirm, at worst nil, with only base-line public provision to make up existences increasingly exiguous by the standards which prevail for the majority.

This marginalized segment of the population is diverse of composition. It will include people wholly out of work for long or for good, when they have little or nothing extra to hand from occupational pensions, golden handshakes or property assets to boost minimum state support. It will include also workers in sectors where effective guardianship from unions or statutory control does not reach; people in and out of jobs according to the vagaries of a labour market now more 'flexible'; and many part-time employees. Women preponderate in these categories, old and elderly people in the first; and 'black' workers in Britain and France, 'guestworkers' in some other European countries, have been designated prototypical members of this quasi-outcaste population. Separately or together, these latter points have quite often been taken in support of some larger thesis that the axes of inequality which matter are now gender, ethnicity and even age, rather than 'class'. Yet the general inferences prompted by such sketches of widening labour market polarization differ considerably. Some commentators, indeed, have read into the trends they see a confirmation of the death of class, if with divergent messages (for example, Gorz, 1982; Bauman, 1982). Others have sought to cling on to one baby, at least, while throwing out the bathwater (for example, Therborn, 1986; Hornemann Moller, 1989). Acknowledging class still as a matter of 'power at the top', they see class for the rest as being reshaped. But the reshaping implied is drastic. For what is postulated, in all logic, is an accelerating dissolution of whatever there once was of a working class of broadly common condition and cause.

There may be echoes here of such familiar categories as the 'reserve army of labour', the 'lumpenproletariat' and, conversely, the 'aristocracy of labour'. But mainstream Marxist hopes have been pinned to eventual erosion of just such divisions within the working class; and to a spread of working-class identity among office and service employees outside the historical proletariat of workers by hand. The new scenarios turn that sort of projection on its head. They see something like middle-class identity spreading 'downwards' among wage-earners who find places in the core labour force: a vision well reminiscent of earlier 'embourgeoisement' theory. They then add a less familiar twist: the spread of salariat-like identity will stop short of a significant minority. Yet as a minority, whose members may share little more than private deprivation, this group cannot have much political clout. It will form, if speculation of this kind proves sound, an 'underclass' – even a 'non-class' – with no larger class to combine with in opposition.

The term 'underclass' indeed has run wild in recent debate, with connotations so diverse that their only similar feature may be use of the word 'class' to deny much of its substance. 'Underclass' in radical-right usage designates a segment of the population whose life-style, of indiscipline, is dangerous; whose precise numbers are less important than the contagious spread of their example; and whose material poverty, in so far as acknowledged, is self-induced. Illegitimate births and single parenthood are the prime signs of such underclass deviance from family morality. Crime, and unemployment in consequence of unreadiness to work, are both main results and proxy indicators of that deviance. And society's defence against the malaise requires encouragement of 'self-government' at local community level instead of counter-productive welfare-state 'social engineering' (see especially Murray, 1990). The argument is reminiscent of the 'culture of poverty' hypothesis of the 1960s, the spin-offs from that into 'cycle of deprivation' theorizing, and many Victorian characterizations of the down-and-out poor. But this newer variant is distinct by the resoluteness of its conception of class as a matter of voluntarily adopted life-styles – good versus evil – essentially unconditioned by economic structure.

Not so the inferences from labour market segmentation to underclass segregation which have loomed larger in British debate of the 1980s into the 1990s. These inferences, moreover, have found support from an influential mode of reading recent trends in the distribution of income. Even government-released figures now put it beyond doubt that inequalities of real income so widened, from about 1980, that effective levels of living stood roughly still among the poorest, and for some even fell; but rose substantially 'on average', while most for the best-off. This new polarization of incomes has not uncommonly been described as marking a shift to a society split between an affluent majority and a poor minority. The point has been summarized by varying choices of illustrative proportions to represent majority and minority: two-thirds versus one-third, three-quarters versus one-quarter, four-fifths versus one-fifth, nine-tenths versus one-tenth. Of such variant sets, the first two listed have the advantage that their second terms – for the minority – broadly indicate the growing proportion of the population 'in poverty' by one frequently used measure ('supplementary benefit level plus 40 per cent', see Piachaud, 1987; Commission on Social Justice, 1993). And the choice matters a good deal if the main purpose of the exercise is dramatic exposition of the underside impact of new government policies and freed-market forces (for example, Field, 1989): of the fact that people by and large left out in the cold number now well over a quarter of the population.

Yet these are still by such figures a minority; and it is on this point that many diagnoses turn which see new overriding division between a peripheralized underclass and the rest. Never mind the exact numbers assigned to the underclass: they are and will stay a minority. Never mind disparities of condition, opportunity and influence among the majority: these are no longer divisions liable to disrupt a common sense of distance from the poor, of participation in advancement, and of virtuous self-effort in the process. Mind, certainly, the complacency so encouraged among the majority; mind, too, the attrition of 'citizenship' which goes with that and with marginalization of the minority: underclass scenarios of this strain have come mainly from commentators of the centre-left who deplore erosion of political concern for commonality in quality of life (for instance, Dahrendorf, 1987; Halsey, 1989). But whatever the means to combat that, working-class combination looks by these accounts pretty much a spent force for progressive change.

The point that much the same was postulated thirty to forty years ago, and then found too light of weight, is not enough to rule out its validity now. Changing circumstances may have given it new weight. Just this is claimed for a complementary line of interpretation which has picked up the theme of 'consumer orientation' that also figured in the mid-century canon of working-class embourgeoisement. New analysis here has seen emergent divisions – among wage earners most significantly – between people with access to private provision of some essential goods in life and others, by contrast, dependent on public provision. The key example has been housing, where in Britain owner-occupation has spread to some two in every three households overall, and to over two in every five even of households 'headed' by people from unskilled jobs (*Social Trends 1992*). It is plausible to posit some conflict of interest between actual and aspiring home-owners on the one hand, on the other those whose housing opportunities and aspirations are practically limited to renting their homes from public or quasi-public authorities. But one interpretation, foreshadowed in an earlier designation of different tenure-groups as 'housing classes' (Rex and Moore, 1967), attaches a weight to such conflicts of interest, and associated differences of life outlook, sufficient to override the older alignments of class rooted in the economy of production (see especially Saunders, 1990). From this viewpoint, home ownership gives personal independence above and beyond material gain. Its acquisition, even the prospect of it, must have done a good bit to turn many working-class people classless and conservative.

When politicians and journalists fall over each other to add share-holding to owner-occupation as another vibrant force for working-class conversion, this should cut no ice. Even the small minority of blue-collar workers – about one in six or seven (cf. *Social Trends 1988, 1989*; also *General Household Survey 1987*) – who have picked up some shares in denationalized enterprises can have packages of little more than lottery-ticket purpose. But there seems more substance to extension of the 'asset-ownership' argument to a range of other key goods or services. Wage-earner households are now commonly car-owners; occupational pensions have proliferated; private health insurance has grown, and now attracts tax relief for older people. Extrapolating from all this, one school of analysis argues that the further 'downwards' access to such private provision spreads, the more people once working-class by circumstance and outlook are likely to be unlocked from their former dependence on public provision and attune themselves to market-place values and centre-to-right policies. One study, indeed, found signs of some such pattern at work in the parliamentary election of 1983 (Dunleavy and Husbands, 1985). And the suggestion is in line with other commentary to the effect that what matters, for both life chances and life-outlook, is less and less 'class', taken as your source of livelihood and your circumstances of work; more and more whether or not you own your own home, have your own car to free you from dependence on public transport, enjoy private pension rights, have insurance to provide private health care, and so on (see especially Saunders, 1984). A good thing too, it has been added, if this trend is matched by effective policies to enlarge popular access to consumption by private choice: measures to 'empower consumers' more widely – to spread personal ownership, to boost demand for key services through public issue of free-choice vouchers, to curb producer monopolies. All this should serve ordinary people's interests far better than can direct supply from the state: the least curbable and most demand-insensitive of all monopolists (Saunders and Harris, 1990).

Of course incomes remain and, vouchers apart, would remain unequal: a sure sign still of familiar class divisions? To this objection class eclipse theory has two kinds of retort. One, of old vintage, is that inequalities of income no longer matter or would matter much, once most people have some degree of effective consumer power in common and fair hope of enhancing it. The other retort is to deny the premise that income inequalities are still a product primarily of class: The money disparities that really count everyday are a product rather of gender divisions and household circumstances which cut across class.

One leg of this argument points to the fact that women generally have distinctly lower incomes than men: from paid work; through wider exclusion from it; because of longer survival into old age; and, to boot, from shorter straws in the division of household budgets. There is nothing in dispute so far; but the second leg of the argument takes a bigger step. It notes the large but still not wholesale movement of married women into the labour market. It points then to the disparities of household income which arise simply from differences in the number of contributing earners. And the crunch comes in a conclusion that inequalities on this score increasingly override the inequalities which come from individuals' – let alone just men's – places in the earnings pecking order of the labour market. When, say, a husband in blue-collar work and his wife with a full-time typing-pool job together take more money home than a couple where the man is a manager but the woman a full-time housewife, then real income distribution can seem to have a good deal less to do with class than with 'domestic strategies' and the phasing of family life cycles (see especially Pahl, 1984). Another nail is driven triumphantly home into the coffin of class.

Approaches to appraisal

Pull the many strands from this overview together: you then have what may look an imperative case for scrapping wellnigh all resort to class analysis, save in relation to times past and perhaps some places far away. At least one eminent British sociologist has proclaimed just such a case (Pahl, 1989); and if there was deliberately provocative hyperbole to his proclamation, there have been other notable converts to some version or another of new class-eclipse theory.

True enough, the converts among academic social scientists seem still well outnumbered by sceptics and critics. Criticism, moreover, has by no means been confined to writers (for example Wood, 1986; Miliband, 1989) whom their opponents find it easy to label unreconstructed Marxists. From an ambitious nationwide survey in the mid-1980s, for example, an Essex University team theoretically attuned far more to Weber than Marx reached conclusions which explicitly rehabilitated class as a continuing prime influence on people's senses of identity and political orientation (Marshall et al., 1988). And much research in sociology and related subjects continues to take class in some form either as a central focus (for instance, Goldthorpe, 1987; see also Clark et al., 1990) or as a main explanatory or descriptive variable. So when the Essex team's study set off a vociferous intra-professional debate (Saunders, 1989; Emmison and Western, 1990; Pawson, 1990; Pahl, 1993 – as against Marshall and Rose, 1990; Goldthorpe and Marshall, 1992), some of the new revisionists no doubt had a point when they described adherence to class analysis from base-points set before the 1980s as still (irritatingly) in the 'mainstream' of British sociology. Yet the debate itself was a sign of how the climate of academic work in social science has been overcast with new doubts about the salience of class analysis. It is hardly fortuitous that, already in advance of this, the climate of media commentary, political manoeuvre and policy formation had ruled virtually all reference to class out of court: except in paradoxically class-denying underclass talk; or when, in still part-acceptable 'wet' terminology, class inequality is renamed innercity deprivation, say, or child poverty.

Should class really be on its deathbed now, its decline must certainly have been rapid for so previously vigorous a social phenomenon. Today's revisionists may praise their forerunners for acumen in long-run prophecy; but they have not sought actively to revive the contention that class went into eclipse already from the 1950s. The evidence still looks firm that the economic structure of class remained potent in broadly familiar shape well into the 1970s – with Britain on this score a typical rather than a unique western case (cf. in general terms Westergaard and Resler, 1975).

Keynesianism, welfarism and corporatism gave labour larger influence, but never to the point of subverting capital power (see chapters 2–3 and 5–6, above). Ownership of property remained heavily concentrated: of business more so, as big firms and financial institutions took steadily larger stakes themselves in corporate shareholding; of housing less so, as owner-occupancy grew, but with no significant effect for ownership-concentration of productive assets. Inequalities of real income, so of personal life circumstances, were moderately compressed during the 1940s. But thereafter, and as against rising living standards for more or less all, their range changed little in relative terms until the late 1970s (cf. also Royal Commission on the Distribution of Income and Wealth, 1979; Fallick and Elliott, 1981; Fiegehen et al., 1977). Occupational shifts steadily reduced the numbers of blue-collar workers, and increased the numbers in non-manual work at all levels including career-salariat levels. So 'upward opportunity' expanded. But just as relative pay differences between broad occupational groups stayed roughly constant, so did relative disparities of opportunity in working life between men of different social origin (Goldthorpe, 1980). So again did relative inequalities of educational opportunity, despite overall growth of access (Halsey et al., 1980; Gray et al., 1983). And while health improved and mortality fell apace, they did so once more across the board: with little change in the ratios of disparity between classes; and with this still for reasons to do more, directly and indirectly, with economic circumstances than with either 'culture *in vacuo*' or genetic inheritance (Townsend and Davidson, 1982; Wilkinson, 1986).

For all this to have changed in just about fifteen years towards some classless flux – flux at least above a new underclass threshold – looks a remarkable proposition. A change of diagnostic mood may be more likely. The proposition nonetheless has to be put to test: against empirical evidence, and on terms set by consideration of the purposes of class analysis. As I see those purposes, and have outlined them in the Introduction to this book, they also set a sequence for the testing. The first step is to identify sources of power – command above all over key economic resources – and the privilege which goes with it. The second is to map effects on the life circumstances and opportunities of people at large. Distinct and interconnected inequalities on these scores will matter in their own right, because they set distinctly unequal parameters for social relations as well as everyday conditions, never mind the outcome of third-step analysis. That last step, and only that, concerns how people disparately placed in class life view their circumstances and prospects, to whatever political effect in response or non-response. Application of the first- and second-step tests will, to anticipate, show in fact a much sharpened constellation of class now. The third step in the sequence will show paradox and ambiguity, but nothing like dissolution of class awareness, discontent and tension.

8 Power, Privilege and Income Inequality

What about the upper class?

For a start, then, it is remarkable how class-dissolution theorizing of the 1980s on has lowered the ceiling for its concerns. Its gaze has been fixed on changes involving, it is said, the great majority of the population – salariat, wage-earners, small entrepeneurs, and the putative underclass outside or on the margins of the regular labour market. But it has had hardly anything to say about the concentration of power, influence and wealth at the very top.

The conventional wisdom of the 1950s and early 1960s, by contrast, did have something to say about this. Its case for forgetting about class rested not just on a postulate of inexorable working-class 'embourgeoisement', and on an addendum claiming the transformation of residual poverty into a product of discrete individual handicaps. It rested also on a thesis that there was no longer an identifiable upper class, let alone a capitalist one: because hitherto concentrated wealth was gradually being diffused away from the top; and because wealth in any case no longer went hand in hand with power. Decision-making was now either democratically responsive or in the hands of a plural diversity of elites; and even business power had come to be exercised benignly, by professional managers swayed by a range of considerations over and above profit optimization. This thesis was a mirage. But I need rehash little of the case for its rejection (cf. for instance, Westergaard and Resler, 1975, part 3). My point here is that the new 'forget-about-class' wisdom from the 1980s just has not been much bothered with dominance and privilege at the top. Revisionists still on the left continue to acknowledge the abiding concentration of power and wealth up above; but even their leading preoccupation has been down below, with what they see as erosion of working-class commonality. Others on the reactivated bandwagon have written, for the most part, as if that concentration were of no great concern. Some equate power and wealth with human excellence and benign effect – a sort of attribution of 'managerial' virtues to tycoons; so they celebrate the 1980s accentuation of top privilege. But there has been no new theorization and assembly of evidence to back this up; nor have bandwagon-riders made any coherent attempts to rehabilitate their predecessors' thesis of upper-class eclipse.

They would in fact have a hard job to do so. Income inequalities in Britain widened during the 1980s both by sag and lag at the broad bottom *and* by ferocious boom at the top. From one of several similar estimates indicative of general orders of magnitude, real living standards after direct tax and cash benefits fell by 6 per cent from 1979 to 1988 for households in the poorest-fifth bracket, but rose by 36 per cent for the best-off fifth – the latter gain nearly triple that even for the next-best-off quintile (Brown, 1989, using calculations by John Hills). Other evidence makes it clear that upper-bracket gains in turn were concentrated in good part on a small minority of very rich people (see later in this chapter). Again, while the concentration of property ownership in the hands of a few had been somewhat moderated during the 1960s and 1970s, the trend virtually stopped thereafter, to leave the share of all personally held marketable wealth owned by just the richest one per cent of adults roughly steady, throughout the 1980s, at a near-fifth of the total (*Social Trends* 1992): this despite continuing spread of personal home-ownership. Indeed, *excluding* the value of dwellings, the share of the richest 1 per cent in marketable wealth rose from 26 to 28 per cent; that of the richest 5 per cent from 45 to 53 per cent. While the notion of upper-class attrition by shrinkage of top income and ownership privilege was hard enough to square with facts before the 1980s, the facts since then have put it quite out of the running.

Recent experience and evidence are no kinder to the complementary argument that saw the upper class waning through pluralism in both economic and political decision-making. Post- war social reconstruction, economic boom and the tripartite corporatism which came in their wake *had* given organized labour new influence as a key pressure group, though not power to displace the primacy of business prescriptions for economic affairs (cf. chapters 2–3). This purported keystone of pluralism has gone now; and if new-right legislation has trimmed the powers of trade union barons over rank-and-file workers – once, ironically, a left-wing aspiration – recessions and new labour market 'flexibility' have countered such popular gains as might have come from that. General wage-earner gains *vis-à-vis* business ownership and control were neither the intention nor the outcome; and no comparable measures have been imposed on private corporations for accountability even to their now more numerous shareholders, let alone to the wider public. Of course, reinvigorated competition in business enterprise is said to offer a more effective alternative to direct public accountability: because it relies on enhanced consumer power to curb producer power, without distortion from insensitive controls by remote and self-interested agencies. The claim may have point to its logic if adduced as an argument for sometimes separating the mode of funding for public services from actual service delivery. But such point is lost when the claim is made in respect of private business for profit, in a context where income inequalities – disparities of effective consumer power – have substantially widened; and where there are no signs of reversal to the long-run trend of concentration in capital control.

Successful business ever seeks to secure its further success by closing out rivals or taking them over; and the spread of giant conglomerates with eggs in many baskets is an additional, rather than an alternative, means to corporate self-protection. As against these pressures, public measures to restrain private monopoly and cartel formation have a continuing record of poor efficacy; and denationalization of state-owned enterprises in this country has replaced public monopoly only by private oligopoly. The vaunted boom of small business has itself been fairly small, moreover; and the increase recorded in self- employment during the 1980s (from about 8 to 12 per cent of the British workforce before the economic downturn of the early 1990s) involved for some part an increase in subcontracting labour. What matters more, a trend to smaller units of production is far from being a sustained trend to smaller units of financial control. In the latter and crucial terms, no return is conceivable to the modest scale of leading business enterprise in the nineteenth century. Neither recent 'workplace fragmentation' nor the steady shift from manufacturing to services has, in continuing prospect, dented the growth of large-corporation hegemony in each sector, across sectors and transnationally. Even as markets become the more effectively worldwide, widening of competition on that score is countered by concomitant spread of multinational corporation networks. With oligopoly in the lead, competition is correspondingly limited and erratic: a means for consumer power to check producer power, but nothing like a dominant or dependable force to that end.

The producer power that makes the running looks, to boot, still less now like the benign and pluralistically responsible governance once celebrated in managerial-school scenarios. Control in large corporations has not been sliding down the management hierarchy, to allow new leeway for objectives other than market supremacy and profit promotion. It remains, for all strategic purposes, at the top: as governance by dominant configurations of financial interest, at and around board level in companies linked into intricate webs through ties of leading capital ownership and credit deployment. The biggest owner-controllers are now, and increasingly, large corporate bodies themselves: with a range of money-fund institutions in key place through their command of credit and brokerage as well as by direct capital ownership. Business power has in that sense become more impersonal and 'anonymous' than it was (see especially Scott, 1988; also 1985, 1986). Yet the power accumulated in and among these organizations is still exercised by, and to large money gains for, small numbers of high executives and directors, top advisers and key dealers, quite often members of family groupings with extensive financial connections. A still smaller number, each usually with a multiplicity of board posts and consultancies across a range of the leading business world, constitute a little visible elite, who add considerable inside influence in political circles to their great wealth (Useem, 1984).

Join with all this a set of well-known changes on the political front in Britain since the turn into the 1980s. These have included zealous government limitation of local authority activity, in the interests of a strong if 'small' central state and directed not least to curbing labour-movement opposition; pervasive enhancement of business representation in the execution of public policy – for health, education and training, for example – with private commercial enterprise thus exempted from a drive against professional and trade union lobby power which might otherwise have had fair popular justification; ministerial pressures on the broadcasting media – none was needed on the business-governed newspaper press – to shift the political 'balance' required under public surveillance to the right of centre; and strident assertion of the needs from national security and integrity to preserve a secrecy of public administration which, subject to selective 'leakage' from government itself, is more sweepingly defined in this than in many other democratic countries. The conclusion then must be plain that visions of a pluralistic dispersal of power from the top have not come out of the 1980s well.

This is bald summary: it is not intended as a new sketch, let alone a full picture, of the composition and character, external affiliations and internal fissures of the upper class (but see Scott, 1982 and 1991, for invaluable essays in comprehensive analysis of the British variant). My concern has been only to point out two matters paradoxical in their conjunction: that there patently is an upper class and one indeed which, through dominance in a still more evidently capitalist economy, enjoys still more power and privilege in Britain now than just a decade or two ago; yet that mode-setting opinion has blithely declared class a thing of the past nonetheless. It has done so, by and large, not by overt denial of the reality; but by ignoring it, or by taking a schizoid stance to it. There is a splitting of minds apparent, for example, when commentators à la mode have noted the heightened extravagances of City money-making and 'yuppie' culture, but read no signs of a class structure into them. And there is plain sociological blindness involved in commentary, purportedly exhaustive, which forgets about the upper class because it is so very small. Tiny relative size by a count of heads is a notable feature of any top class, whatever the particular defining assumptions. (One suggestion, if by tight criteria, puts the figure for Britain at just one or two per thousand of the total population: Runciman, 1990.) It is the intense concentration of power and privilege in so few hands that makes these people top. Their socio-structural weight overall, immensely disproportionate to their small numbers, makes the society they top a class society, whatever may be the pattern of divisions beneath them.

I need to add only a couple of extra notes to round off the gist of my argument on this front. One concerns the scale of the privilege concentrated in few hands. Just how few hands to take into account when it comes to making quantitative assessments is a rather arbitrary business: it turns on the figures available and the way they happen to be classified. When for reasons much more to do with class than with gender or age, an estimated 1 per cent of the adult population own around a fifth of all marketable wealth in personal hands, and just 5 per cent as much as two-fifths, this clearly points to an immense concentration of measurable privilege. But it is a crude indicator. The precise shares of the few in all wealth are thus liable to fluctuate, when the stock market for trading in the paper assets which make up most of top wealth is unstable; and there will be adults related to the 1 or 5 per cent 'registered' top rich who have benefit from the privilege that goes unrecorded: fewer of these over time, however, as the prime holders of large capital have increasingly spread their holdings among other family members (women as well as men) to reduce taxation. In any case neither arithmetical cut-off point – 1 per cent or 5 per cent of adults – provides an analytical definition of the 'upper class'; and the latter fraction especially will include many people, such as well-established professionals and business managers, whose place is only in the foothills surrounding peak privilege and power. For all this, the available figures of ownership concentration show beyond dispute that the slice of the nation's wealth vested in tiny-minority hands is a fat one: not a matter, as often believed, just of incidental top-up luxury from wealth too small in aggregate to add much to other people's lives if, somehow or other, means were found to share it out a good deal more evenly.

There are, moreover, other data to much the same effect. Take incomes in 1988/9 as they were recorded after deduction of income tax. Among all 'tax units' (at that time still most married couples, apart from a few wealthy ones for whom it paid husband and wife to opt for separate taxation, together with all free-standing adult individuals), the richest 5 per cent between them then had at least as large a share of all income in aggregate as did the entire poorest one-third. Rather over 15 per cent of the total pool went to the one-in-twenty few, against under 15 per cent to the one-in-three many (estimated from *Social Trends 1989*, table 5.11). Even as they stand, these figures leave out of account real income that goes unrecorded to escape taxation, more of it among the rich than the poor. There is plainly a large mass of every-year purchasing power at and near the tiny top to spread down, hypothetically, in some radically different system of distribution. Add another comparison possible from the same source: if directed right to the bottom of the pile, a quarter taken off the post-tax incomes of just the richest 5 per cent would have been enough by itself almost to double the incomes of the very poorest one-eighth: those who, unit for unit, had less than £5,000 to live on that year by contrast with sums from £35,500 upwards after income tax for the top one-in-twenty. Much of the quarter-portion lopped from the top in this imaginary exercise could have come, moreover, from quite a small fraction of the 5 per cent, since high monetary privilege is very skewly peaked even within itself.

Wealth, it may be said however, is not all of privilege; and privilege is not of itself power. The other note I still need to make about 'upper-class' dominance is to meet this sort of objection. Distinct though the three are in abstract, in practice high wealth stretches to become all-round privilege; and such privilege at the top in turn goes hand in hand with large power. For one thing, while riches and high status do not fully coincide within top circles, such disjunctures – classically, for example, between new money and old 'blood' – are matters of rarefied finesse. In longer perspective, prestige and connections, know-how and know-whom, accrete generally to great wealth to boost its societal influence. For another thing, and quite straightforwardly, great wealth is great purchasing power. It can buy the scarcest 'positional goods' not least (Hirsch, 1977). And when as much profit may be got from a small number of rich buyers as from many more buyers with small purses, this does a lot to shape patterns of market supply and production. Proportionately per user head, far more re- sources go into up-market than down-market supply; and proportion- ately also far more diversity of provision. Third, great wealth in an economy like Britain's most often goes with – and comes from – significant shares in active command over large corporate resources: resources which, with formal ownership in good part corporate itself and otherwise quite scattered, are usually very much larger still than the stakes in them that the top-rich hold directly and personally. If they are multi-*millionaires* in their own names – and still better placed by a count also of their family connections' wealth – Lord This, Sir Roland That and Mr Still Untitled will typically, as directors and dealers, fund-swingers and men-to-be-listened to, have a large say in the deployment of multi-*billion*-pound assets: assets on a scale, even, that can rival the budgets of small nation-states.

But lurking behind the power which the rich command in these ways – more or less directly and actively – there is another sort of power they enjoy more passively, and by way of collective class benefit: because the 'rules of the game' are set in their favour. These are the taken-for-granted assumptions which any society has for the ongoing conduct of its general affairs, and which constitute the half- hidden cornerstones of inequality and so of privilege. In British so- ciety, as with variations in other capitalist societies, they include the routine expectation, in particular, that resources be generally de- ployed to optimize long-run private capital profit; and that public intervention, even to quite other ends, should not substantially offset that main presumption (see chapters 2 and 4). There is room for plenty of dispute and shift of tack about how best to comply with the rules; and about the salience of such other ends as, pursued 'too far', might transgress the first. When reigning interpretations of the rules have shifted in our time through slides of political climate, first with social reconstruction in the 1940s and then to reverse effect with new-right ascendancy in the 1980s, those shifts had significant impact; and they were accompanied, especially on the latter occasion, by more explicit assertion of leading principles than in the ordinary run of affairs between transitions. Yet in that ordinary run the rules need little proclamation aloud, or active direction, to ensure compliance with them. They are, instead, taken by and large without question: as guidelines for managing things as they are; and as limits to manage- ment change, public or private. So they set rough limits also to the effective range of most policy debate and most contest between any conflicting interests. To go against the grain of the rules will, in the routine order of affairs, seem to involve more trouble than is practically worthwhile, especially when resources for resistance are meagre. On this argument then (and I am here rehashing old words of my own – Westergaard and Resler, 1975, part 3 – while also of Lukes, 1974) those whom such pre-set assumptions favour have power of a sort just from that: power from the relative inertia of political-economic structure, to underpin the power which they exercise more actively and directly.

Critics find fault with this argument because it ascribes power to impersonal processes and practices; not just, as ordinarily, to people who can be shown to get their way over others who can be shown to oppose them, when decisions are made or agendas are set or strings are pulled quietly behind the scenes. But if it is proper to use the word 'power' only in the latter senses, then some other term is needed to describe the ways in which rarely contested rules of the game give privileged players advantage over others. This retort, in turn, the same critics dismiss by questioning the implications of the very words 'privilege' and 'advantage' alike. Both terms, they say, arbitrarily impute a conflict of interests to a relationship between people which those people themselves have not defined as conflictual. There is by this contention no conflict, when the rich have neither actively invented the rules nor had to impose them against demonstrable resistance; and if all or most others, excluded from wealth, have not contested the rules as, in a democracy, it is open for them to do. The conflict of interests, so this criticism concludes, is a figment of my imagination, if I can adduce no hard evidence of it from observably opposed actions or audibly conflicting aspirations on the part of the people concerned (see for instance, Hindess, 1987). But it is not very arbitrary, I suggest, and makes good analytical sense, to assume that the rich have an inherent interest in maintaining their wealth, even when they do not have to assert it vigorously; and that those people who are patently well excluded from wealth have no less inherent an interest in changing the balance, even if they have also countervailing interests – not least in just getting on with their lives more or less as things are – that may inhibit them from thinking and saying, let alone doing, much about it.

How far and in what spirit ordinary people do actually accept the unequal rules of the game is a separate issue. In fact they seem to do so quite a lot more as a matter of humdrum necessity than by way of positive endorsement. There is evidence enough of widespread resentment of current inequality for no mere analytical invention to be involved in positing popular interest in 'fairer shares'. But consideration of that evidence comes later (see chapter 11). There is another and substantial agenda item before it: to trace the patterns of unequal life experience, across the social scale, which go with the bunching of power and privilege at the top.

Income trends from around 1980

The most obvious information with which to start to test fashionable conjecture about the erosion of class as a significant influence on most people's experiences in life concerns trends in the distribution of real income. In fact the evidence on this score points incontrovertibly to widening class fissures since the end of the 1970s: not just between top and bottom, but across the entire range.

Growth of the gap between rich and poor is now so well known that it needs little underlining. Signals accumulated steadily over the 1980s that, while levels of living improved 'on average' and people already well off became very much better off, material circumstances for the poor at best stayed much as before and at worst actually deteriorated (for instance, Walker and Walker, 1987; Brown, 1989; Department of Social Security, 1990). Estimates for the full decade 1979–89 confirmed the trend by showing real increases in disposable income to the order of nearly 40 per cent on balance for the wealthiest one-fifth of households, but a mean fall of some 4 $1/2$ per cent for the poorest one-fifth (Townsend, 1991). So much for 'trickle down' of new wealth to the bottom. True, figures of this sort are open to revision at their edges; and they cannot, by the nature of their compilation, show changes in the situation of individual people or households over time. They leave the polarization of incomes since around 1980 beyond dispute, however (cf. also Jenkins, 1991); and they run plainly counter to the notion that class as a force for unequal life experience is on its way out. They do so, at least, unless class concomitantly has come to play much less part than before in shaping income inequalities. Counter- intuitive though that suggestion may be, it still needs checking as we go along (see especially chapter 9). But it finds little support from the estimates just summarized which show, for example, that the fall in real levels of living recorded for many households in the poorest-quintile category – concentrated especially on families with children – was not an artefact of shifts in household composition during the period.

Yet if class by these signs is still very much a force to keep the poor poor, selective reading of the same signs has been taken often to support one version of revisionist conjecture: the thesis of emergently overriding division between new underclass and affluent classless majority. Yes, the poor have lost out, and their numbers have grown. But, so the argument goes, most households have gained; and the prodigious rate of their gains is evident from the growth of 'average' real incomes: by about a quarter from 1979 to 1989; by upwards of a third perhaps to 1991, according to a recent if somewhat overstated figure (Department of Social Security, 1993).

The inference, however, proves feeble once the 'average' is picked apart. Averages mislead when the variations around them are very wide and skew; and just this is the case here. Take the latest available official estimates of household incomes 'below average' just mentioned (DSS, 1993). They show that, *after* deduction of housing costs, disposable post-tax incomes fell by fully 14 per cent in real terms for the poorest one-in-ten of all households over the years 1979–90/1; stayed level without gain for the next-poorest tenth; but rose by well over 30 per cent 'on average' across the population as a whole. Yet no decile-category in the entire lower half of the population gained anything like that notional-average improvement of material living standards. Even the fifth decile up the scale – households up to mid-point – saw their real incomes rise over the twelve years by only a little more than a fifth; and for the third and fourth decile-groups, below them, real incomes after housing costs grew on balance by no more than about 7 and 16 per cent respectively, very much less than the average on which revisionists have pinned their postulate of phenomenally growing mass prosperity. Alternative calculations of real-income changes *before* deduction of housing costs show less actual loss for the very poorest; some little gain for the next-poorest one-in-ten; smaller differences in outcome, overall, among the five lower-half deciles. But the point remains, all the firmer, that for at least 50 per cent of the population, household incomes in real terms grew at best far less than the artefactual average; and at rates only modest by the standards of the fairly even-spread growth that had prevailed in the much-maligned 1960s.

The average so exceeded even mid-level experience, of course, because there were formidable gains for people in the higher reaches of the income scale. Just how formidable is not visible from the official report cied above; for this is, ingeniously, confined to losses and gains among households 'below average income'. But as noted already, parallel analysis for the 1980s alone – when gains 'on average' came to nearly 25 per cent over eight years but to less than half of that, by generous measure, even for the fifth decile-category up the scale (Department of Social Security, 1990, Annex 1) – indicates an almost 40 per cent growth of real incomes for the best-off one-fifth of households from 1979 to 1989 (Townsend, 1991). Taken up to 1991, a minis-terial answer to a parliamentary question gives a corresponding fig-ure of well over 50 per cent, and of more than 60 per cent for just the richest one-in-ten (*The Independent*, 11 October 1993). Concentration of enhanced advantage within this upper cluster has been still more marked, and appears to have continued despite renewed recession. Directors of the top 100 companies in Britain thus, on balance, more than doubled their own pay in real terms from 1983 to 1992, the rise proceeding apace even after business profits went into decline again at the end of the 1980s (Commission on Social Justice, 1993).

To summarize, it is not just the poor who have drawn short straws, if any, from economic growth since 1989. Even people up to mid-point incomes, and a number some way above that level, have gained quite little either by comparison with the rich or by past standards of rising prosperity. The poor are much less a minority by virtue of exclusion from benefit of radical-right market boom than are the wealthy by virtue of high-boosted privilege from it. What then explains the dras-tic widening of income inequalities over the past fifteen years or so, right across the board as this process has worked?

Two main sets of factors were involved: changes in public policy, and market changes which in turn received extra boost from policy changes. I have discussed the former earlier (chapters 3 and 5–6). To sum up, the successive governments under new-right leadership in Britain have not (at least yet) dismantled 'the welfare state' in the radical fashion to which their most vocal ideologues aspire. But if what they have done is more like tinkering, it is tinkering on a large scale as the results have accumulated. The details on either side of the ledger – benefits and taxes – need not hold us up here. It is enough to look at the net impact of changes under the two headings together. An estimate is available of the consolidated effects on disposable house-hold incomes of these changes over the ten years 1979–89, so calcu-lated as to exclude the effects both from other sources and of differences in composition between households at different levels of income (Johnson and Stark, 1989). This points to some real-term gain of money-in-hand for most households in consequence of shifts in direct-tax-cum-benefit provision during the decade – to an average tune of about £7 a week per household. But single people living on their own sustained a mean loss; there was, on balance, neither gain nor loss for pensioners relying mainly or exclusively on state support, or for unemployed couples without children; and while a majority of other households did gain something, this was little except for those high up the income ladder. In fact, of the total net addition to privately disposable incomes that came from the decade's changes in direct-taxes-cum-benefits, little short of half (some 46 per cent) went to just the richest one-in-ten of all households; and another third (34 per cent) to the next three decile-groups down the scale. This then left only one-fifth of the bounty to be shared out among the entire sixty per cent of households with incomes from 'good middling' down to the poorest; and among these, indeed, the 40 per cent with incomes from below middle and downwards got barely 8 per cent of the total. On this score again, near-exclusion from financial gain in the 1980s was *not* confined to a minority in poverty. It extended well up the ladder, and the very poorest, in fact, drew just a little more than those a step or two above them.

So the cumulative package of changes in taxation and benefit provision during the period gave overwhelming weight to favouring those already well favoured. That bias must indeed have been rather greater than even these figures show since, concerned with money-in-hand before personal spending, they leave aside the effects of indirect taxes that fall on money only when it is spent. Such taxes generally have a regressive edge, and have been stepped up as income tax has fallen. Running to 1989, moreover, the estimate used here stops just short of the extension, in 1990, of local poll tax from Scotland to England and Wales: a measure which added yet another, and very visible, twist to regression. But then this record also stops short of 1990's replacement of Mrs Thatcher by Mr Major, and of the tortuous unwinding of poll tax which followed. Save for the coming of council tax instead, however, the change in cabinet leadership involved no government retreat from the line of regressive redistribution, pursued in social policy during the 1980s. It would in any case take far more than some moderate softening to erase the stark imprint which that decade's shifts of tax–benefit provision left on class structure in Britain. Moreover market changes then – and since, during the second deep recession of the new era – have left at least as stark an imprint.

Take the pattern of earnings in paid employment as offering the simplest sign – high unemployment apart – of these changes in the labour market. Polarization was here again to the fore in the 1980s. Over the ten years from 1980 to 1990, pre-tax salaries for full-time non-manual work thus rose by about 40 per cent in real terms for the highest-paid decile among both men and women in such work, even disregarding non-cash perks which also boomed at the top. But wages at the bottom increased only little in purchasing power during the same period: by barely 8 per cent over ten years for the lowest-paid decile among women in full-time manual employment; and indeed by under 2 per cent for their male counterparts, in this case a near-standstill of real wages for a decade. (Calculated from data in the *New*

Earnings Survey 1990, by application of the Retail Price Index, All Items.)

Yet, once more, polarization cannot be taken as evidence for increased segregation of an impoverished underclass from a well-set 'middling mass'. As in respect of income distribution at large, so too in respect of earnings from employment many people 'in the middle' experienced only modest gains from the 1980s' growth of pay packets. Median earnings from full-time work rose, it is true, by one-fifth in real terms for men; and by well over one-quarter for women. (Women's pay disadvantages *vis-à-vis* men in fact diminished in respect of full-time employment. This was the only trend contrary to the polarization otherwise at work, though – with men's earnings from full-time work generally still half as high again as women's in 1990 – gender differentials by no means vanished.) But even the best-paid manual workers – fashionably seen as hyper-prototypical of a new middling mass – found their real wage increases from 1980 to 1990 short of the notional median rise. Here again, gross averages are a misleading statistic when, as during this decade, a great deal of the total gain went to the already well-paid. Among men, upper-quartile salaries from full-time *non-manual* employment thus rose in real terms by fully 33 per cent over the period: a rate of gain nearly twice that even for the best-paid decile of manual workers; well over twice that for the best-paid quartile among the latter, and some three times that for the 'average' male manual worker, whose real wages rose only by 10 ½ per cent during the decade. Among women the ratios of differential gain were much the same, if in a pattern a little sharper still in its contrasts between high boom towards the top, modest rises in the middle and only slow growth further down the range.

The point that needs emphasis about those contrasts is, to repeat, that they applied up and down the whole range: they set no distinct line of division between excluded minority and commonly thriving mass majority. Certainly the lowest-paid lagged furthest behind in real-term rise of earnings. But many others' shares in growth – while bigger for each step up the scale – were still quite small by earlier post-war standards. Those of almost all manual workers, and of low-grade office workers too, fell well short of the 'average' rises on which commentators tend to fasten. It was the higher and highest echelons of salary- earners who drew the long straws in the pay growth of the decade: a minority at the top rather than at the bottom. As pointed to by such data from summary national statistics these constituted a sizeable minority, it is true. They ranged over business managers, administrators, professionals and entertainers of diverse kinds – much of the 'service class' (cf. for example, *Social Trends 1989*, table

5.6). But leading the way among them were very much smaller numbers of high executives in private enterprise. Their privileged salaries, typically swollen well into the six-figure range, in turn prompted pressure for competitive part-emulation at the peaks of the public sector (see *13th Report on Top Salaries*, Cmd 938, 1990) and among top management of newly privatized public facilities.

In short, pay stratification simply grew sharper across the board, except as between women and men in full-time employment. And while limited in impact both by continuing gender discrimination at large and by many women's dependence on part-time work, the exception itself underlines the pattern of class stratification associated with accentuated pay stratification. When inequalities of pay widened so much in the 1980s, it was in main part because differentials grew between different types and levels of employment: between the broad and crude categories of manual and non-manual work distinguished in the summary official statistics; between wage-earners of different skills, trades, sectors or corners of the labour markets, salaried people on career paths of greater though varying dependability, and top-flight professionals and executives or dealers in business and finance especially. And when the latter gained so much more than others overall, it was because they could add to their golden pay rises also good chunks of property income – including spin-off from the share-option schemes that proliferated on corporation boards – and, not least, the benefits of large cuts in top-rate taxation: all privileges distinctly of a class character.

9 Class-Confounding Inequalities?

Life-cycle disparities and women's work

Like the further concentration of power and privilege in top-circle hands, the gross widening of income inequalities since about 1980 provides, then, signal evidence that material class structure has been hardening, not softening. Not really so, some critics will counter, if disparities of income are now less and less a product of class; more and more a reflection of differences of household composition and domestic strategies, of age, stage of life and gender. I turn now to take general stock of that proposition: also to examine related views, outlined in chapter 7, which similarly postulate that alternative lines of social division have come to prevail over older lines of class division; but first the contention that income inequality has in good part now floated free of class.

All the pointers from the evidence summarized in the previous chapter tell against that contention. So again does much in the causation of greatly increased poverty over the past decade and a half: high rates of unemployment, under-employment and non-employment, which hit hardest at people otherwise dependent on low-grade routine work; and the succession of regressive shifts in the fiscal and benefit-dispensation system which, in net effect, have served privileged-class against lower-class interests. So in turn does the fact that several of the analyses on which I have drawn to show the widening of income inequalities have been subject to meticulous, if technically controversial, attempts to 'cleanse' the data of effects from one significant set of 'non-class' factors: variations in household composition. Even so, there is more to be said to dispose of the proposition that inequality of income now has little to do with class.

To challenge that contention is not to deny its every premise. It is obvious that some substantial part of the totality of disparities in effective incomes arises from circumstances which are not, in principle, of a class character: in particular from differences of household make-up, including the ratio of earners to dependents; and from variations in both income and demands on it over the life-cycle of individuals. In practice, nevertheless, there are often significant class twists to the patterns of income disparity from such sources that, conceptually, seem 'class-free'. Thus when money-in-hand varies by age and stage of life within class, it does so in turn variably between classes. The regular increments in pay on which most professionals and many managers can count, together with larger promotion opportunities, help to make for a diversity of earnings by seniority within these groups that is not paralleled among wage-earners in routine jobs. By contrast, incomes generally fall to sharper effect in retirement for the latter than for the former, since careers in business and the professions commonly yield a spin-off by way of occupational pensions, accumulated savings and often cash-handshakes unmatched in retirement from rank-and-file jobs.

There is nothing very new to this, seen in broad terms. Just such inter-class differences of pattern to intra-class disparities of financial circumstance explain why, for example, the 'poverty cycle' described by social surveyors around the last turn-of-century was in essence a working-class phenomenon. Wages that rose little after the early years of working life combined with still relatively large though incipiently contracting family size to sharpen the risks of poverty in childhood and young-to-middle parenthood. A third trough came in late life, when income from wages dwindled away and, given women's greater longevity then as now, made working-class widows a majority among the old poor. The peaks of the cycle came in between: for young adults on full wages before they had children; and for parents whose children-turning-adult could help towards their own keep before they left home. For most middle- and upper-class couples, by contrast, incomes than as now commonly grew as families grew; family limitation had in any case spread earlier and further among them than among working-class couples; while investments and support from kin (if regular pensions more rarely then) gave relative protection in old age.

Things have changed in some respects that matter on these scores. And they have changed even apart from the rise in levels of living that has raised standards of expectation for everyone, so also conceptions of 'poverty'; apart, too, from the dramatic decline of private domestic service which has made palatial living much less an attribute of wealth than it once was. Most striking has been the near-common adoption of a 'small family' pattern, with class differences in fertility now quite limited and, in some part, inverted by comparison with the past. In direct consequence – except for 'new' poverty associated with the last two decades' rise in lone parenthood – two of the three troughs in the classical wage-earner family life-cycle are less marked overall than they were even half a century ago: the troughs in childhood and in young-to-middle parenthood. Real-income disparities on that score have thus been reduced: both intra-class and inter-class. By indirect consequence however – because lowered fertility has been the main cause of the 'ageing' of population common to industrial countries – there are now many more elderly and old people to experience the relative decline of income that typically, though class-variably, occurs in late life. The risk of hardship in old age thus looms larger than it did before: the more so, too, because retirement now comes earlier; and because even old people, women more than men, have recently come to live rather longer than they previously did. There is increased disparity of incomes on that score: in part intra-class, between households of earners and the retired in broadly the same class. Yet inter-class inequalities of financial circumstance in retirement too remain very sharp.

This latter point needs emphasis for two reasons: first, because, already from the 1950s, it became part of standard commentator-patter to describe the risk of poverty in retirement as a phenomenon of old age, a product of demographic process rather than of class structure; second, because, more recently, commentators from centre to right have claimed that a spread of occupational and personal pesions is well on its way to erode any such significant class inequalities of circumstance in retirement as still survive. Both assertions are false. Poverty or near-poverty in later life is *not* a classlessly common risk of old age. It is a risk concentrated on those who retire, and on dependent wives and widows of men who retire, with little or no income other than from the base-line state pension. These people – towards the end of the 1980s still over half of all the retired (cf. for example, Johnson and Stark, 1989) – are by large preponderance those who in working life depended on wages or low salaries. People who retire with sizeable incomes from employers' or similar pension schemes to add to the basic state benefit are, by contrast, in largest measure former professionals and semi-professionals, managers and executives: the top-paid in working life getting also of course the top-grade pensions. True, membership of occupational pension schemes has indeed spread – and this well before the 1980s – so that more of tomorrow's retired than of today's will draw some advantage from them. But the spread still leaves the unequal incidence of provision by class – and by gender even within class – very distinct.

Not only are the terms of effective benefit the better and more secure the higher a member is up the occupational scale. But sheer membership of any employer-provided scheme, whatever the terms, is still patently uneven (*General Household Survey 1988*, 1990). Among *male* full-time employees in 1988, it ranged from about 75 to 80 per cent in the case of professionals, managers and also the 'intermediate' grade of white-collar workers just below them, down to only 50–5 per cent in the case of manual and personal service workers almost regardless of skill. Membership was lower among *female* full-time employees – to say nothing of the many part-timers, for whom it is very rare – at every occupational level: on the whole only a little lower for professional and intermediate-grade women; at an enrolment rate of just 45–50 per cent in the case of the many women in 'junior' clerical work and the far fewer in skilled manual jobs; but at barely 30 per cent among those in semi-skilled and personal service work, while quite insignificant among the unskilled. Personal pension policies outside employer-provided schemes have grown much recently with help from tax inducements; but their benefits also, of course, depend on incomes in working life, and are beyond effective reach of the low-paid. The prospect remains clear that class will continue to divide incomes in retirement on much the same general lines as hitherto; and at least as sharply as incomes in working life.

Gender indeed divides too. Yet with respect to employment earnings (chapter 8) and retirement provision alike, it does so in a pattern of occupational disparities *among* women which roughly parallels that among men. Gender is a dimension of inequality distinct from class; and it has long been so. But its effects, from the analysis thus far, are to compound class divisions rather than to neutralize them. Such a conclusion is disputed, however, by those commentators who see the very growth of women's – overwhelmingly married women's – employment as the prime factor in a postulated progressive displacement of class from its former role in shaping inequalities of income. For most couples of working age across much of the board, so this argument runs, household income now depends more on whether they have two full-time pay packets between them, or one-and-a-half, or just one or even less, than it does on the precise class-graded pay rates from which each is made up. The contention is again that intra-class differences – here in domestic 'strategies' and personal opportunities, varying both by choice and by stage of life – have been taking over much of the significance that class once had for determination of material inequality.

Even now, in Britain, nearly one in every three wives of working age is still out of the labour market at any one time, while half of those in it work only part-time (*General Household Survey 1988*, 1990). So household incomes certainly do vary substantially, at whatever level of class, according just to the wife's employment status. But important though the point is in many ways (explored in pioneering manner by Pahl, 1984), it will not do by itself to clinch the inference to a grand historical shift away from class salience. For that inference to hold, either or both of two conditions would need to hold. The increase in married women's employment would need to have pulled proportionately more working- than middle- and upper-class wives into 'dual earning', so adding more over time to the household incomes of the former than the latter. Alternatively or complementarily, it would need to have had much the same effects by placing the wives of low-paid men often in relatively high-paid work, and vice versa. The facts, however, meet neither condition.

To the contrary, in respect of the first, at the time when rather few wives had paid work it was those married to blue-collar workers who did so more often than others. The notion of 'marriage as a career' was, in practice, something of a bourgeois prerogative. That notion has since been widely eroded. The continuous upward trend in married women's employment – starting from a low point among middle- and upper-class wives especially – has in consequence been steeper for these than for working-class wives, who were never so fully disengaged from the world of paid work (Westergaard and Resler, 1975, part 2, chapter 6; Joshi, 1985). By the 1980s in fact it had become at least as much the norm for women living in partnership with men in high and middling occupations to work for pay, outside the phases of child-bearing and early child-rearing, as for the wives of blue-collar workers to do so (Bonney, 1988a and b). Indeed it is now the female partners of unskilled and especially unemployed men who are rather less likely than other married women to have regular paid work. The reasons for that, moreover, almost certainly have more to do with lack of opportunity and with force of social security rules – both class-skew influences – than with domestic strategies and personal choices somehow floating free of class.

Historically, then, the shift to dual earning has changed life circumstances more in the upper and middle ranges of the class structure than further down. The effect – towards rather greater instead of smaller class inequality of income distribution – could be offset to a degree, if working women married to middle- and upper-class men

more often than others took only part-time work. The size and security of their husbands' earnings might be imagined to encourage
them to do so. But this does not seem to be the general case. It appears
rather that the greater latitude for choice that goes with material
comfort or wealth – and with correlated higher education – may help
now to foster somewhat fuller engagement in paid work on the part
of married women from relatively well-off homes. There are, to my
knowledge, not as yet comprehensive analyses on the matter across
Britain as a whole. But data from a few local studies have shown
earning wives whose partners are professionals, managers or the like
to be a little more likely to have full-time employment than those
married to blue-collar workers (Pahl, 1984, from reworking of table
8.3, p. 208; Bonney, 1988c; Noble et al., 1989). Better opportunities for
help with child care may have something to do with this; so may the
nature, rewards and satisfactions of the work available itself. Certainly some tendency this way fits the well-established fact that, over
the country as a whole, full-time work on the part of women is far
more common in professional and managerial posts than in the more
mundane office, personal service and other wholly or partly routine
grades of employment to which most women are still confined (for
example, Martin and Roberts, 1984). Wholly unskilled work on the
part of women is indeed almost exclusively part-time (*Social Trends
1992*, table 4.8).

The question remains whether there may be some criss-cross pattern
of employment among married women, through which many wives
with partners in lower-paid jobs themselves work at higher-paid
levels, and vice versa. The suggestion sounds implausible, given the
fact known from research on social mobility that marriage partners
are more likely to come from fairly similar backgrounds than from
very different ones. It has nevertheless attracted some attention, from
findings that many marriages can be described as 'cross-class' partnerships, when the spouses are separately categorized by reference to
their own individual occupations. Just how many depends, of course,
on the categorization of occupations used. But on the basis of a three-
way grouping into 'service, intermediate and working' classes, a
rough 40–50 per cent of all marriages in this country then cut 'across
class' in the mid-1980s (Marshall et al., 1988; Goldthorpe, 1987). In
fact, however, such findings in their further detail leave the supposi-
tion legless that marriage partners' respective earnings might often
'compensate' each other, to an overall effect of much diminishing class
inequality of household incomes. The levels at which working wives
and their husbands work are in statistical terms quite closely connected. Thus some two in every three among the minority of earning

wives whose work is professional, managerial or the like, are married to men whose work is similarly of a 'service-class' type; only few (about one in seven) to manual workers. Conversely, over half the partners of married women in manual and equivalent low-grade jobs are themselves blue-collar workers, while very far fewer are in service-class work (under one in five and down to one in nine, according to details of classification procedure that need not hold us up here). Marriage between spouses of whom one has a manual job and the other a service-class career is thus uncommon; and among the relatively few women who, as yet, combine marriage with a record of work experience showing a 'professional profile', the overwhelming majority have partners themselves in well-heeled occupations. (See again Marshall et al., 1988; Goldthorpe, 1987; also McRae, 1986; Dex, 1987.)

When nevertheless so many marriages can be described as partnerships 'across class', this comes chiefly from the concentration of much female employment in intermediate-range work – in clerical, secretarial, auxiliary-administrative or service-oriented employment that is neither distinctly working-class nor professional-cum-managerial. Work of this sort draws on women married to men from virtually all levels of the male hierarchy of class. It is plausible, though as yet not well demonstrated, that wives of blue-collar workers may be over-represented on the lower job rungs of this 'intermediate' range, with service-class wives correspondingly better placed within the range. But even if this should not be so, women's work within that range is in general modestly paid – distinctly lower-paid than men's work at broadly the same occupational levels. True, a wife's earnings from such employment will boost the income from her partner's pay proportionately more if the man is a manual worker than if he is a professional, an executive or the equivalent. But the man's pay will commonly still be the larger element in either case; and over the family life-cycle distinctly so. So it will continue to set the material circumstances of the one couple clearly apart from those of the other. The growth in incidence of 'cross-class' marriages through married women's employment has complicated the impact of class structure on inequality of household incomes. But it has in no way cancelled it out: far from it, when we remember that the past four decades' trend from 'marriage as a career' to 'dual earning' has been – by historical default, so to speak – more a middle- and upper-class phenomenon than a working-class one.

To look across the balance sheet as a whole, there is certainly some new shape to a number of those conceptually 'class-free' factors that have always made for additional disparities of income side by side with the disparities set by class structure. These are factors – collectively designated 'features of civil society' in a study of poverty in Denmark (Andersen and Elm Larsen, 1989) – that turn in essence on the number (and gender) of effective earners relative to total household size and needs, at whatever level of the class structure as formed by market and associated policy forces. But it should be plain from the foregoing analysis that those forces remain highly potent in generating disparity of incomes – so of decisive circumstances in life – by class, now as before. Indeed, in Britain at least, their potency in this respect grew sharper in the course of the 1980s, as both market inequalities widened and their moderation by measures of state policy was curtailed.

Gender, race – and class

I am aware that critics are still likely to accuse me of playing down gender inequality, and of wholly ignoring ethnic inequality. Let me therefore add some comments here to counter misconceptions on this score, even though the matter concerns issues wider than the immediate one of influences on income distribution.

Class, gender and race (or more broadly ethnicity) may be described as distinct dimensions of inequality. Unreconstructed Marxist interpretations are unconvincing when they seek to derive subordination of women to men, or oppression of blacks and browns by whites, primarily from the workings of capitalist economies. They offer, at best, a limited mode of description; but no inherent explanation why, in the first place, women and this or that ethnic minority are singled out for selective segregation under property and market processes (see, for example, Carling, 1992). Comparative-historical evidence as well as logic tell against such reductionist interpretations, in ways that need no elaboration here. But if the three broad dimensions are better depicted as *distinct* than as one package with class at its centre, they are also *different* in their modes of social operation, each *vis-à-vis* each other.

For one thing, very obviously, women commonly cohabit with men in households which – whatever their form and durability – join the everyday lives of underdogs and overdogs generally across the gender division. Gender inequality operates domestically, privately, within households – as well as in the public sphere – to a degree and in an arguably formative manner that has no parallel in the cases of class and ethnic inequality. Concomitantly – though the point is incidental to my purpose here – the inhibitions to collective underdog mobilization-in-opposition are wider of range in the former than in the two latter cases. So far old hat – nothing new, at least, after two decades of vigorous challenges from feminist analysis and debate. But less commonly noted is a difference that sets class inequality apart from both gender and ethnic inequality. This is that, in the public sphere and in general principle alike, the latter two operate in large measure through the former. Inequalities between women and men, between blacks/browns and whites – for that matter between Catholics and Protestants in a Protestant-dominated society, and so on – come to major expression as inequalities of class; but not vice versa.

If the point sounds indecently abstract, it is in reality quite straight-forward. In the public sphere, women experience their social subordination especially – though not only – by way of poor placement in the structure of class. Overall, by comparison with men, their economic 'life chances' are more limited: that is, their chances of full access to paid work; of advancement and high reward in work; of achieving influence and authority, command and power. Gender discrimination actively, and gendered foreshortening of aspirations, so operate as to place women 'by their own right' comparatively low in the economic order of class – and, still today, to make household partnership with a better-placed man a significant alternative means to good class circumstances. The last point apart, much the same goes for discrimination by skin-colour or ethnicity. It too so operates – in large part, though not only – as to place blacks-and-browns lower in the order of production and distribution than whites. This overall again, while to variable effects; and even the class achievements of a black or brown bourgeoisie turn to a degree on the parts such people play as 'agents' – whoever accredits them – or as 'service caterers' for their own minority groups more widely.

The reverse relationship, of course, is virtually inconceivable. Gender inequality presses women into the routine- grade slots of the class structure of work; but class inequality cannot turn male routine workers into women. Skin-colour discrimination pushes blacks and browns downwards in the hierarchies of employment, housing, access to credit and so on; but class inequality does not usually mean that whites at the same levels of those class hierarchies are designated 'coloured'. If the asymmetry here is self-evident to the point of banality, I have spent time underlining it nevertheless because its implications seem to escape notice in current conventional reference to 'gender, race and class', as if these were essentially parallel (as well as distinct) dimensions of inequality; and the asymmetry seems also to have been underplayed in ferocious, more specialist debate about 'women and class' (see for instance, the protracted discussion in volumes 17–19 of *Sociology*, November 1983 – May 1985, reviewed by Roberts, 1993; and Crompton and Mann, 1986).

The implications are not, to repeat, that class inequality 'explains' gender or ethnic inequality. Nor are they that the two latter would vanish *ipso facto* if, somehow, the former were to be abolished. Subordination of women to men, or of blacks/browns to whites, in no way operates only in and through the economic order of class. But note first, as one patent implication, that a hypothetical near-classless society would give both gender and ethnic inequality less room for play: discrimination could not sizeably take the form of segregation in low-rewarded work or poor housing, to exemplify the matter crudely, if work rewards and housing were near-equally spread. A second implication has more real-world weight. This is that it makes little sense to say, as many commentators seem to say, that divisions by gender and/or ethnicity now 'cut across' or even 'submerge' divisions by class. They cannot really do so, given both the point that they work through class, in the sense I have just argued, and a set of associated facts.

Of course you may conjure with scenarios that could give such commentator-talk force. Imagine, for example, that most or all men were high-placed in the world of work and power, most or all women low-placed. Class division would still exist as a conceptual principle. But gender division could seem to have 'submerged' it as a practical reality, *if* women continued to cohabit with men in household partnerships. These partnerships would then, most or all, involve 'cross-class marriages' very distinctively; and inequality – of gender now coincident with class – would very sharply divide spouses within households, but not mutually divide households as between different levels of class. The speculation, however, bears no resemblance to the real-world interaction between class inequality and gender inequality described earlier; and that is what matters.

It takes no wild speculation to postulate, on the other hand, a society where most blacks are low-placed in the world of work and power, most whites better – though far from all high-placed. South Africa comes close to this pattern; the United States has features of it, significantly countered by very different 'ethnicity ratios' and much else. Even in the former case, racial division has not in analytical terms displaced class division. But with the two so near-coincident, ethnic inequality is extraordinarily visible as a divider of economic life circumstances; and correspondingly potent, now, for mobilization of underdogs-in-opposition. Again, however, realities in Britain today bear little resemblance to those even in the USA; and this for one very crude reason above all others. Internally diverse as in any case they are, even in aggregate black-and brown-skinned people in Britain make up too small a proportion of the population – some 5 or 6 per cent – either to give the pervasive inequalities of class an American-format imprint of ethnic inequality; or, more modestly, for dark skin-colour to be a near-defining feature of real or imagined 'underclass' membership.

No word here is intended to gloss over the sadly salient facts of inequality by gender and race, or the violence of the affront they constitute to human dignity. My point has been only to challenge, as I see it, the analytical myopia involved in talk which takes 'gender, race and class' as conceptually parallel dimensions of inequality; and which goes on then to pose gender and race as forces, today, towards displacement of class. Class inequality remains potent in itself: and just so also in constituting one prime structure through which the distinct inequalities of gender and ethnicity are articulated.

'Underclass' versus 'middle mass'

The continuing potency of class inequality is, in sum, starkly evident from disparities in the economic means to life that cannot be explained away as progressively classless in character; from disparities in ownership of private property still crasser than in income, ownership especially of financially productive assets; and from a concomitant concentration of power – not only consumer privilege – in tiny minority hands. Inequality on all these scores has grown sharper since around 1980: this in remarkable contrast both to the broad pattern of relative constancy from the 1950s into the 1970s, and to now clamorously revived assertions of 'class eclipse'. It is not surprising to find some evidence that class disparities in the risks of sickness and death, in relative terms long resistant to diminution even before 1980, may also have widened since (Whitehead, 1987; see also Wilkinson, 1986a and b). Of course these indicators do not exhaust the full range of class influences on life circumstances. I shall take up other features of the material configuration of class in turning now, and throughout the following chapter also, to the question where the main lines of class division run today – for the moment the main lines of economic division irrespective of the political divisions to which, as a matter for later discussion, these in turn may or may not give rise.

That question can never yield a simple answer, by way of some neat categorization of classes precisely enumerated. The term 'class structure' may seem to imply this. But it is just a shorthand phrase – a metaphor – for such consistency of pattern as can be discerned in a multiple array of inequalities that concern people's places in, and life-courses through, the order of production and distribution. There is the more sense to the term 'structure', the more the various facets of inequality coincide to mark off the same people across the board from the same other people; and there is the clearer-cut a structure the more distinct such pervasive class demarcations are. But to talk of 'structure' remains part-metaphorical talk for several reasons. The various facets of inequality will never fully coincide; and they often show at least semi-continuous gradations rather than clear-cut categorical breaks. On both scores, then too, the scope expands for conceptual dispute: about the relative significance of this facet of inequality versus that, and about boundary lines in the hierarchy or hierarchies of inequality. Above all perhaps, the information available falls inevitably short of what an ideally comprehensive job of class cartography – even at one time, let alone over changing times – would take. I shall not pursue these matters into detailed consideration of the relative merits of recent rival advanced schemes for class categorization. My first point here is just that any such scheme can be only a rough approximation. But secondly, this is no argument against attempts to identify the main divisions of class in empirical, while only approximate, terms; and no argument against use of the metaphor of 'structure'. Class is still plainly a live force when, by way of crucial example, the mass of evidence points to entrenched conjunction of privilege with power at the top, even if the precise boundaries of 'the top' elude practical definition. So also there is plainly sense to talk of a 'structure' of class when the sheer chances of life versus death continue to differ, over many decades, in a pattern that corresponds with the categorization offered even by an acknowledgedly crude and outmoded scheme of occupational stratification.

Fashionable 'class eclipse' wisdom in the 1980s–90s has ignored the formative division between 'top' and all others. But in averting its gaze resolutely from this – and when not throwing all conception of class to the winds – it has fixed instead on a new line of division said, 'emergently', to be superseding whatever other lines there were before: between an 'underclass' minority and a 'classless' mass majority. Of the two main versions in which the thesis comes, one can be dismissed quite summarily. This is a 'moral turpitude' version, which depicts underclass circumstances as a socially corrosive package of deliberate if weak-willed personal disengagement from paid work, from nuclear family morality, from conformity to legal order, and from independence of public welfare provision (see especially Murray, 1990). As a range of critics have pointed out (for instance, J. C. Brown, 1990; Macnicol, 1990; Walker, 1990 and 1991), this postulate eschews factual evidence in its diagnosis of unemployment and resort to state benefits as significantly 'voluntary'; in its close linkage of these with marital instability, illegitimacy and crime, as if all were common products of a single condition of cultural malaise; and, over-all, in its indifference to structural explanation either of poverty or of the other components of such postulated malaise.

The alternative main version of current 'underclass' theory cannot be so easily dismissed. It highlights structural causes of poverty and dependence on public welfare provision by describing underclass formation as the result of enforced exclusion from labour markets: exclusion either altogether or from their secure core. Some variant or other of this has taken a firm hold in present-day British commentary; and it has found a degree of support from professional analysts (for example, Dahrendorf, 1987; Field, 1989; Halsey, 1987; even Townsend, 1993, though he properly notes the enhanced privileges of an 'over-class' side by side with seemingly increased segregation of an 'under-class'). Moreover the thesis is plausible at first sight, because it starts from observation of the trends to sharpened income inequalities and labour market disparities that have indisputably marked the end-of-century era. Indeed, underclass-talk has an understandable appeal when used only as ready rhetoric to sum up the downside impact of those trends to polarization, or to give snapshot descriptions of life today in localities of concentrated deprivation.

For all this, the thesis does not stand up well to closer examination, once it goes beyond summary rhetoric. Correspondingly also, scepticism seems so far to have prevailed over enthusiasm among academic sociologists (see, for instance, Bagguley and Mann, 1992; Gallie, 1988a; Mann, 1992; Westergaard, 1992.) It is odd, to start with, that so allegedly salient a new line of main structural division should be so variously drawn as to yield markedly different assessments of under-class-minority numbers. Still more cogent is the point – emphasized earlier (chapter 8) but widely neglected – that the people excluded from large participation in the 1980s' growth of 'average affluence' comprise no minority, let alone a clearly distinct one; but a good half of the population. This was evident from several measures – of earnings in full-time work and of spin-off from tax – benefit shifts, as well as of real incomes overall. It is similarly evident from a further estimate that shows quintile shares in all disposable 'equivalized' income dropping, between the late 1970s and the late 1980s, from 10 to 7 per cent of the total for the poorest one-in-five of households, but by one percentage point also for each of the next three quintile groups up the scale. Only the richest one-in-five increased their share – from 37 to 44 per cent of the total (*Social Trends 1992*, table 5.19). In these terms, 'minority segregation' is at least as striking in the high reaches as in the low reaches of the class structure.

The thesis of new 'outcast poverty' need assume no homogeneity among the underclass save by way of common economic deprivation. (So too it need assume no significant potential for political mobilization of the underclass *per se*, an issue on which a good deal of commentary has focused to different conclusions: see e.g. Bauman, 1982; Gallie, 1988a; Giddens, 1973; Gorz, 1982.) But it necessarily assumes a marked attenuation of links between the world of solid employment and the world on or below employment-fringes. This assumption too is at the very least dubious.

It is certainly hard to apply to one large component cluster of the postulated underclass: the retired poor, who in Britain today make up some two-fifths or more of the poor, wherever within realism one may decide to draw the 'poverty line' (*Social Trends 1992*, table 5.17). For while these people will not return to the world of work, they cannot easily be seen as a species apart from the rank-and-file wage-earners most of them once were, or from the prospectively pension-poor wage-earners that a good many of their younger relatives, acquaintances and neighbours must be (cf. earlier this chapter). There is, provisionally, more clout to the assumption in application to the unemployed and the tenuously employed of working age. A range of research into the impact of recession in the early 1980s has thus confirmed earlier work in showing long-term unemployment, especially, to be a profoundly isolating condition; its victims, moreover, to be drawn disproportionately from among people previously low-placed in the world of work (see, for example, Allen et al., 1986; Colledge and Bartholomew, 1980; Daniel, 1981; Fryer and Ullah, eds., 1986; Harris, 1987; Marsden, 1982; Moylan et al., 1984; Showler and Sinfield, 1981; Sinfield, 1981; Warr, 1987; Westergaard et al., 1989). Even so, protracted joblessness does not mark off a distinct group. There seems too much movement between the spheres of work security and insecurity for so clear-cut a conclusion. Deep recession tends, for example, to press redundant skilled workers into lower-grade and in turn more vulnerable jobs on re-employment – if they do not take early retirement, on much the same small-pension terms as the less skilled. Economic recovery, if and when it comes, will work the other way: to pull both skilled and less skilled some way back up, even though it will leave many more people out in the cold today than earlier. Given continuous 'de-industrialization', moreover, renewed recession in the early 1990s appears to have spread risks of redundancy rather wider: to affect more employees in the ostensible labour market 'core' than before, and to make uncertainty of employment less distinctly a feature of lowest-stratum location in the class structure.

Labour markets are to a degree segmented; and changes over the past two decades or so have indeed increased labour insecurity and enlarged those reaches of the markets whose employees are ill-protected. But quite extensive research into these shifts has still failed to identify any clear, or a notably accelerating, pattern of segmentation between core and periphery, primary and secondary sectors, with workers locked as fairly distinct sets into one or another of these over increasingly long durations (see, for instance, Brown, R. 1990; Burchell and Rubery, 1989; Gallie, 1988a; Rubery, 1988.) The point is not that the scenarios of deep-set labour market cleavage on which some 'outcast poverty' theorizing has drawn are inherently implausible, or that trends further in their direction can be firmly ruled out for the future. But the evidence so far is against them rather than for them.

Still less robust is the assumption that people above the circumstances of 'outcast poverty' increasingly constitute a classless 'middle mass', more or less united in life circumstances and prospects by common participation in generally rising prosperity and consumer power. That proposition plainly falls foul of the data I have already adduced about the share-out of the proceeds from such uneven economic growth as there has been since around 1980. The proposition has even so continued to attract wide support, by reference especially to consumer opportunities supposedly enlarged by the current era's release of market forces. The very wide spread of owner-occupation in housing has come to be taken as the prototypical case on which the assertion of new 'middle-mass empowerment' turns. Reams of loose talk apart, the assertion has been most cogently made in a professional study, whose author argues that acquisition of home-ownership constitutes a qualitative break in life which distances beneficiaries decisively from the one-time working-class world of tenancy-dependence (Saunders, 1990). Whatever financial advantages it offers, so the key thesis here runs, home-ownership satisfies an inherent human desire for possession of property: for such self-control over private life as this confers, whether or not it may also amount to acquisition of a politically resonant 'stake in the country'.

There is persuasive force to the general argument for personal autonomy, even though its particular formulation and the strength of the survey evidence on which it partly rests are contestable; and though personal control over household homes might be more equitably achieved through a system of lifelong public leaseholds than through inheritable full building-and-land ownership (cf. chapter 6 above). But what matters for the present purpose is the inference drawn for class structure: an inference drawn with some caution by the author here; but with abandon by many other enthusiasts for the postulated social magic of owner-occupation. To put the matter bluntly, it by no means follows that acquisition of home-ownership constitutes so decisive a break in life as to quench the salience of class inequalities at large: the salience either of persistent inequality among home-owners; or of the class circumstances that more of these owners now continue to have in common with the fewer who now remain tenants of public landlords. Inequality in respect of housing itself is all the more evident as owner-occupation has spread (see especially Forest et al., 1990). Lower incomes buy cheaper homes in poorer locations, and leave owners more vulnerable to maintenance bills; they yield lower, while still arbitrary, capital gains on sale in a buoyant housing market or on transmission to heirs; and they entail more risk of irreversible dispossession, despite new spread of capital losses, when the market loses buoyancy as in the early 1990s. Add to this the plain points that the jobless stay jobless, wage-earners stay wage-earners, careers-people stay careers-people, and tycoons stay tycoons whatever, generally, the form of tenure by which they occupy their homes; and that inequalities in the means of livelihood have sharpened apace between such class-categories of people over the last decade and more. 'Consumer power', quite simply, is income power. It is more stratified than it was, not less. Home-ownership confers no immunity from shortage of it: no 'mass-majority' immunity from the divisive pressures of a class structure which remains firmly in place, for all underclass-talk assumption that class is now only a sad fringe phenomenon.

10 Careers versus Jobs

Harder set though it now is, however, the class structure has also changed shape to more complex consequences. In particular, the 'working class' as it once was has continued to shrink in size over the past half-century, while groups on its conventional margins *and* well above them have grown. In addition, by whatever conception of its boundaries, the working class has come to be more diverse of conditions within itself, notably during the last two decades or so.

Take the second point first, as it leads immediately out of the preceding discussion. Increased labour market fragmentation has not led to segregation of a distinct underclass. But it has sharpened differences of circumstance among people whose lives depend on present, past or prospective wage-earning. So it has reversed, in some part, a set of trends over much of this century earlier towards greater working-class homogeneity of condition. In long historical perspective, the factors behind these trends had included the dramatic decline of employment in private domestic service; the decline, too, of casual unskilled labour; and the growth of semi-skilled industrial work: all processes of upgrading, but towards 'homogenization'. The displacement over time of craftsmen, artisans and mechanics by skilled production-line operatives also made for wider similarity of industrial employment circumstances: never mind the degree to which it might or might not involve 'de-skilling' (among an extensive literature on this subject following Braverman, 1974, see, for instance, S. Wood, 1982); and never mind the fact that 'Fordist' assembly-belt processes never came to prevail nearly as far as often stereotypically assumed. From the Second World War into the 1970s, moreover, long boom gave further impetus towards significant commonality of labour conditions: because unemployment was low, and trade unions were well placed enough for corporatist collective bargaining to set some framework for a nationwide labour market to standardizing effects.

These previous long trends to class-homogenization of industrial labour were in broad line with classical Marxist expectations – though they went, not with 'immiserization', but with generally rising absolute levels of living for all. Recent trends, by contrast, have included a twist to tangible immiserization for some by present-day standards; and larger disparities of life circumstances within the working class. Leave political implications for later; the material facts are little in doubt. High unemployment now even in phases of growth, and wider unevenness of wages down the scale – as well as of salaries up the scale – plainly denote less commonality of labour conditions. Trade union activity is substantially weaker than it was fifteen years ago, again to part-fragmenting effect.

True, the evidence here is not all of one piece. (See, for instance, Bagguley et al., 1990; Batstone, 1984 and 1988; Gallie, 1989; Martin, 1992; Millward, Stevens et al., 1992; Winchester, 1988.) Union presence survived the traumas of the early 1980s in Britain with sufficient resilience to achieve some bargained growth of real wages over the decade; within still unionized establishments, workplace organization also seemed to stay fairly firmly in place; 'market-based' unionism in business-supportive style has not caught on so widely as was once forecast; and popular support for unions in their role of protecting employees appears, if anything, to have grown. Yet these are points of qualification, no more, against the overall diminution of that role. While the wheel of industrial relations has not been turned back fully to the 1920s, little more than half of Britain's workplaces are now covered by union agreements, by comparison with some two in every three around 1980; the range of issues included in agreements has narrowed; and the aggregate density of union membership among employees is down from percentages in the mid-to-high 50s before 1980 to percentages in the 40s in recent years. It matters little for the immediate consequences that the causes can be traced more to the conjunction of high unemployment with shifts of economic activity from well-unionized to poorly unionized employment than to concerted aggression of employer policies. The outcome in any case has been to magnify labour market subdivisions which – while forming no clear pattern of 'core' versus 'periphery' – leave growing zones of wage work, in the lower reaches of private service employment especially, increasedly ill-protected.

Sharper diversity of economic experience within the working class has not, however, eroded the divide between wage-centred life and well-heeled salary, let alone profit-centred life. But it is now harder to say just where that divide sets in, on a class map constructed from the varied yet still far from exhaustive information available.

The 'old' working class – comprising people in or out of jobs conventionally labelled 'manual' – are undoubtedly, together with now growing numbers of people in or out of low-grade service jobs, in all generality below the line, when supervisors and technicians are excluded from this bloc. And it is a 'bloc', with much still in common to life experience despite the recent growth of economic disparities within it. Data on social mobility thus continue to show little salience for individual occupational prospects to the distinction between skilled and non-skilled manual labour – in this country, by some contrast to Germany, for example (Erikson and Goldthorpe, 1992; Goldthorpe, 1987; also Marshall et al., 1988; Noble et al., 1989). To come from a skilled working-class home, or to start working life in a skilled job, gives in general little extra chance of advancement to distinctly better employment over comparable beginnings from non-skilled origins. As the manual working class has continued to contract in numbers, moreover, so those people who live all or most of their adult lives as 'members' of it have come to be very largely recruited from families of the same kind. These points in turn chime with the fact that there is a good deal of individual movement between the skilled and non-skilled layers of this working class. The frequent combination of the levels into one broad cluster, for purpose of summary classification, remains empirically well justified. Above all, of course, employment in manual work at any level is overwhelmingly employment in plain *jobs*. So on balance is employment in low-grade personal service work, though markedly poor wages and high labour turnover here may find some – and unionization-resistant – compensation from opportunities for 'fiddling' and from face-to-face relations with customers and managers (Ditton, 1977; Marshall, 1986). Neither kind of employment, at all events, carries the signal advantages in pay long-term, in promotion and pension prospects, and in degrees of autonomy in everyday work, which distinguish salaried managerial or professional employment on well-set *career* paths.

The distinction between 'jobs' and 'careers' has a good deal more to tell about inequalities of employment-related class circumstances today than has tradition's distinction just between 'manual' and 'non-manual' work. As elaborated in some recent research, it well confirms the conjunction of work-and-life advantages that usually go with employment at 'service-class' levels. So a large nationwide survey in the mid-1980s (Marshall et al., 1988, see especially pp. 78, 118–120) asked employees to describe a variety of features to their work, concerning scope for personal initiative, individual control over work-timing and pace, freedom from direct supervision and so on. Managers and professionals of service-class status 'scored' overall while not uniformly high, though women even at this level lower than men. Manual workers scored distinctly low – in a good many respects close to nil – almost regardless of skill or gender. Of those in service-class employment, again, the great majority described themselves as on 'career ladders' – women a little less often than men – by contrast with only a third of skilled workers, a quarter of non-skilled men, and very few non-skilled women even if in full-time work.

This so far is only useful re-emphasis of the broadly familiar. The crunch concerns the situations of people at employment levels between 'service' and 'old' working class. From the same data, they are in aggregate intermediately placed; but with some noteworthy differences among them. Men in 'non-routine', though nominally manual work – supervisors and technicians, a predominantly male category – came halfway up or better on the scores concerning work-discretion and the like, while most said they were on promotion ladders. But the picture is a good deal more ambiguous for routine non-manual employees: especially for that large majority of those who are women – secretaries, typists, clerical and sales assistants and so on. True, when in full-time work, upwards of half such women said they had a place on a career ladder, and many reported some degree of autonomy to their work. But their scores in respect of self-perceived decision-making and freedom from direct supevision were low: overall little above those of manual workers.

Information of this sort is broad-brush. But because it is so far rare in fairly large-scale quantitative form, it is worth adding some findings from a sizeable 1986/7 survey in Sheffield, by then far more a recession-depressed service economy than the steel-manufacturing centre it had been earlier (Noble et al., 1989). In pursuit of the distinction between 'jobs' and 'careers', this focused on pay systems and on perceptions of employment security and promotion prospects, rather than on features of discretion and initiative in everyday work. Not surprisingly at that time and place, a sense of job insecurity proved quite widespread among male manual workers (33 per cent); but considerable even among men in managerial posts (19 per cent); much lower among both professionals and routine-grade non-manual workers of either sex. Perceptions of promotion possibilities varied from pervasive optimism among professionals to very much less of it among non-skilled as well as part-time workers. But in this instance managers, routine-level white-collar or white-blouse employees if in full-time work, and skilled blue-collar workers came out much on a par: around half of all these saw at least some prospect of advance-

ment, though this in answer to an arguably loose question that failed
to distinguish between institutionalized career ladders and less regular opportunities for promotion.

Overridingly evident, however, were marked employee-class differences in modes of pay. The issues here were how far pay varied
from one pay packet to the next, as proved common in manual work
but quite rare otherwise; whether full pay was provided on sick leave,
as was near-universal for full-time employees at all levels of non-
manual work, but available only for just above half of all manual
workers regardless of skill, and for still fewer women in part-time
clerical work; especially whether pay rose regularly on an incremental
scale. On this latter score the contrasts ranged from near-absence of
incremental pay rises among manual workers to around 75 per cent
prevalence among people in professional, semi-professional or similar
work. For managers, the figure was somewhat under half: barely
higher than for men in routine-grade non-manual employment. It was
much the same in aggregate for women in work of the latter kind, but
with a notable difference according to employment status: of full-
timers three in five were paid on incremental scales, of part-timers
only a third.

These various measures of salariat versus wage-earner employment
conditions neither coincide very neatly with each other nor allow
assignment of this and that group, as defined by various current
occupational classifications, wholly to one side or another. The degree
of discretion in everyday execution of work, the advantages of place
on a recognized promotion ladder, of regular increments in pay, of
continued full payment when off sick, and so on, differ to an extent
even among professionals; more so among 'managers' – a broad category of rather mixed work circumstances, at least as separately
defined in the Sheffield study. Conversely, even among manual workers quite many get full sick-pay and some are on promotion ladders,
though very few enjoy incremental pay scales or significant discretion
over how to do their work. Yet, taken together, such measures do a
good deal – over and above wide disparities of actual earnings – to
mark out class differences in the circumstances, in and from work, of
that great majority of the working population who are all nominally
'employees'. Moreover, the contrast so fleshed out between wage-
earner jobs and salariat careers is not a mere artefact of academic
analysis, little visible to wage-earners or the career-salaried themselves. It is a contrast which most people seem to recognize and can
apply to their own circumstances.

This is certainly the case to judge from the Sheffield study. Asked to
look back over their work-life experience and to describe it, if they

could, as involving work mainly either in 'jobs' or in 'career' employment, almost all employees were prepared to do so; and on the whole their descriptions tallied pretty well with the records they gave of their work, as it was now and as it had been over time. The descriptions so tallied in the sense, for example, that over three in every four of those men and women alike, whose current and longest employment was non-manual above routine level, took 'career' as the appropriate tag; while just as many blue-collar and low-grade personal-service workers said 'job'. Significantly, women in full-time 'white-blouse' work at routine level divided almost equally – but with an edge towards choice of the term 'job', especially if they saw little chance of promotion ahead; and nearly all the part-timers here said 'job'. Of course, nominal labelling of this sort might be one thing, such perceptions of advantage or disadvantage as may go with it another. But overall more than half of those questioned thought the difference between job experience and career experience 'important for life', outside work as well as in work itself. Careers were seen to carry advantages for the quality or range of life, leisure or social contacts, even over and above advantages for living standards or work satisfaction. And while people who described their work experience as mainly confined to jobs were – perhaps by way of self-consolation – somewhat less inclined to attribute importance to the distinction than were those who saw themselves on career paths, they implied disadvantage enough to their experience by usually ascribing it to lack of opportunity on their part – from family, educational or other social circumstances – rather than to lack of ability, let alone to any preference for a job-life over a career-life.

The world of prime dependence on jobs remains, then, distinct from the world in which employment takes career-shape. Job-dependence involves not just lower and less predictable pay overall, less security of work and very little say in work; but also more limited advancement prospects, and common exclusion from the regularity of pay growth by seniority which goes, even without promotion, with place on an incremental salary scale. It is hardly surprising if, among a number of 'class-cultural' differences, life is harder to plan ahead for working-class people than others (cf., for example, Anderson et al., 1992). All this applies plainly enough still in general to individuals, couples and families at blue-collar or menial personal-service level – in skilled as well as non-skilled work, still more if out of work or past it. But it applies also to many women – if much less to the rather few men – whose work is rank-and-file office employment or the like. At least it applies to many of these women by virtue of their own work itself, if not by reference to their family circumstances when their household partner's work is in the career mode.

I may be accused here of reviving the thesis of progressive 'white-collar proletarianization' despite considerable, though not wholly uniform, evidence against it (cf. for instance, Lane, 1988 and Marshall et al., 1988, as against Crompton and Jones, 1984). But my comments do not concern male clerks and their kind, a small and ambiguously situated category, often transients between other class locations. And in focusing on *'white-blouse'* workers – who indeed account for some three in every four routine-grade non-manual workers by common current classifications – I assert no general trend to 'downgrading' of their conditions over time. My point is, instead, that their common categorization as a single and ostensibly 'intermediate' group obscures a range of disparities in employment circumstances: from quasi-career status, to little or no better than plain job status for a majority among them.

For a start, around 40 per cent or more of all women in routine-category non-manual employment work *part-time*. This may not generally entail lower hourly rates of pay (Gallie, 1991). But it does exclude the majority of part-timers from full sick-pay, for example; and more importantly from promotion ladders, from incremental pay scales and from perception of their work as any more than jobs. The evidence summarized in the last few pages is clear to this effect. It looks more ambiguous in respect of women in *full-time* clerical or similar employment. But what looks like ambiguity here must rather be disparity. When somewhere around half of such full-timers report that they are on promotion ladders or incremental pay scales – maybe often rather short or small-stepped, yet ladders and scales to some past or prospective advantage nonetheless – this is significant. Yet it is surely not a pointer to some unitary category of full-time employees all more or less part-way in these terms between rank-and-file wage-earners and salariat proper. It suggests, rather, noteworthy subdivisions of employment circumstances within the category – subdivisions which are not unfamiliar from everyday knowledge of the range, for example, from senior secretarial to office-assistance work; which have been meticulously explored in a few illuminating case studies (for example, Crompton and Jones, 1984); but which have still not been adequately mapped across the board, notwithstanding efforts in recent categorization to separate out more clearly the poorer-placed personal-service workers from routine-level employees in administration and commerce.

In fact, it seems that up to half of all women with full-time work in routine-grade non-manual employment are much on a par with most of their part-time colleagues in exclusion from the formal ladders and scales for advancement; and are correspondingly inclined to see their work experience as confined to jobs. Add the points that, by inference from the nationwide survey cited before, at least similar proportions appear to have little say over how to do their work; that, from both this and the Sheffield survey, women who start working life in clerical or similar employment are indeed – in contrast to their male counterparts – more likely to move down later into manual jobs than to achieve promotion up the occupational scale; and also that, from official earnings data, full-time pay at this ostensibly 'intermediate' level is for women generally still lower than are men's wages in *manual* work. The implication then follows that some good majority of all women with routine-grade 'white-blouse' work – say upwards of half the full-timers, over and above most part-timers – have jobs which, the 'office milieu' apart, are just about as far from career-mode work in their terms of everyday employment as is the generality of blue-collar work.

If 'career-mode' work is taken to correspond roughly with the 'service-class' employment of main current British classifications (originated by John Goldthorpe and colleagues), it is nevertheless also more mixed of character than incautious use of either label implies. For one thing such categorization fails to mark off top-elite privilege and power. But below that peak too, there are not only gradations of salariat advantage, as recognized in part when higher- and lower-grade service-class employment are distinguished. There are also subdivisions which cannot readily be seen as differences of level on a vertical scale. From everyday observation and from a variety of evidence, 'professions' and 'management' constitute two partly separate spheres of career employment.

Both have their internal gradations of level, of course – the former especially between small elite professions and large 'auxiliary' professions, each in turn with their own hierarchies of seniority; the latter in the form of multiple grades of managerial authority. But en bloc professional employment – together with much administration in public service – looks distinct from business management by way of more uniform, institutionalized provision of promotion ladders and incremental pay scales; more security of employment, still backed even at high level by collective bargaining; so more clearly demarcated career paths, with recruitment often direct into them from appropriately qualifying higher or further education; and of course, since many professions are primarily in the public sector, varying degrees of detachment by work role from the world of private enterprise. The converse of these features applies to business management, including more recruitment from below salariat ranks. But if career paths there overall are less certain, they also offer perks at middle level and above unmatched in most professional work; and they may nourish individual hopes – wild though these will be for all but a few managers – of a rise to high success, with rewards well above those on offer from the best of secure professional ladders.

So, on this and other scores, the economic structure of class is more complex than before. It never was, nor tended to become, just bipartite – 'capital' versus 'labour'. It is closer to tripartite – 'hightop' versus 'careers' versus 'jobs', then, rather than 'service' versus 'intermediate' versus 'working' classes. But this, too, over-simplifies. It is hard, moreover, to put any but fairly rough numbers against the main divisions which the evidence suggests. The most relevant overall categorizations for the purpose (Goldthorpe, 1987; Marshall et al., 1988) do not fully fit the lines I have tried to sketch; and lines drawn will be only approximate. Yet some approximate quantification is needed to conclude this discussion.

Start at the top. Extreme power and privilege are concentrated in the hands of a tiny minority: only a small fraction of 1 per cent, if we take just its high-capitalist core (Scott, 1991); at most, say, 2 or 3 per cent of the population if we include those people, from the peaks of government and professional hierarchies as well as business, who are pretty close to that core. At its nether edge this upper class then shades into the best-placed stratum of the salariat. The latter cluster as a whole – executives and managers, administrators, professionals, semi-professionals and so on – has been growing. Excluding top-elite circles, it now numbers around 30 per cent of the population on a count of households rather than individuals. These are people somewhere in the broad sphere of careers, whether by their own employment circumstances or by their marriage-partner's if clearly better. But they form a cluster rather than a single class. More of them are – or were – before retirement – on modest career paths than on high ones; about half of them are involved in public service employment as distinct from private business (estimated from Gallie, 1988b, table 6).

This leaves some two-thirds of the population below both top class and internally diverse salariat. But they in turn make up no single group. Employers in very small business and own-account workers too – jobbing craftsmen, petty shopkeepers and the like – work directly for profit, if quite often precariously and over long hours; not for wages, under others' authority. Technicians, industrial supervisors even if nominally 'manual', and a fair number also of routine-grade non-manual workers, while low in authority and by place on ladders up, not very far in employment circumstances from rank-and-file wage work, have a foot even so into the world of salaried management and career specialism. They and their families are to some real extent 'betwixt and between'. Add their numbers to those of the independent 'petite bourgeoisie': all told another near-30 per cent of the population by an approximate count of households.

As against these, people whose economic lives indubitably centre overall on mere jobs and mere wages – now, or before if they are no longer at work – remain a very large bloc of the population. But at barely 40 per cent they are no longer a majority. True, very nearly half the population have or had when they last worked no more than a rank-and-file job – whether 'blue-collar', 'white-blouse' or in low-level personal service – if we count individuals by their own employment circumstances alone: up to some six-in-ten women, then, though little more than four-in-ten men. But if we count by households instead, and allow for 'cross-class' marriages – marriages especially between women in plain routine work and men some way higher up the scale – the overall figure for the world of jobs-only drops to some four in ten. It seems likely to fall rather further still, unless continuing growth of low-grade office and service work comes to outpace continuing contraction of older-style manual work. If that might happen, it has not from the balance of evidence happened yet.

11 Politics and Class

Voting patterns

The long trend towards predominance of diverse 'middle-class' over plain 'working-class' employment is usually taken to imply a general process of levelling-up. Yet there has been no levelling-up of incomes to match. The ostensible paradox needs to be emphatically noted, for it means that the impact of 'occupational embourgeoisement' on economic class structure has been far from straightforward. It also needs to be explained. When relative inequalities of real income stayed broadly constant in Britain from the 1950s into the 1970s, despite 'upward' occupational shift, this must in good part reflect the simultaneous ageing of the population. One signal consequence of that process has been to increase the numbers of older people in or near poverty through retirement from jobs yielding meagre pensions. Explanation is more obvious, and gross, in respect of the past decade and a half when, very far from levelling-up as employment on or nearer career paths continued to grow, incomes have reached a pitch of inequality in distribution unknown since at least the interwar years. The conjunction now of harsher and more freely working market forces with regression of tax–benefit provision has, over and above much larger unemployment, formidably sharpened disparities of money between *all* levels, in as well as out of employment.

One consequence of this, in turn, is to accentuate the ambiguities of 'middling' place in the class structure: that of many modest salary-earners, for example, on low-set career paths. There are, fairly steadily over time, more of these people; and the widening of income gaps since the late 1970s has added its bit to setting them apart from the poor and the rank-and-file of wage-workers. But it has also set them still further apart from those people well above them, in the upper echelons of business or professional life, whose shares in income growth have vastly outstripped all others'. Even if political inclinations could in general be readily deduced from economic class circumstances – to begin to move to this thorny final topic – it would be hard to do so in their case. Their recent economic experience could have turned such modest salary-earners more to the right than before, in a renewed and maybe self-congratulatory sense of distance from the depressed and declining world of job-and-jobless life below them. But it might instead have turned them leftwards, in resentment at their now more pronounced exclusion from high-rising bourgeois affluence. Or it might then have done neither on balance, pull one way countered by push the other.

Ambiguities in the middle stretches of the class structure apart, however, economic polarization could well have been expected to bring political polarization in its train: if to confirm the well-placed in allegiance to the right, then to swing the ill-placed more firmly left. Not so in fact, to judge by voting trends in general elections, which have left the Labour Party in Britain with only just about a third of the total poll even at 1992's recession-election; and with much weaker support at all levels of class than in the corporatism-cum-boom mid-1960s, when Labour's vote reached a peak little short of half the total. It is this phenomenon, especially, which has triggered incessant talk about eclipse of class. Commentary of that ilk assumes, first, that the decline of support for Labour signifies a steady whittling away of class as an axis of political division; second, that this must signify an underlying erosion of class as a matter of significant divisions in economic and associated social life. The second assumption is patently false, from all that I have said before. The first could still be true since, even in capitalist societies, marked divisions of economic class may come to only blurred expression in prevailing political divisions: the United States, Ireland and Japan are, in their different ways, examples of this to quite long-standing effect. But the first assumption, too, needs at least qualification; and this even in respect of the voting patterns on which it is focused.

Despite Labour's decline, class location is still the prime externally visible influence on how people in Britain vote; and, in *relative* terms, differences of class location make for differences of voting as marked as ever. Credit for first establishment of that fact goes to a study following the 1983 election, which – applying the better-discriminating Goldthorpe classification of occupational class in place of the crude alphabetical-letter categorization standard in everyday market research – reconstructed the record of class voting patterns deposited in sample surveys from the elections of the 1960s onwards (Heath et al., 1985, chapters 2 and 3). Comparison of the data for 1966 and 1983 makes the point cogently. The former year was Labour's peak: 48 per cent of all votes; 72 per cent of blue-collar votes as against 19 and 25 per cent of 'petty bourgeois' and 'salariat' votes respectively; between these extremes, 42 and 61 per cent support respectively from routine non-manual workers and from technicians and supervisors, the latter cluster still predominantly behind Labour. By contrast the election of 1983 was Labour's nadir: a mere 27 V_2 per cent of all votes; 49 per cent of blue-collar votes as against 12 and 14 per cent of petty bourgeois and salariat votes; around 25 per cent of the votes now from people in both 'intermediate' categories.

In short, Labour's support had dropped drastically overall: proportionately most among technicians and supervisors – but *not* so among the much larger group of rank-and-file skilled manual workers, with whom market-research categorization and common commentary misleadingly confuses them; proportionately least in fact, though still by a dramatic factor of one-third, among blue-collar workers of whatever skill-level. But with this pattern of general decline in support for Labour across the class board, the ratios of class difference in voting had stayed broadly, and remarkably, steady: the more so from this study's full analysis of all elections over a near-twenty-year period, to confirm a pattern of 'trendless fluctuation' in respect of relative class differentials in electoral allegiance. Rough continuity on that score was evident again at the 1987 election (by recalculation from Heath and Evans, 1989, table 4.4), now at a higher level of overall support for Labour (32 per cent); and comparable analysis for the 34 per cent Labour-share election of 1992 will probably show much the same once more.

By such relative measures, then, class is still highly salient for electoral politics in Britain. There has been no trend to a growth of 'cross-class' voting in the manner implied by the notion of class de-alignment – instead a long trend of general decline in support for Labour: gradual from the mid- 1960s; precipitate from 1979 to 1983; reversed in 1987 and 1992 but still up to only a one-third share, well short of past post-war levels or of the level needed for a parliamentary majority. Yet in *absolute* terms, this loss of support does represent a decline in the salience of class for British politics at large. It does so, at least, for institutionalized politics, since the Labour Party has been the major agency for overt articulation of class and class interests in British politics. The Conservative Party in fact pursues class politics, and has done so very assiduously over the last two decades. But, like its counterparts almost always and everywhere, it covers that pursuit with an appeal in rhetoric and ideology to unity across purportedly trivial or outmoded class divides. The centre party grouping – which under its changing names of Liberals, Alliance and Liberal Democrats has taken almost all the net gain from Labour's decline, to achieve poll-shares of 25, 23 and 18 per cent respectively in the elections of 1983, 1987 and 1992 – pursues policies rather hard to distinguish from those now advanced by Labour. Yet it is loud in express denial of class ties, and indeed draws its support pretty evenly from all levels, with only a modest top-up from the salariat and from routine-grade non-manual workers.

Why has Labour support so shrunk, and so swung the balance to predominance of parties which take 'class' to be a dirty word? A fair part of the ultimate answer may hang on the point that the Labour Party, too, is now much inclined to see class as a dirty word. But my argument to that effect must wait. Meanwhile, the first half or more to an immediate answer looks deceptively simple. It is that the party was set to lose quite steadily anyway, as the structure of employment has shifted away from the core Labour constituency of industrial workers. Assume no changes in the way that people at any given level of class cast their votes by comparison with the mid-1960s; assume only that 'occupational embourgeoisement' proceeded as in fact it did: then Labour's vote would still have dropped to some 37 per cent of the total by 1983 – roughly halfway down to the 27 $1/2$ per cent the party actually scraped in then (Heath et al., 1985, pp. 36–7). This hypothetical figure, moreover, is only a few points above Labour's actual 34 per cent share of votes in 1992. Given some further occupational shift over the intervening years, many commentators have it that the party's recent electoral performance is now around its current 'natural' level, and will inexorably fall more as ostensible 'embourgeoisement' continues.

Persuasive though this part-explanation is within its own assumptions, those assumptions pose further conundrums. One is an old one: why, even at the best of times for Labour, did a sizeable minority from its prime blue-collar constituency vote fairly consistently against 'their own' party – a minority, fluctuating around one-third, larger than commonly then in Scandinavia to take perhaps the most relevant cross-national comparison? Whatever the much-debated reasons – in crude overview a lack of labour movement coherence inherited from the long and slow character of Britain's industrial development, from the gradualism of political reform here, and/or from cultural patterns of social deference strengthened maybe by the nation's past imperial role – the fact certainly gave Labour a smaller historical base than otherwise from which to move into the last quarter of the twentieth century. Yet as influences from the past were likely to fade, after all, this could have signalled scope for Labour growth rather than the predestined decline now glibly read into occupational shift. Another conundrum is also familiar, but looms steadily larger precisely as occupational shift proceeds: why has Labour – again even at the best of its times, now still more evidently than before, and this for all the party's congenital moderation – failed to recruit substantial support at least from the near-wage-earner groups that rank as intermediate between salariat and old working class in current classifications? Indeed, as I noted earlier, even modest salary-earners could have been thought to come within Labour's net in some larger numbers, as recent economic polarization has underlined their distance from privilege and power still more than from routine wage-earning dependency. That they did not is a puzzle that deserves to be explored; not just a *fait accompli* to be sealed away in the psephological assumptions of common commentary.

In any case, support for Labour had fallen class-for-class to 1983, never mind the shrinkage of its old blue-collar base. And partial recovery since then has not much affected the picture in its most significant features: the electoral appeal of the party now only to some half of all manual workers, and to somewhere around a quarter of the technicians, supervisors, routine-grade office workers and so on, who are even at best only a step away from rank-and-file wage-earning. The prime conundrum of all is that defection from Labour at these levels came when the main signs from the economics of class pointed the other way; when only the rich and the well-placed among the salariat were making substantial gains from such material growth as there was.

Among the more plausible attempts at explanation are those which posit new or accentuated structural divisions across the working class (for example, Dunleavy and Husbands, 1985). General debate as well as some academic research has ascribed great importance to distinctions of housing tenure especially (see chapter 7 and 9). While home-ownership does not somehow insulate its beneficiaries from the larger economic inequalities of class, its spread has made for new disparities of material circumstance and potential interest among wage-earner households. Working-class owner-occupiers generally do incline less to Labour, and more to conservative social views, than their council-tenant counterparts, though this in no way elides class differences of party allegiance within tenure groups. Yet it is hard here to sort out chicken and egg. Home-ownership and/or its neighbourhood milieux may encourage acceptance of the status quo; but, conversely, workers already inclined to favour the status quo may also be those who are keener, or for that matter financially better placed, to move to owner-occupation given a chance. The balance of still uncertain evidence points the latter way: so against ascribing much political effect to the shift of housing tenure by itself. Moreover, the growth in numbers of working-class home-owners looks too small to count for much towards the overall fall of Labour votes (see especially Heath et al., 1985, chapter 4; cf. also Marshall et al., 1988). It is another matter that Tory championship of owner-occupation and sale of public housing may, more generally in the 1980s, have boosted the credibility of radical-right claims for privatization as a means to personal 'emancipation': this when set against Labour ambivalence over housing policy, and that party's long failure to look for measures to 'emancipate' council tenants without permanent loss of public asset-ownership. Even if so, however, popular trust in privatization on this score must have taken some knocks since, in the 'negative equity' mortgage crisis accompanying early 1990s recession.

There might be more to learn about Labour's decline from the weakening of trade unionism. Certainly non-unionists, like home-owners, lean more to the political right than their opposites at each broad class-level of employment. And there is little of a chicken-and-egg problem here. Non-unionists have not increased in number by way of large-scale opting-out in growing hostility to trade unionism – a swing of opinion that would have offered no independent explanation for a parallel swing of votes. The decline of union density has come mainly instead from higher unemployment and from shifts of economic activity towards poorly unionized types of employment. Work circumstances in employment of this kind – where workplaces are often relatively small, everyday contacts among similarly placed colleagues are limited, contacts with superiors and/or 'the public' loom concomitantly larger – may themselves militate against such sense of 'underdog identity' as arguably goes with political inclination to the left. They certainly hamper union organization; and the absence or frailty of a trade union milieu may then militate against formation or maintenance of Labour Party loyalties. Either way, newly accentuated structural fault-lines within and around the working-class – whether the division between presence and absence of collective bargaining by itself, or divisions of workplace environment at large that also tell for or against collective bargaining – could then go some way to explaining Labour's loss of support. It could do so, moreover, without resort to underclass theory's extravagant postulate of an emergent all-overriding divide between the marginally-if-at-all employed and the securely employed; and without resort either to the implication of such theory that skilled workers would desert Labour in far larger numbers than the non-skilled. This latter implication is indeed notably belied by the fact that skill level continues to make little difference for the way plain working- class people vote: now at only some 50 per cent figures of Labour support, but much as when the figures were around 70 per cent.

Explanation by reference to union decline and shifts of workplace relationships still poses some problems, however. It raises issues about class and political 'identity' which I shall take up a little later. It also runs into trouble over timing. Both the fall in union density and the particular shifts of employment structure that principally account for it came to large effect only in the course of the 1980s. The electoral shifts that are here supposed to be their consequence in fact set in rather earlier. Both Conservatives and Labour lost votes sizeably to the Liberals already in 1974; and while Mrs Thatcher's first victory in 1979 was more at Liberal than at Labour expense, Labour's cataclysmic loss of support came in 1983. De-industrialization had bitten hard by then, it is true. But it would still be early days for its workplace-environmental consequences to have had much rightward political effect against such leftward political effect as might have been anticipated from high and still rising unemployment. Positive moves of employment structure in fact gathered more pace later, with revival of economic growth in the second half of the 1980s: now, however, together with some limited recovery for the Labour Party, and with no further loss of wage-earner votes either in 1987 during boom or in 1992 during slump again. Whatever may prove to be the longer-run consequences of employment shifts for voting patterns, matters of politics itself must have much to say about the dramatic changes of party fortune in the years up to and shortly after 1980.

Popular perceptions of particular events and episodes have no doubt played a part in swinging votes at the margin at this time or that: among these, and to disadvantage for Labour, perhaps (if dubiously) the Falklands War before 1983; more certainly the 'winter of discontent' before the 1979 election; the following years' confirmation of the impotence of trade union militancy still more in hard recession; the split-off of Social Democrats from Labour, and the much-publicized disunity and alleged 'extremism' of Labour leadership which went with that. All this, outside a very short run, strengthened leading moderate opinion in the party that salvation lay in firm steerage to the centre: in effect a good deal rightwards, as neo-liberal-cum-authoritarian ascendancy in the Conservative Party had moved the foci of everyday political contest to the right. Yet discussion in this vein does not help much towards understanding why, then, more votes than before seemed to swing under influence from particular events and episodes; why the seismic swing of 1983 went so heavily against

Labour; how far voters have forced the opposition parties into policies of a now rightward-turned 'middle way', as party spokespeople and conventional commentators claim, or conversely it is rather opposition politicians who have pulled the electorate that way in their perennial chase of elusive 'floating voters'; above all, how it is that the radical right have triumphantly captured top policy agendas yet have signally failed to capture popular hearts and minds for their philosophy.

Outlooks, values and interests

The radical right set out to marketize and privatize. Their successes on these scores made for inevitable sharpening of class inequalities. That gave a further objective still more importance. This was to re-educate the public: into acceptance of inequalities as no more than necessary incentives for enterprise, and of class as a dead concept; into reliance on private resources for welfare provision, with only minimal and stigmatized resort to state support; and into acquiescence that government responsibilities must be strictly limited, while strongly exercised where they do apply. The general failure so far of the radical right's campaign to re-educate the population at large – by contrast with its relative success in re-educating policy-makers and policy-agents – has some curious light to throw on the twists and turns of electoral politics. But that failure has to be demonstrated first.

Survey evidence leaves it in no doubt: cumulative evidence especially from the annual reports on *British Social Attitudes* (starting in 1983/4), from other nationwide studies (notably Marshall et al., 1988) and from some local inquiries in depth (Westergaard et al., 1989; Noble et al., 1989; also Edgell and Duke, 1991); not just from everyday opinion polls of fairly surface-skimming kind. So far as perceptions of class disparity in general are concerned, data from these sources have quite consistently shown substantial majorities of the population as a whole – up to two-thirds or even three-quarters from the mid-1980s onwards – to believe that wealth in Britain is too heavily concentrated towards the top; that it should be a government responsibility to reduce income inequalities in favour of the worse-off; that it is hard for people to move from one social class to another – and that things have either not changed on this score, or have actually got worse in recent years. So far as views on relevant measures of policy are concerned, there seems understandably more uncertainty or ambivalence. But overwhelming majorities of survey respondents are definite in assigning responsibility to government for health care and decent living standards for old people. Decent housing for those who cannot afford it by themselves also figures high though not so firmly in popular notions of proper public policy; and far more people look to government in some way to ensure work for everyone who wants it than would leave this off the agenda.

Support for public measures towards fairer shares has indeed grown; and by the early 1990s, rather more than half the population overall expressed themselves in favour of a rise in taxation to fund better public welfare provision. Hardly anyone then wanted cuts in welfare to allow cuts in tax; and in general, radical-right aspirations have found little or quite limited popular resonance. Majorities have opposed reliance on market forces to resolve the country's economic difficulties, for example. Again in common, as against top-level right-ist, opinion the view that unemployment benefit is too low and causes hardship has long prevailed over the view that it is too high and discourages a search for work: this in a ratio of two to one by 1990. And the notion of a two-tier health system has throughout proved anathema for the bulk of the electorate, in recent years for some three in every four people overall.

There are, of course, class differences of perspective on a number of these matters. In respect of welfare provision, one analyst in particular has underlined a contrast between high levels of support, with only little variation by class, for public services of at least as much absol-ute-term benefit to 'middle-class' as to working-class people – notably NHS health care, retirement pensions and education; and on the other hand considerably lower levels of firm support, both overall and especially among people of non-manual category, for state provision of kinds that would in practice benefit mainly working-class people – for example, decent housing for those short of means to it, decent living standards for the unemployed, jobs for all who want them (see especially Taylor-Gooby, 1991, among several publications in which he has advanced this argument). One implication is that provision of the latter sort, while more directly because more narrowly geared to redistribution, is less likely to find general political backing. When even working-class support for it is less definite than might be ex-pected *in vacuo*, this may reflect – rather than explain – ambivalence about it even on opposition party agenda, perhaps just in conse-quence of relatively low concern with it in 'tone-setting' middle-class opinion. Nonetheless it needs to be stressed that – from the same data, and quite out of line with radical-right philosophy – large majorities of people at all levels still see it as at least a 'probable' (while not so commonly a 'definite') responsibility of government to make base provision for fair living standards, jobs and housing. Market forces are not generally trusted to do that by themselves. It is also worth noting that the class differences evident in the degree of firmness with which such views of government responsibilities are held point to a continuing political salience of rational, and so class-divided, appraisals of material self-interest.

On the whole, by contrast, class differences look small when it comes to very general perceptions of the economic shape of British society. With minor variations from one study to another, and from one form of question posed to another, remarkably large majorities across the social scale express shared views that the dice are loaded unfairly in favour of the rich and against the poor. Where there are shades of difference, one is most consistently apparent: small employers and own-account workers – the petite bourgeoisie in old but now revived parlance – incline less to critique of this sort than others. As against that, however, technicians and manual supervisors come out much on a par with rank-and-file blue-collar workers in firmly jaundiced perception of the socio-economic structure as unjustly skewed to top advantage. Add the point that much the same goes for their survey-reported opinions on most matters of policy for fairer shares. The question then looms still larger why so disprotionately many people from this small category abandoned their former majority habit of Labour-voting around the early 1980s; and why few of them seem to have returned so far since. Whatever the answers to that unresolved puzzle, the information now accumulated about people's socio-political views surely points to this group as one promising target for Labour Party or more radical-left mobilization: little less so than are the greater numbers though smaller proportions of blue-collar workers at humdrum wage-earner level whose support for Labour has also wilted.

Survey respondents from the other supposedly 'intermediate' category of routine-grade non-manual workers matter more numerically than technicians and supervisors. They come out indeed as rather betwixt and between so far also as their reported opinions go. They are only a touch less prone than manual workers – non-skilled, skilled, even technicians or foremen – to see wealth, income or power as unfairly skewed. But they are closer to the salariat on a number of scores – though not all – concerning what might or might not be done about it by means of public policy. These people, however, are quite a mixed cluster in economic terms. By reference just to individual employment circumstances perhaps about half, including most part-timers, are at no more than basic job level. But count by households instead, with allowance for 'cross-class' marriages, and the scales tip towards some majority of routine-grade non-manual workers as a step or two away from the world of plain jobs (see chapter 10). Even so, cross-class marriage need not always have the political effects it so far seems to have most often: to bring the ways married women vote into broad line with the ways their husbands vote, if not directly through male 'ideological dominance' then rather because household economic circumstances continue by and large to hang more on husbands' than on wives' places in employment. A major analysis on that topic has in fact shown – though it did not stress – one deviation from this common pattern. In partnerships between 'intermediate-category' men and 'working-class' women, twice as many – while still only a good third – of the wives as of the husbands said they would vote Labour (Marshall et al., 1988, p. 133, table 5.22). This could be just a fluke. But it could instead be an incipient sign that married women may come to view their political interests rather more by reference to their own employment circumstances and prospects than mainly to their domestic partnership circumstances. Any spread of female 'emancipation' in this form should, over time, boost support for Labour – or for left-radicalism in some future reinvigorated guise – among the large numbers of married women in low-level jobs, white-blouse as well as manual. The political effects of gender inequality and class inequality would then come closer to going hand in hand.

Be that as it may, at only around 25 per cent, voting support for Labour among routine-grade non-manual workers remains for the present well below the level one might expect from survey findings about such people's general socio-political views. More 'mixed' though their opinions are than those of blue-collar workers, office workers at this level still lean predominantly centre-left in outlook. This sort of gap between actual voting and apparent potential is evident too, of course, in the case of the 'old' working class: the point glares out from the evidence summarized so far. To a degree it applies even within the salariat, the 'service class' by another name.

When about two-in-three or even more people in some sort of business or professional work, so classified, say they think wealth in Britain too concentrated, income inequality too extreme, class disparities of opportunity as wide as ever, then this shows at least a clear sense of unease over social injustice that spreads widely across classes. True enough, views about what governments should do about it are here more divided, in ways I have already partly indicated. Nor is it surprising to find support for incomes policies in favour of the low-paid dropping, from around 80 per cent among both routine-grade white-collar people and all levels of manual workers interviewed in one nationwide study, to some 60 per cent among the salariat (Marshall et al., 1988, p. 180); to find only 30 per cent support in their case for the idea of taxes on company profits in order to create jobs, as against percentages otherwise from around 50 upwards except among petty bourgeois respondents (ibid.); or again to find, from a large local study, general endorsement of measures to redistribute income and wealth towards 'ordinary working people' confined to some 45 per cent of professionals, managers and employers, by contrast with 65–70 per cent of all in lower grades of work whether manual or non-manual (Noble et al., 1989). Here is evidence, nonetheless, of at least considerable and sometimes pretty high-figure salariat sympathy for policies – over and above looser rhetoric about injustice – that run distinctly against the grain of right-wing radicalism. So too and very firmly, as discussed earlier, in respect of public provision for health, pensions and education – services which are not in fact just 'middle-class benefits' but go across the class board, with proportionately more ultimate advantage for the very many at lower class levels who could otherwise ill afford them.

Such potential as this suggests for recruitment among the salariat to at least corporatist class-redistributive political programmes differs by level of 'service-class' employment. It differs also by sector of employment and, in fair parallel with this, between managers and professionals. Of that near-half of the salariat whose work is in public-sector service, fewer than one in three declared an intention to vote Tory in the mid-1980s for example; the majority divided their preferences more or less equally between the Alliance and Labour (Marshall et al., 1988, p. 251). Many such public-service employees are professionals and semi-professionals. It is these especially, in contrast to managers, whose general opinions show a sympathy for moves to fairer social shares which Labour has so far tapped only to limited extent, in rivalry now with the Liberals for command of an ill-defined 'middle way'. An egalitarian tilt to socio-political perspectives and policy priorities among this cluster within the salariat, by comparison with business people, was thus evident from a Sheffield study in the second half of the 1980s (Noble et al., 1989). Though professional and/or public-sector work often offers more regular promotion ladders and incremental pay scales than does employment at similar 'service-class' levels in enterprise management, it must tend also to nurture a particular set of interests in protection of public service activity, often as well in professional 'autonomy', in conflict with the thrust of government policy over the past decade and a half in Britain.

When, furthermore, the salariat prove strongest in support of the so-called 'new agenda' in politics (for example, Heath and Evans, 1989) – as a whole more inclined than others to favour 'green' priorities, women's, 'black' and civil rights, moderation in penal pol-

icy, nuclear disarmament and/or conciliation in international relations – it is from among public-service professionals especially that
such support comes (cf. also Parkin, 1968). 'New agenda' issues find
distinctly less sympathy among all other work-defined groups, including ordinary wage-earners quite notably (Noble et al., 1989). This
need not put leftward-leaning professionals wholly out of political
kilter with working-class people. The former share, in moderation, a
number of the latter's pre-eminent concerns with the matters of class
inequality that comprise the 'old agenda'. The issues on the new
agenda, though ever liable to evoke illiberal and especially racist
backlash in populist vein, seem in any case to have rather low salience
for voting patterns currently; and, in forward perspective, their general
logic is not at odds with the logic of much fairer class shares. Equality
of both gender and ethnicity would be harder to obstruct if inequalities
of economic class were substantially reduced (see chapter 9). The case
for civil rights and penal moderation is a case also on behalf of class-
underdogs. Green goals to curtail economic growth must be coupled
with measures for fairer distribution of economic output, if their
achievement is not to hit ordinary people and the poor – even within
affluent countries, let alone elsewhere – insupportably hard.

Priorities can nevertheless clash between old and new agendas. And
to make my own value judgements more explicit at this point, I put no
plea for a 'rainbow coalition' of the sort it became fashionable to
advocate on the revisionist left in the 1980s: certainly not if pursuit of
that should mean tempering class-redistributive objectives in order to
court professional-group favour at all levels. In the upper echelons of
professional life, even the radically inclined will in common with
colleagues have their own furrows still to plough in defence of substantial career advantage, vocational authority and effective influence
on recruitment towards 'closure' of their occupations. Those vested
interests may well find accommodation within liberal-centrist programmes of reform towards both some range of new agenda aims and
moderate economic redistribution – provided that neither is pursued
much beyond trimming of that privilege and power at the very top in
which even the well-established professions have little share. Not so
with a programme that sought to combine the new agenda with the
drive to comprehensive economic redistribution needed both to give
it cutting edge and to evoke wage-earner commitment in place of
distrust. A programme of this kind could not on grounds of political
efficacy – and, in my own view, should not on grounds of social
equity – look to sustained appeal to people in professional life above
the lower echelons. Moreover – and as a note pertinent to the central
place of gender equality on new agendas – it is at rather low levels

of professional life that women with careers of their own are concentrated: careers especially in such mass-number professions as schoolteaching, social work, nursing and other medical-auxiliary employment, where advancement prospects for the many are limited, professional discretion is curbed by authority from on high, and salaries remain often not far above wage-earner pay.

In summary then, popular perceptions both of class inequality and of its injustice are spread wide in Britain – wider by far than could be expected from the facts that a still radical-right inspired Conservative Party retained well over 40 per cent of the popular vote in 1992; and that a long-run decline of Labour votes has been matched by new electoral prominence for a centre party which expressly disavows class politics. Commentators sometimes dismiss the puzzle with an argument that surveys can show little about real opinions. Take exactly the 1992 election, this kind of assertion has it: when the polls predicted Labour victory, the reality came out as Labour defeat; and that, to boot, was much because voters took fright over Labour tax-rise plans of just the sort surveys had said voters favoured. Loose-shot critique in this vein is misguided. Never mind here common press distortion of Labour's tax plans, in fact *both* that party and the Liberals in 1992 proposed tax increases to fund better social provision; and at some points over 50 per cent, their combined majority of votes was, as it happens, of much the same level as the majority then found by surveys to favour this option. The size of 1992's discrepancy between poll predictions and eventual votes was unusual, and probably arose from factors with little bearing on more intensive social surveys: a combination of slightly skew sampling, 'last-minute swing' and – worryingly for electoral democracy – a rise in abstention, even non-registration, on the part of poorer people. Above all, the findings from the surveys on which I have drawn look remarkably robust in their broad similarities – similarities from one source to another; across varying forms, sequences and contexts of questions; and by way of some gradual trend of opinions, from the mid-1980s onwards, to further distaste for radical-right perceptions and prescriptions.

Yet surveys do show apparent inconsistencies of individual opinion (see especially Heath, 1986). And when there is a pattern of consistency itself to such apparent inconsistencies, this can have quite a lot to suggest for explanation of puzzles like the current contrasts in Britain between voting at general elections and survey-probed evidence on popular social ideology. What it has to suggest is a wide spread of disillusion with the efficacy of established political processes for social change; and not least working-class disenchantment on this score with their 'own' labour movement.

This is a point which my colleagues and I have tried to explore through two studies in Sheffield: the first a survey, in the early 1980s, of nearly 400 people who had lost their work in a local steel firm some three years earlier (Westergaard et al., 1989); the second involving interviews with 1,000 adults across the city, in the latter half of the 1980s, about their lifetime economic experiences and their socio-political views (Noble et al., 1989). Sheffield may seem too atypical for conclusions to be drawn for the country more widely; and both studies indeed showed rather larger electoral support for Labour, present as well as past, than across Britain as a whole – this at every level of class, in what may be confirmation of some effect from local or regional culture on party allegiances. Yet, strikingly, voters interviewed in both studies had defected from Labour over the early 1980s in much the same ratios, class-level for level, as in the country overall. Experience of redundancy and unemployment seemed not by itself to have held back that trend. Opinions on a wide range of social and economic issues proved closely in line with those reported in nation-wide surveys of the kind on which I have so far mainly drawn, with only a slight edge towards more 'egalitarianism'. And these opinions showed very much the same oddities, of discrepancy between ostensible Labour potential and actual Labour voting at the time, as have stood out from other work.

As the first study especially underlined, near in time to the events, former party supporters appeared to have defected from Labour in the years running up to the 1983 election, for two sorts of reason in the main. In part, they had come to distrust Labour's competence: the party's leadership was divided and ineffectual; and while respondents by and large preferred distinctly corporatist and centre-to-left policy prescriptions for the revival of employment and growth to which they gave priority, they were evidently sceptical of a Labour government's ability to bring hard sense to that business of public economic management. In larger part still, they saw trade union leaders as out of touch; industrial militancy as counter-productive and too narrowly self-seeking; Labour's efficacy as thus suspect also from the association they ascribed to the party with such things. Views of this kind – of the latter kind in some tune with the government's campaign against unions – found moderate degrees of endorsement also among those people who had stayed with Labour.

Yet, crucially and at first sight quite 'inconsistently', old-style Labour values remained strongly entrenched. There was, for example, majority agreement even among defectors that trade unions are an essential defence for workers against employers' power otherwise to have their own way; and that strikes arise from basic conflict within

industry. It seemed 'other people's' trade unions and strikes that were
the target for many respondents' unease over mindless militancy: at
any rate rarely their own unions – which critics found remote, when
at all, then rather through too cosy a relationship with management –
and not strikes with whose circumstances they could empathize. Blue-
collar workers in particular proved still firm in loyalty to the principles of trade unionism and collective organization to protect
employees' interests – just as in overwhelming proportions they rejected the radical-right beliefs that the poor are to blame for their own
poverty, and the unemployed in the main too lazy to look for work.
But many now had little or only uncertain faith in old means of
industrial action to back up collective bargaining; little faith either in
political parties to do much for ordinary people like themselves. It
was, moreover, manual workers especially among whom this discon-
solate tension between aspirations for fair shares and practical means
to them was most evident.

The same goes for the second and more comprehensive Sheffield
study. In reinforcement of the first, and of the general run of findings
from nationwide surveys of the mid-1980s onwards, this showed a
wide groundswell of popular opinion to the effects that British society
unjustly privileges top people; that contrasting poverty is the result of
'an unfair system' in general or of personal misfortune against which
there is too little protection – a majority diagnosis well worth noting
in contrast to a minority view that poverty is an inevitable consequence of modern progress and change or, as very few respondents
believed, a sign of individual failure; that measures therefore ought to
be set in hand to reduce inequality of wealth, income and power. But
there was less agreement about just what measures; and much less
trust that any measures would be taken which would really change
things.

This was not for lack of some shrewd assessment of policies: on the
contrary. Attitudes to taxation provide the most telling case. Cutting
personal tax was at the time – and is in principle still – high on the
Conservative agenda. How then, respondents were asked, should
taxes be cut if they were cut? Offered a list of options, over 60 per cent
– with little variation by class – chose one or other of a progressive
character, which would shift some of the weight away from low
incomes: increasing base allowances to take more people out of the
income-tax net; reducing VAT; or, though a much rarer choice, raising
the rate of child benefit. Only 30 per cent of respondents picked the
regressive options listed: cutting basic rates of income tax or, as hardly
anyone wanted, cutting the highest rate. People here seemed to prove
well aware of the different effects of alternative tax prescriptions;

certainly a clear majority favoured prescriptions in line with their general endorsement of fairer shares.

But matters are quite different when it comes to political realities. These were hypothetical options: though all were technically feasible, and the progressive ones quite humdrum, only the regressive ones proved to be on offer in practice. The survey was conducted in the run-up to the 1987 election. The 1988 Budget which followed was notable for its adoption of just that regressive package which the majority of survey respondents here had rejected: cuts in both basic and, very dramatically, higher rates of income tax. This was as the Tories had promised. But there was no clear alternative in sight from the oppositon parties. Labour's tax proposals at the 1987 election, in particular, had been fatally muffled for fear of giving offence to anyone at all. The story was almost repeated in 1992, though not quite. Labour's Shadow Chancellor did then offer a package for moderately progressive change through selectively directed tax increases to im- prove benefits which, according to an estimate from the Institute for Fiscal Studies (Webb and Dilnot, 1992), would actually have improved circumstances for the lower-income half of all households – the poor most – and trimmed real incomes only for the 15 per cent or so best-off families. But this 'alternative budget' came a bare three weeks before the election: with enough time for the overwhelmingly Conservative press to campaign loudly against it as an agenda for tax increases on everyone across the board; but with none of such long preparation of voters' minds as a Labour switch from anodyne rhetoric to measures with some teeth would, in all probability, have required of a party widely suspected of inefficacy. Indeed, the 'Shadow Budget' seemed to drop out of sight again in the course of those intra-party exchanges of recrimination that followed Labour's fourth successive election defeat.

In political circumstances of this nature even a radical-right tax package, in the style so far most sharply exemplified by the Budget of 1988, may find a good measure of pragmatic popular acceptance, although it flagrantly breaches the principles endorsed by the ma- jority of people. The Sheffield survey again helps to explain how. Respondents were asked how they would view a cut in income tax for *all* people – and 'all' must in logic of course include the rich. In answer to other questions a majority, blue-collar workers especially, advo- cated heavier taxes on the wealthy: this, incidentally, just as far more people believed the rich to engage widely in tax-dodging than be- lieved (as many did nonetheless) benefit-scrounging to be common – 80 per cent versus 50 per cent. Yet despite majority concern to put greater tax pressure on at the top, rather more than half of all respondents expressed approval for income-tax cuts across the board; and the figure was nearly two in three among manual workers. It is too glib to take all this just to discredit survey-polling of opinions. Contradictory as they may seem, the findings make sense in suggesting that rank-and-file wage-earners, especially, are caught in a trap over tax policies as these are in practice on offer. Just because the tax system is inequitable, as they plainly recognize, the system bears heavily on themselves. When no opposition party has set out a sustained strategy to change it in comprehensively progressive direction, it is hardly surprising that many of them then welcome what can readily look like a small mercy: some cut in their own immediately visible tax payments, even though the effects over a little longer run will go against both their material interests in public provision and their larger social hopes for fairer shares.

They certainly do recognize their material interests in public provision, though here too there can be ostensible inconsistencies of opinion. Take the National Health Service: from these survey findings as well as others, the most widely and warmly endorsed of all state-benefit services. Questioned in some detail on this subject, moreover, Sheffield respondents were equally firm in seeing private health care as a breach of NHS purposes and principles. Four in every five thought that private provision both takes resources away from the NHS and makes for unfair advantage on waiting lists for treatment. Given also a set of options for the general organization of health care, hardly anyone (only 7 per cent) chose more private provision; over 40 per cent, and fully half of all manual workers, chose instead a radical option – on no current party agenda – to rely exclusively on public funding. It is awareness of electoral risks from just such remarkable strength of support for 'socialized medicine' in Britain that has held successive governments since 1979 back as yet from radical-right recipes in this field.

Even so, opinions in this survey wavered in answer to another and logically connected question: what about 'encouragement' of private health care? The majority against was still clear – yet now smaller, at only 60 per cent. In fact some 20 per cent expressed positive approval; and this minority in favour rose to about one in four among two groups of people at humdrum levels of the class structure – routine-grade non-manual workers and non-skilled manual workers, though both were otherwise among those near-unanimously dedicated to the principles of public provision for health. The 'inconsistency' here is arguably minor. But it could be taken as a small sign to similar effect as the larger sign from attitudes to taxation: that people in rank-and-file work (though here not so much the skilled) are more liable than others to find themselves caught in a thought-trap between their socio-political values and a lack of political response to them. Private health care is growing, with government backing. Almost all think it wrong. But then, some seem to say, this is the way things are going: maybe some good could come of it after all? Far more evidently a risk in respect of taxation, such creeping acceptance of small or uncertain mercies in the absence of live alternatives could make eventual leeway for a regressive shift even of popular values. There has remarkably, however, been no proven sign of this yet.

Speculation aside, the larger point stands firm that very many people – wage-earners and near-wage-earners especially – expect little to their good to come from politicians and parties. It might be thought just a reflection of Northern distrust of the South when views of this kind were voiced by respondents in the Sheffield study. Three in every four there, and fully four in every five blue-collar workers, said they felt people like themselves to have 'little say in how the country is run'; nearly as many thought the wealthy to have too much power and influence; and four out of ten manual workers, though fewer among others, endorsed a view that voting in elections 'will never really change things for the better'. But disillusion on the latter score, ominous in a country whose conventions include particular pride in parliamentary democracy, looks widespread also from survey evidence across the nation. A large study at roughly the same time as the one in Sheffield thus showed some half of respondents to believe that all parties are 'the same when in power' or that each is 'as bad as another'; and the same proportion of manual workers, supervisors and technicians to feel that 'it makes no difference which party runs the government', with the percentage taking this view down to about 30 only among the salariat (Marshall et al., 1988, pp. 161 ff, 255). The sanguine may take heart that probably a majority of people overall, if a bare one, still think elections matter; and that a good many more actually turn out to vote at general elections. It is nonetheless hardly comforting that a sense of exclusion from significant political influence is spread wide and, if unsurprisingly, affects those at low-to-lowish levels of the economic class structure most.

Why this should be so could be explained – or restated – just by gloomy reference to an inevitability of *de facto* oligarchy and/or unresponsive 'bureaucracy' within the formal processes of representative democracy. Now as earlier (Westergaard and Resler, 1975), however, I see more mileage for understanding by reference – if gloomy again – to the ways in which class politics has come to be 'institutionalized'. With such institutionalization, both in Britain and widely elsewhere in western Europe, labour-movement parties were admitted to the stage of high politics; and class contest came for long to form the recognized main theme around which parties mobilized. But the conflict between classes, whatever its pitch and character earlier, also came to be regulated, moderated and tamed in consequence. Compromise might be pursued as a tactic first; but it became usually, in due course, a virtual end in itself. Labour movements – sooner in some countries, later in others – sought reform because it was easier to achieve, and did indeed bring tangible benefit for labour interests, without head-on challenge to the established order. But as head-on challenge then generally dropped from sight, and as reform over time came closer to its limits without it, the class substance of institutionalized politics tended to drain away. Rival parties contested in elections for the 'middle ground' and for 'floating voters', still confident that they could retain the support of their original constituencies nonetheless. And with this, the parties came to base their claims increasingly on purported instrumental competence in governance, more than on principled and long-run pursuit of class-constituency interests. So politics became, and appears now to be pretty commonly seen as, 'dull' or trivial, even when not mean-spirited or corrupt. And as politicians and parties have lowered their sights, voters at large have come not to expect much of them.

It is not that people think governments *could* do little to better common welfare (cf. also Young, 1985). It is instead that very many now think they *will* not, as cynicism about parties and elections shows. If only in that rather perverse sense, popular disillusion has some congruence with one feature of radical-right doctrine: the assertion that governments should do much less of what they once did or purported to do. True enough, in pursuing that end to market-freeing effects, the radical right have also sought strenuously to 'break the mould' of class compromise as institutionalized over the decades to the 1970s. Yet the Conservative Party's retention of more than 40 per cent of votes during this process has not, from the evidence now summarized, come from anything like a matching conversion of voters to the 'new' right's mould-breaking philosophy. It appears, ironically, to have come very much more from the party's long-entrenched claim to superior competence in governance, when governance means management of the established economic order. The Conservatives, radical-right or not, are after all the party of 'practically minded' business. When their assertion of natural expertise in economic management has continued to pull in election-decisive votes even across two deep recessions, it is scarcely a sign that the assertion is intrinsically credible; rather that Labour's efficacy by comparison is widely

trusted *neither* in that sphere *nor*, crucially, in the sphere of class-redistributive policy which was once its own. The spread of disillusion-
ment with politics and politicians has damaged the left in political
practice far more than the right, I suggest, because the former have the
emptier hands the more they set pursuit of a rightward-shifted
'middle way' above pursuit of the fairer class-shares which a clear
majority of the population still either actively want or – above modest
class level – would evidently at least tolerate in preference to the
patent injustices of the socio-economic order as it has become since
around 1980.

To argue for Labour to break the mould leftwards – in tune with
popular aspirations, not out of tune with them as conventional commentary has it – is not to see radical socialist transformation ahead.
Aspirations for *fairer* shares are not, as they emerge from successive
survey findings, aspirations for *equal* shares. They might perhaps
come closer to that over time, were the parameters of practical politics
once to be shifted left of centre. But just to achieve a shift of this sort,
and sustain it to election successes, could well entail a long haul of
character transformation and image reversal for Labour: perhaps also
the prods from such new party formation on Labour's left as a change
to proportional representation in Britain might allow. These are prospects unlikely to appeal to the party's establishment, without larger
active pressure from below: a double-bind when such pressure itself
is liable to run out of steam through activist enticement into 'one-
more-short-haul' pursuit of the middle way.

A long-haul appeal, however, neither has to be nor plausibly could
be an appeal to class allegiances in old style. Labour has historically
drawn much on a sense of 'working-class identity' which in turn
identified the party with the class. It still seems to do so to quite a high
degree, among its reduced number of supporters (Marshall et al.,
1988); and the continuing role of such a sense of identity may be
inferred also from the facts that birth, upbringing and/or early-to-
midlife employment experience in blue-collar circumstances continue
to exercise some leftward influence on individuals' political views
and their class-characterizations of themselves, even when they have
reached salariat position later (ibid.; also Noble et al., 1989). But it is
another matter just what a respondent's statement of 'class identity'
means, even when it is properly separated in measures of the concept
from expressions of socio-political opinion (cf. especially Evans,
1992). It looks wellnigh certain, anyway, that personal identification
with 'the working class' will become gradually rarer. For one thing,
the general association of the term with the manual working class
seems to persist, notwithstanding parallel economic circumstances

among low-level non-manual employees; and the sheer numbers of manual workers are falling.

For another thing, people's political orientations are likely to come to hang progressively more on explicitly rational appraisals of self-interest, rather than on emotional identification with their class as some sort of 'community'. Working-class solidarity has never involved only affective loyalty to kith and kin – to neighbours, 'work-mates' or trade-fellows – at the expense of calculated pursuit of mundane common interest (e.g. Marshall et al., 1988, chapter 8). The two have rather intertwined. But they have also historically been at odds to a degree. Working-class identities forged in good part from social relations of proximity – from commonalities of family, locality, workplace or work-sector – have had a sentimental and 'particularistic' character to them that could inhibit rather than promote mobilization for wider class interests (for example, Westergaard, 1975). Appeal to such wider interests requires precisely a 'universalistic', and rational-calculative, appeal to the very concrete self-interests which people of similar class location have in common, never mind whether or not they feel emotionally tied together in some class 'fratemity' of whatever label. Rational calculation of this mode is well in key with the trend of present-day politics. Labour and the left could, and in my view should, make use of it to mobilize widespread and evidently well-perceived popular self-interest in fairer shares.

Might there, finally, be a barrier from radical-right claims to have enhanced individual opportunity? It is improbable. Rather few voters seem to be impressed by these claims, when two in three or more survey respondents have said they thought social mobility to be hard to achieve; or that social class affects opportunities 'quite a lot' to 'a great deal', with no change for the better either recently or in near prospect (Marshall et al., 1988, p. 167; Young, 1985). And such views are in good accord with reality. True and interestingly enough, the leadership of the Conservative Party itself has come to be drawn from lower down the social scale in some step with radical-right ascendancy. Mrs Thatcher and Mr Major are prominent examples though the House of Commons continues to include virtually no Tory MPs of manual working-class origins (Borthwick et al., 1991). Perhaps, too, high-financial boom in the 1980s drew some new recruits into City of London business, of more mixed social origins than before. But if so, it has yet to be shown; and this or that shift of intake to tiny elites hardly matters for opportunities in the population at large. Research on social mobility in general, continued into the 1980s, has shown no break yet of trend or pattern from the past – except the distinct *loss* of opportunities suffered by the many people now pitched into unemployment (Goldthorpe, 1987). And if these are still early days to judge ultimate outcomes on this front, differential class recruitment to higher education has shown only little change despite overall growth of access since the 1960s (Halsey, 1992). Student numbers have been further stepped up from the late 1980s especially. But intake is now to a system which, while unitary *de jure*, is increasingly stratified *de facto* into levels of provision that differ substantially in respect of funding, of character, and so of quality by any usual standards. It seems inevitable that these different levels of provision will recruit students in correspondingly different mixes of social origin and, in turn, deliver them as graduates to correspondingly different levels of employment.

It would indeed be against the signs from comparative research on social mobility (Erikson and Goldthorpe, 1992) to expect any diminution in relative inequalities of opportunity between classes, when inequalities of economic class condition have sharpened as they have so dramatically in Britain since around 1980. Radical-right talk about 'opportunity' is in any case notable for careful abstention from reference to *equal* opportunity even as an aspiration. Associated proclamations of the coming of a 'classless' society sound bizarre against the record of the past decade and a half. If taken seriously, however, they seem to envisage a dispensation in which acute inequality of economic outcomes in life is rendered morally and politically innocuous by free opportunity for individuals to make the best they can for themselves of their endowments, however they may have come by these. But, essentially unspecified, this notion of '*free*' opportunity propounds no need to offset the further impetus of freed market and property processes themselves towards transmission of advantage and disadvantage by class from one generation to the next. It seems enough for opportunity to be labelled 'free' if only some visible number of people make it to better things from humbler beginnings – although this has been the case always in any capitalist society. Sociological exercises in the calculation of class mobility ratios are then ignored on a bland assumption that their disparities show, not inequality, but mere differences of personal capacity or private concern for occupational achievement. Even – in practice indeed especially – increased wealth on the part of those already wealthy is acclaimed as proof of newly freed opportunity.

It is a consolation that, in unfurling this banner for a 'classless' society, neo-liberalism in Britain has not been able to add to its triumphs in policy the victories in re-education of the public which it has sought at the same time. Even this could come: it is a risk, in my view at least, if Labour and the left stay sucked into electoral contest for rightward-tilted so-called central ground. As yet, however, class as a matter of distributive injustice still figures high among popular social concerns. That is one reason why it should return to a high place on both political and social-scientific agendas.

References

In addition to all works cited, the following list includes a small number of the many others relevant, among these a few published too late for specific reference in the text.

Abbott, P. and Sapsford, R. 1987: *Women and Social Class*. London, Tavistock.
Allen, S. Waton, A. Purcell, K. and Wood, S. (eds) 1986: *The Experience of Unemployment*. London, Macmillan.
Andersen, J. and Elm Larsen, J. 1989: *Fattigdom i Velfaerdsstaten* (Poverty in the Welfare State). Copenhagen, Samfundslitteratur.
Anderson, M., Bechhofer, F. and Kendrick, S. 1992: *Individual and Household Strategies* (SCELI Working Paper 24). Swindon, Economic and Social Research Council.
Arblaster, A. 1984: *The Rise and Decline of Western Liberalism*. Oxford, Blackwell.
Atkinson, J. 1986: *Changing Work Patterns*. London, National Economic Development Office.
Bagguley, P. and Mann, K. 1992: 'Idle thieving bastards: scholarly representations of the "underclass" '. *Work, Employment and Society*, 6.
Bagguley, P., Mark-Lawson, J., Shapiro, D., Urry, J., Walby, S. and Warde, A. 1990: *Restructuring: place, class and gender*. London, Sage.
Barker, R. and Roberts, H. 1993: 'The uses of the concept of power'. In D. Morgan and L. Stanley (eds), *Debates in Sociology*, Manchester, Manchester University Press.
Batstone, E. 1984: *Working Order: workplace industrial relations over two decades*. Oxford, Blackwell.
Batstone, E. 1988: 'The frontier of control'. In D. Gallie (ed.), *Employment in Britain*, Oxford, Blackwell.
Bauman, Z. 1982: *Memories of Class*. London, Routledge & Kegan Paul.
Bauman, Z. 1992: *Intimations of Postmodernity*. London, Routledge.
Bonney, N. 1988a: 'Gender, household and social class'. *Brit. J. Sociology*, 39.
Bonney, N. 1988b: 'Dual earning couples: trends of change in Great Britain'. *Work, Employment & Society*, 2.
Bonney, N. 1988c: 'Women's two roles: choice and constraint' (mimeo). Paper for an ESRC–SCELI Workshop at Warwick University.
Borthwick, G., Ellingworth, D., Bell, C. and MacKenzie, D. 1991: 'The social background of British MPs'. *Sociology*, 25.

Braverman, H. 1974: *Labor and Monopoly Capital*. New York, Monthly Review Press.

Brittan, S. 1978: 'Inflation and democracy'. In F. Hirsch and J. H. Goldthorpe (eds), *The Political Economy of Inflation*, London, Martin Robertson. See also *idem*, 1983.

Brittan, S. 1983: *The Role and Limits of Government*. London, Temple Smith.

Brown, G. 1989: *File on Fairness*, no. 3. London, House of Commons.

Brown, J. C. 1990: 'The focus on single mothers'. In C. Murray.

Brown, R. K. 1990: 'A flexible future for Europe?' *Brit. J. Sociology*, 41.

Bryson, V. 1992: *Feminist Political Theory: an introduction*. London, Macmillan.

Burchell, B. and Rubery, J. 1989: *Segmented Jobs and Segmented Workers* (SCELI Working Paper 13). Swindon, Economic and Social Research Council.

Burnham, J. 1945: *The Managerial Revolution*. Harmondsworth, Penguin Books (first published in USA 1941).

Burrows, R. and Marsh, C. (eds) 1992: *Consumption and Class: divisions and change*. London, Macmillan.

Carchedi, G. 1975: 'On the economic identification of the new middle class'. *Economy and Society*, 4.

Carling, A. 1992: *Social Division*. London, Verso.

Castles, F. G. 1978: *The Social Democratic Image of Society*. London, Routledge & Kegan Paul.

Cawson, A. 1986: *Corporatism and Political Theory*. Oxford, Blackwell.

Clark, J., Modgil, C. and Modgil, S. (eds) 1990: *John H. Goldthorpe: consensus and controversy*. London, Falmer Press.

Colledge, M. and Bartholomew, R. 1980: *A Study of the Long-Term Unemployed*. London, Manpower Services Commission.

Commission on Social Justice 1993: *The Justice Gap*. London, Institute for Public Policy Research.

Craig, C., Rubery, J., Tarling, R. and Wilkinson, F. 1985: 'Economic, social and political factors in the operation of the labour market'. In B. Roberts, R. Finnegan and D. Gallie (eds), *New Approaches to Economic Life*, Manchester, Manchester University Press.

Crewe, I. 1984: 'The electorate: partisan dealignment ten years on'. In H. Berrington (ed.), *Change in British Politics*, London, Frank Cass.

Crewe, I. 1986: 'On the death and resurrection of class voting'. *Political Studies*, 34.

Crewe, I., Särlvik, B. and Alt, J. 1977: 'Partisan dealignment in Britain 1964–1974'. *Brit J. Polit. Science*, 7.

Crompton, R. 1993: *Class and Stratification: an introduction to current debates*. Cambridge, Polity Press.

Crompton, R. and Gubbay, J. 1977: *Economy and Class Structure*. London, Macmillan.

Crompton, R. and Jones, G. 1984: *White-Collar Proletariat: deskilling and gender in clerical work*. London, Macmillan.

Crompton, R. and Mann, M. (eds) 1986: *Gender and Stratification*. Cambridge, Polity Press.

Crosland, C. A. R. 1973: *Socialism Now*. London, Cape.

Crouch, C. 1977: *Class Conflict and the Industrial Relations Crisis: compromise and corporatism in the policies of the British state*. London, Heinemann.

Crouch, C. 1979: *The Politics of Industrial Relations*. London, Fontana/Collins.

Crouch, C. and Dore, R. P. (eds) 1990: *Corporatism and Accountability: organised interests in British public life*. Oxford, Clarendon Press.

Crouch, C. and Marquand, D. (eds) 1989: *The New Centralism: Britain out of step in Europe?* Oxford, Blackwell.

Dahrendorf, R. 1987: 'The erosion of citizenship'. *New Statesman & Society*, 12 June.

Daniel, W. W. 1981: *The Unemployed Flow*. London, Policy Studies Institute.

Dennis, N. and Halsey, A. H. 1988: *English Ethical Socialism*. Oxford, Oxford University Press.

Department of Social Security 1990: *Households below Average Income*. London, HMSO.

Department of Social Security 1993: *Households below Average Income: a statistical analysis 1979–1990/91*. London, HMSO.

Dex, S. 1987: *Women's Occupational Mobility*. London, Macmillan.

Ditton, J. 1977: *Part-Time Crime: an ethnography of fiddling and pilferage*. London, Macmillan.

Dunleavy, P. and Husbands, C. T. 1985: *British Democracy at the Crossroads*. London, Allen & Unwin.

Edgell, S. and Duke, V. 1991: *A Measure of Thatcherism*. London, Harper Collins.

Edwards, R. 1979: *Contested Terrain: the transformation of the workplace in the twentieth century*. New York, Basic Books.

Emmison, M. and Western, M. 1990: 'Social class and social identity'. *Sociology*, 24.

Erikson, R. and Goldthorpe, J. H. 1992: *The Constant Flux: a study of class mobility in industrial societies*. Oxford, Clarendon Press.

Esping-Andersen, G. 1985: *Politics against Markets*. Princeton, Princeton University Press.

Evans, G. 1992: 'Is Britain a class-divided society? A re-analysis and extension of Marshall *et al.*'s study of class consciousness'. *Sociology*, 26.

Fallick, J. L. and Elliott, R. F. (eds) 1981: *Incomes Policies, Inflation and Relative Pay*. London, Allen & Unwin.

Fiegehen, G. C., Lansley, P. S. and Smith, A. D. 1977: *Poverty and Progress in Britain 1953–73*. Cambridge, Cambridge University Press.

Field, F. 1989: *Losing Out: the emergence of Britain's underclass*. Oxford, Blackwell.

Forest, R., Murie, A. and Williams, P. 1990: *Home Ownership, Differentiation and Fragmentation*. London, Unwin Hyman.

Fryer, D. and Ullah, P. (eds) 1986: *The Experience of Unemployment*. Milton Keynes, Open University Press.

Fulcher, J. 1987: 'Labour movement theory versus corporatism: social democracy in Sweden'. *Sociology*, 21.

Fulcher, J. 1991: *Labour Movements, Employers and the State: conflict and cooperation in Britain and Sweden*. Oxford, Clarendon Press.

Gallie, D. 1988a: 'Employment, unemployment and social stratification'. In *idem* (ed.), *Employment in Britain*, Oxford, Blackwell.

Gallie, D. 1988b: *Technological Change, Gender and Skill* (SCELI Working Paper 4). Swindon, Economic and Social Research Council.

Gallie, D. 1989: *Trade Union Allegiance and Decline in British Urban Labour Markets* (SCELI Working Paper 9). Swindon, Economic and Social Research Council.

Gallie, D. 1991: *The Social Change and Economic Life Initiative: final report to the ESRC (part 2)*. Swindon, Economic and Social Research Council.

Gamarnikow, E., Morgan, D., Purvis, J. and Taylorson, D. (eds) 1983: *Gender, Class and Work*. London, Heinemann.

Gamble, A. 1979: 'The free economy and the strong state'. In R. Miliband and J. Saville (eds), *The Socialist Register 1979*, London, Merlin Press.

Gamble, A. 1981: *Britain in Decline: economic policy, political strategy and the British state*. London, Macmillan.

Gamble, A. 1988: *The Free Economy and the Strong State: the politics of Thatcherism*. Basingstoke, Macmillan.

Gellner, E. 1988: *Plough, Sword and Book: the structure of human history*. London, Collins Harvill.

Giddens, A. 1973: *The Class Structure of Advanced Societies*. London, Hutchinson.

Glass, R. 1979: 'Verbal pollution'. *New Society*, 29 September.

Goldthorpe, J. H. 1978: 'The current inflation: towards a sociological account'. In F. Hirsch and J. H. Goldthorpe (eds), *The Political Economy of Inflation*, London, Martin Robertson.

Goldthorpe, J. H. 1980: *Social Mobility and Class Structure in Modern Britain* (in collaboration with C. Llewellyn and C. Payne). Oxford, Clarendon Press.

Goldthorpe, J. H. 1983: 'Women and class analysis'. *Sociology*, 17. (The debate which followed this paper is well reviewed in Roberts, 1993.)

Goldthorpe, J. H. 1987: *Social Mobility and Class Structure in Modern Britain* (with assistance of C. Llewellyn and C. Payne; 2nd edn). Oxford, Clarendon Press.

Goldthorpe, J. H., Lockwood, D., Bechhofer, F. and Platt, J. 1968/9: *The Affluent Worker* (3 vols). Cambridge, Cambridge University Press.

Goldthorpe, J. H. and Marshall, G. 1992: 'The promising future of class analysis'. *Sociology*, 26.

Gorz, A. 1982: *Farewell to the Working Class*. London, Pluto Press (original French edn, 1980).

Gough, I. 1979: *The Political Economy of the Welfare State*. London, Macmillan.

Gray, J., McPherson, A. F. and Raffe, D. 1983: *Reconstructions of Secondary Education: theory, myth and practice since the war*. London, Routledge & Kegan Paul.

Halsey, A. H. 1978: *Change in British Society*. Oxford, Oxford University Press.

Halsey, A. H. 1989: 'Social trends since World War II'. *Social Trends*, 17.

Halsey, A. H. 1992: 'Opening wide the doors of higher education'. *National Commission on Education Briefings*, no. 6.

Halsey, A. H., Heath, A. F. and Ridge, J. M. 1980: *Origins and Destinations: family, class and education in modern Britain*. Oxford, Clarendon Press.

Harris, C. C. 1987: *Redundancy and Recession in South Wales*. Oxford, Blackwell.

Hayek, F. A. 1973: *Law, Legislation and Liberty: the mirage of social justice*. London, Routledge & Kegan Paul. See also *idem*, 1988.

Hayek, F. A. 1988: 'The weasel word "social" '. In R. Scruton (ed.), *Conservative Thoughts*, London, Claridge Press.

Heath, A. 1986: 'Do people have consistent attitudes?'. In R. Jowell et al. (eds), *British Social Attitudes: the 1986 report*, London, Social and Community Planning Research.

Heath, A. and Evans, G. 1989: 'Working-class Conservatives and middle-class socialists'. In R. Jowell et al. (eds), *British Social Attitudes, 5th Report*, London, Social and Community Planning Research.

Heath, A., Jowell, R. and Curtice, J. 1985: *How Britain Votes*. Oxford, Pergamon Press.

Hills, J. 1989: *Changing Tax*. London, Child Poverty Action Group.

Hills, J. (ed.) 1990: *The State of Welfare: the welfare state in Britain since 1974*. Oxford, Clarendon Press.

Hills, J. 1993: *The Future of Welfare: a guide to the debate*. York, Joseph Rowntree Foundation.

Himmelstrand, U., Ahrne, G., Lundberg, L. and L. 1981: *Beyond Welfare Capitalism*. London, Heinemann.

Hindess, B. 1987: *Politics and Class Analysis*. Oxford, Blackwell.

Hirsch, F. 1977: *Social Limits to Growth*. London, Routledge & Kegan Paul.

Hobsbawm, E. J. et al. 1981: *The Forward March of Labour Halted*. London, Verso.

Holloway, J. and Picciotto, S. (eds) 1978: *State and Capital: a Marxist debate*. London, Edward Arnold.

Hornemann Møller, I. 1986: '*Arbejderflertallet og 70'ernes Socialreform* (The 'Labour Majority and the Social Reform of the 1970s). Copenhagen, Socialistiske Økonomers Forlag.

Hornemann Møller, I. 1989: *Samfundet Polariseres* (Society is being Polarised). Copenhagen, ATA Forlaget.

Jenkins, S. P. 1991: 'Living standards and income inequality in the 1970s and 1980s'. *Fiscal Studies*, 12.

Jessop, B. 1978. 'Capitalism and democracy: the best possible shell?' In G. Littlejohn et al. (eds), *Power and the State*, London, Croom Helm.

Johnson, P. and Stark, G. 1989: *Taxation and Social Security 1979–89*. London, Institute of Fiscal Studies.

Joshi, H. E. 1985: 'Motherhood and employment: change and continuity in postwar Britain'. London, Office of Population Censuses and Surveys (Occasional Paper 34).

Kinsey, R. 1993: 'Innocent underclass'. *New Statesman & Society*, 5 March. See also S. Anderson, R. Kinsey, I. Loader, and C. Smith: '*Cautionary Tales': a study of young people and crime in Edinburgh*, 1990. Centre for Criminology, University of Edinburgh.

Korpi, W. 1978: *The Working Class in Welfare Capitalism: work, unions and politics in Sweden*. London, Routledge & Kegan Paul.

Lane, C. 1988: 'New technology and clerical work'. In D. Gallie (ed.), *Employment in Britain*, Oxford, Blackwell.

Le Grand, J. 1982: *The Strategy of Equality: redistribution and the social services*. London, Allen & Unwin.

Lewis, J. 1992: *Women in Britain since 1945*. Oxford, Blackwell.

Lockwood, D. 1988: 'The weakest chain in the link'. In D. Rose (ed.), *Social Stratification and Economic Change*, London, Hutchinson.

Lockwood, D. 1989: *The Black-Coated Worker* (2nd edn). London, Allen & Unwin.

Lukes, S. 1974: *Power: a radical view*. London, Macmillan. See also Barker and Roberts, 1993.

McEachern, D. 1990: *The Expanding State: class and economy in Europe since 1945*. London, Harvester Wheatsheaf.

Macnicol, J. 1990: 'Nightmare on Easy Street'. *Times Higher Education Supplement*, 29 June.

McPherson, A. and Willms, J. D. 1987: 'Equalisation and improvement: some effects of comprehensive reorganisation in Scotland'. *Sociology*, 21.

McRae, S. 1986: *Cross-Class Families*. Oxford, Clarendon Press.

Mann, K. 1992: *The Making of an English 'Underclass'.* Milton Keynes, Open University Press.

Marsden, D. 1982: *Workless.* London, Croom Helm.

Marshall, G. 1986: 'The workplace culture of a licensed restaurant'. *Theory, Culture and Society,* 3.

Marshall, G. and Rose, D. 1990: 'Out-classed by our critics?' *Sociology,* 24.

Marshall, G., Rose, D., Newby, H. and Vogler, C. 1988: *Social Class in Modern Britain.* London, Unwin Hyman.

Marshall, T. H. 1950: 'Citizenship and social class'. In *idem, Citizenship and Social Class, and other essays,* Cambridge, Cambridge University Press.

Martin, A. 1979: 'The dynamics of change in a Keynesian political economy: the Swedish case and its implications'. In C. Crouch (ed.), *State and Economy in Contemporary Capitalism,* London, Croom Helm.

Martin, J. and Roberts, C. 1984: *Women and Employment: a lifetime perspective.* London, HMSO.

Martin, R. 1992: *Bargaining Power.* Oxford, Clarendon Press.

Meidner, R. 1976: *Kollektiv Kapitalbildning genom Löntagarfonder.* Stockholm, Prisma/LO. English translation, *Employee Investment Funds: an approach to collective capital formation,* London, Allen & Unwin, 1978.

Middlemas, K. 1979: *Politics in Industrial Society: the experience of the British system since 1911.* London, André Deutsch.

Miles, S. and Middleton, C. 1993: 'Markets, ideologies and primary initial teacher education'. *Internat. Studies in Sociology of Education,* 3.

Miliband, R. 1969: *The State in Capitalist Society.* London, Weidenfeld & Nicolson.

Miliband, R. 1970: 'The capitalist state: reply to Nicos Poulantzas'. *New Left Review,* no. 59. This and the article to which it was a reply (Poulantzas, 1969) were reprinted in J. Urry and J. Wakeford (eds), *Power in Britain,* London, Heinemann, 1973.

Miliband, R. 1978: 'A process of desubordination'. *Brit. J. Sociology,* 29.

Miliband, R. 1989: *Divided Societies: class struggle in contemporary capitalism.* Oxford, Clarendon Press.

Millward, M., Stevens, N., Smart, D. and Hawes, W. 1992: *Workplace Industrial Relations in Transition.* Aldershot, Dartmouth Publishing.

Mishra, R. 1984: *The Welfare State in Crisis.* Brighton, Wheatsheaf.

Mishra, R. 1990: *The Welfare State in Capitalist Society: policies of retrenchment and maintenance in Europe, North America and Australia.* London, Harvester Wheatsheaf.

Moylan, S., Millar, J. and Davies, R. 1984: *For Richer for Poorer: DHSS cohort study of unemployed men.* London, HMSO.

Murray, C. 1990: *The Emerging British Underclass.* London, Institute of Economic Affairs (Health and Welfare Unit).

National Commission for Education 1993: *Learning to Succeed* (Paul Hamlyn Foundation). London, Heinemann.

Noble, I., Walker, A. C. and Westergaard, J. H. 1989: *Socio-Political Consciousness and Economic Experience in Sheffield.* End-of-award report to the Economic and Social Research Council, award no. G00232211. (No other general account has yet been published of this 1,000-interview sample survey, from which relevant results are reported at several points of the present book.)

Nove, A. 1983: *The Economics of Feasible Socialism.* London, Allen & Unwin.

Offe, C. 1984: *Contradictions of the Welfare State*. London, Hutchinson.

O'Higgins, M., Schmaus, G. and Stephenson, G. 1990: 'Income distribution and redistribution'. In T. M. Smeeding, M. O'Higgins and L. Rainwater (eds), *Poverty, Inequality and Income Distribution in Comparative Perspective*, New York, Harvester Wheatsheaf.

Pahl, R. E. 1984: *Divisions of Labour*. Oxford, Blackwell.

Pahl, R. E. 1989: 'Is the emperor naked?' *Internat. J. Urban and Regional Research*, 13.

Pahl, R. E. 1993: 'Does class analysis without class theory have a promising future?' *Sociology*, 27.

Panitch, L. 1976: *Social Democracy and Industrial Militancy: the Labour Party, the trade unions and incomes policy, 1945–1974*. Cambridge, Cambridge University Press.

Panitch, L. 1980: 'Recent theorisations of corporatism'. *Brit. J. Sociology*, 31. Reprinted in *idem, Working-Class Politics in Crisis: essays on labour and the state*. London, Verso, 1986.

Panitch, L. 1981: 'The limits of corporatism'. *New Left Review*, no. 125.

Parkin, F. 1968: *Middle Class Radicalism*. Manchester, Manchester University Press.

Parkin, F. 1979: *Marxism and Class Theory: a bourgeois critique*. London, Tavistock.

Pawson, R. 1990: 'Half-truths about bias'. *Sociology*, 24.

Payne, G. 1987: *Employment and Opportunity* and *Mobility and Change in Modern Society* (2 vols). London, Macmillan.

Piachaud, D. 1987: 'The growth of poverty'. In A. C. and C. Walker (eds), *The Growing Divide*, London, Child Poverty Action Group.

Pinker, R. 1979: *The Idea of Welfare*. London, Heinemann.

Piore, M. and Sabel, C. 1984: *The Second Industrial Divide*. New York, Basic Books.

Pontusson, J. D. 1984: 'Behind and beyond social democracy in Sweden?' *New Left Review*, January/February.

Poulantzas, N. 1969: 'The problem of the capitalist state'. *New Left Review*, no. 58. (See also Miliband, 1970.)

Poulantzas, N. 1973: 'On social classes'. *New Left Review*, no. 78.

Poulantzas, N. 1975: *Classes in Contemporary Capitalism*. London, New Left Books.

Poulantzas, N. 1977: 'The new petty bourgeoisie'. In A. Hunt (ed.), *Class and Class Structure*, London, Lawrence & Wishart.

Rawls, J. 1972: *A Theory of Justice*. Oxford, Clarendon Press.

Reisman, D. A. 1977: *Richard Titmuss: welfare and society*. London, Heinemann.

Rex, J. and Moore, R. 1967: *Race, Community and Conflict*. Oxford, Oxford University Press.

Roberts, H. 1993: 'The women and class debate'. In D. Morgan and L. Stanley (eds), *Debates in Sociology*, Manchester, Manchester University Press.

Roche, M. 1987: 'Citizenship, social theory, and social change'. *Theory and Society*, 16.

Roche, M. 1992: *Rethinking Citizenship*. Cambridge, Polity Press.

Rooker, J. 1993: 'Opportunity and achievement: a discussion paper on higher education'. *Times Higher Education Supplement*, 12 November.

Royal Commission on the Distribution of Income and Wealth 1979: *Report No. 7* (Cmnd 7595). London, HMSO. See also *idem, An A to Z of Income and Wealth*, London, HMSO, 1980.

Rubery, J. 1988: 'Employers and the labour market'. In D. Gallie (ed.), *Employment in Britain*, Oxford, Blackwell.

Runciman, W. G. 1990: 'How many classes are there in contemporary British society?' *Sociology*, 24.

Sabel, C. 1982: *Work and Politics*. Cambridge, Cambridge University Press.

Saunders, P. 1984: 'Beyond housing classes: the sociological significance of private property rights in means of consumption'. *Internat. J. Urban and Regional Research*, 8.

Saunders, P. 1989: 'Left write in sociology'. *Network* (British Sociological Association newsletter), no. 44.

Saunders, P. 1990: *A Nation of Home Owners*. London, Unwin Hyman.

Saunders, P. and Harris, C. 1990: 'Privatisation and the consumer'. *Sociology*, 24. (See also Burrows and Marsh, 1992.)

Scase, R. 1977: *Social Democracy in Capitalist Society: working-class politics in Britain and Sweden*. London, Croom Helm.

Schmitter, P. C. 1974: 'Still the century of corporatism?' *Review of Politics*, 36.

Schmitter, P. C. (ed.) 1977: *Corporatism and Policy Making in Contemporary Western Europe*, special issue of *Comparative Political Studies*, 10.

Scott, J. P. 1982: *The Upper Classes: property and privilege in Britain*. London, Macmillan.

Scott, J. P. 1985: *Corporations, Classes and Capitalism* (2nd edn). London, Hutchinson.

Scott, J. P. 1986: *Capitalist Property and Financial Power*. Brighton, Wheatsheaf.

Scott, J. P. 1988: 'Ownership and employer control'. In D. Gallie (ed.), *Employment in Britain*, Oxford, Blackwell.

Scott, J. P. 1991: *Who Rules Britain?* Cambridge, Polity Press.

Showler, B. and Sinfield, A. (eds) 1981: *The Workless State*. London, Martin Robertson.

Sinfield, A. 1981: *What Unemployment Means*. London, Martin Robertson.

Sinfield, A. 1993: 'Reverse targeting and upside-down benefits: how perverse policies perpetuate poverty' (British Association, Section N Presidential Address). Edinburgh University, Department of Social Policy and Social Work.

Skidelsky, R. (ed.) 1988: *Thatcherism*. London, Chatto & Windus.

Solomos, J. 1989: *Race and Racism in Contemporary Britain*. London, Macmillan.

Stephens, J. D. 1979: *The Transition from Capitalism to Socialism*. London, Macmillan.

Stewart, A., Prandy, K. and Blackburn, R. 1980: *Social Stratification and Occupations*. London, Macmillan.

Taylor-Gooby, P. 1985: *Public Opinion, Ideology and State Welfare*. London, Routledge & Kegan Paul.

Taylor-Gooby, P. 1991: 'Attachments to the welfare state'. In R. Jowell et al. (eds), *British Social Attitudes: the 8th report*, London, Social and Community Planning Research.

Therborn, G. 1986: *Why Some People are More Unemployed than Others*. London, Verso.

Thompson, E. P. 1978: 'The poverty of theory: or an orrery of errors'. In *idem*, *The Poverty of Theory and other essays*, London, Merlin Press.

Titmuss, R. M. 1958: 'The social division of welfare'. In *idem*, *Essays on the Welfare State*. London, Allen & Unwin. (See also Walker, 1981.)

Titmuss, R. M. 1962: *Income Distribution and Social Change*. London, Allen & Unwin.

Titmuss, R. M. 1968: *Commitment to Welfare*. London, Allen & Unwin.

Titmuss, R. M. 1973: *The Gift Relationship*. Harmondsworth, Penguin Books.

Titmuss, R. M. 1974: *Social Policy: an introduction*. London, Allen & Unwin.

Townsend, P. 1979: *Poverty in the United Kingdom*. Harmondsworth, Penguin Books.

Townsend, P. 1991: *The Poor are Poorer*. Bristol, Bristol University (Department of Social Policy and Social Planning).

Townsend, P. 1993: 'Underclass and overclass: the widening gulf between social classes in Britain in the 1980s'. In G. Payne and M. Cross (eds), *Sociology in Action*, London, Macmillan.

Townsend, P. and Davidson, N. (eds) 1982: *Inequalities in Health: the Black Report*. Harmondsworth, Penguin Books.

Tylecote, A. 1992: *The Long Wave in the World Economy: the present crisis in historical perspective*. London, Routledge.

Useem, M. 1984: *The Inner Circle*. New York, Oxford University Press.

Uusitalo, H. 1989: *Income Distribution in Finland*. Helsinki, Central Statistical Office of Finland (Studies, no. 148).

Walker, A. C. 1981: 'Social policy, social administration and the social construction of welfare'. *Sociology*, 15.

Walker, A. C. 1984: *Social Planning: a strategy for socialist welfare*. Oxford, Blackwell.

Walker, A. C. 1990: 'Blaming the victims'. In C. Murray.

Walker, A. C. 1991: 'Poverty and the underclass'. In M. Haralambos (ed.), *Developments in Sociology*, vol. 7, Ormskirk, Causeway Press.

Walker, A. C. and Walker, C. (eds) 1987: *The Growing Divide: a social audit 1979–1987*. London, Child Poverty Action Group.

Warr, P. 1987: *Work, Unemployment and Mental Health*. Oxford, Oxford University Press.

Webb, S. and Dilnot, A. 1992: 'A carefully crafted package'. *The Independent*, 17 March.

Westergaard, J. H. 1970: 'The rediscovery of the cash nexus'. In R. Miliband and J. Saville (eds), *The Socialist Register 1970*, London, Merlin Press.

Westergaard, J. H. 1975: 'Radical class consciousness: a comment'. In M. Bulmer (ed.), *Working-Class Images of Society*, London, Routledge & Kegan Paul.

Westergaard, J. H. 1977: 'Class, inequality and corporatism'. In A. Hunt (ed.), *Class and Class Structure*, London, Lawrence & Wishart.

Westergaard, J. H. 1978: 'Social policy and class inequality: some notes on welfare state limits'. In R. Miliband and J. Saville (eds), *The Socialist Register 1978*, London, Merlin Press.

Westergaard, J. H. 1992: 'About and beyond the underclass'. *Sociology*, 26.

Westergaard, J. H. 1993: 'Class in Britain since 1979: facts, theories and ideologies'. *Hitotsubashi Journal of Social Studies* (Tokyo), 25. (Japanese translation, by M. Watanabe, with additional commentary in press for publication, Tokyo, Aoki, 1993.)

Westergaard, J. H., Noble, I. and Walker, A. C. 1989: *After Redundancy: the experience of economic insecurity*. Cambridge, Polity Press.

Westergaard, J. H. and Resler, H. 1975: *Class in a Capitalist Society*. London, Heinemann (Penguin Books, 1976).

Whitehead, M. 1987: *The Health Divide: inequalities in health in the 1980s*. London, Health Education Council.

Wilkinson, R. G. 1986a: 'Occupational class, selection and inequalities in health'. *Quarterly J. Social Affairs*, 2.

Wilkinson, R. G. (ed.) 1986b: *Class and Health: research and longitudinal data*. London, Tavistock.

Winchester, D. 1988: 'Sectoral change and trade-union organisation'. In D. Gallie (ed.), *Employment in Britain*, Oxford, Blackwell.

Winkler, J. T. 1975: 'Law, state and economy: the Industry Act 1975 in context'. *Brit. J. Law and Society*, 2.

Winkler, J. T. 1976: 'Corporatism'. *Europ. J. Sociology*, 17.

Winkler, J. T. 1977: 'The corporate economy'. In R Scase (ed.), *Industrial Society: class, cleavage and control*, London, Allen & Unwin.

Wood, E. M. 1986: *The Retreat from Class*. London, Verso.

Wood, S. (ed.) 1982: *The Degradation of Work: skill, deskilling and the labour process*. London, Hutchinson.

Wright, E. O. 1976: 'Class boundaries in advanced capitalist societies'. *New Left Review*, no. 98.

Wright, E. O. 1978: *Class, Crisis and the State*. London, New Left Books.

Wright, E. O. 1979: *Class Structure and Income Determination*. New York, Academic Press.

Wright, E. O. 1985: *Classes*. London, Verso.

Wright, E. O. 1989: 'Re-thinking, once again, the concept of class structure'. In *idem* (ed.), *The Debate on Classes*, London, Verso.

Wright, E. O. and Martin, B. 1987: 'The transformation of the American class structure, 1960-1980'. *Amer. J. Sociology*, 93.

Wright, E. O. and Shin, K.-Y. 1988: 'Temporality and class analysis'. *Sociological Theory*, 6.

Young, K. 1985: 'Shades of opinion'. In R. Jowell and S. Witherspoon (eds), *British Social Attitudes: the 1985 report*, London, Social and Community Planning Research.

Several series of statistical reports on which I have drawn are not listed above. These include the regular official reports on the *General Household Survey*, the *New Earnings Survey, Top Salaries* and *Social Trends*; as well as the reports on annual unofficial surveys of *British Social Attitudes*, conducted by Social and Community Research (ed. R. Jowell et al.), from which specific articles cited are listed above, however, by authors' names.

Author Index

Subject Index